Lecture Notes
in Business Information Processing   136

Series Editors

Wil van der Aalst
  Eindhoven Technical University, The Netherlands
John Mylopoulos
  University of Trento, Italy
Michael Rosemann
  Queensland University of Technology, Brisbane, Qld, Australia
Michael J. Shaw
  University of Illinois, Urbana-Champaign, IL, USA
Clemens Szyperski
  Microsoft Research, Redmond, WA, USA

T0240724

Esther David   Christopher Kiekintveld
Valentin Robu   Onn Shehory
Sebastian Stein (Eds.)

Agent-Mediated Electronic Commerce

Designing Trading Strategies and Mechanisms for Electronic Markets

AMEC and TADA 2012
Valencia, Spain, June 4th, 2012
Revised Selected Papers

 Springer

Volume Editors

Esther David
Ashkelon Academic College
Department of Computer Science
Ashkelon, Israel
E-mail:
astrdod@acad.ash-college.ac.il

Valentin Robu
University of Southampton
School of Electronics
and Computer Science
Southampton, UK
E-mail: vr2@ecs.soton.ac.uk

Sebastian Stein
University of Southampton
School of Electronics
and Computer Science
Southampton, UK
E-mail: ss2@ecs.soton.ac.uk

Christopher Kiekintveld
University of Texas at El Paso
Department of Computer Science
El Paso, TX, USA
E-mail: cdkiekintveld@utep.edu

Onn Shehory
IBM Haifa Research Lab
Haifa, Israel
E-mail: onn@il.ibm.com

ISSN 1865-1348
ISBN 978-3-642-40863-2
DOI 10.1007/978-3-642-40864-9
Springer Heidelberg New York Dordrecht London

e-ISSN 1865-1356
e-ISBN 978-3-642-40864-9

Library of Congress Control Number: 2013947195

Typesetting: Camera-ready by author, data conversion by Scientific Publishing Services, Chennai, India

Printed on acid-free paper

Springer is part of Springer Science+Business Media (www.springer.com)

AMEC/TADA 2012 Preface

The last few decades have seen a rapid development and widespread proliferation of electronic commerce. Advances in technology and increasingly ubiquitous connectivity allow businesses to perform transactions both with customers and with each other electronically, leading to ever faster and more efficient business processes. The far-reaching consequences of this shift in commerce are evidenced by the multitude of businesses that offer their goods and services through virtual shopfronts on the Internet, by the large-scale adoption of business-to-business (B2B) standards and systems, and by the rise of electronic marketplaces that connect buyers and sellers, facilitating the exchange of goods or the placement of online advertising.

In tandem with the development of electronic commerce, new autonomous software components have also started to emerge, which participate in electronic marketplaces on behalf of organizations or individuals. These so-called software or trading agents interact autonomously and proactively with electronic markets to meet the objectives of their owners, for example, by placing orders to replenish stocks within complex supply chains, buying and selling stocks for profit, or managing online advertising campaigns by bidding for ad placements on popular websites. Such agents are capable of handling and analyzing vast amounts of data, and can respond almost instantaneously to changing market conditions or operating constraints. Thus, they promise great improvements in efficiency over relying solely on human-mediated commerce.

Yet, a shift toward an increasing reliance on software agents creates a range of pressing new research challenges. These include the design of appropriate agent decision algorithms, approaches to predict the complex behaviors and interactions of multiple agents, including the computation of equilibria, and the engineering of protocols and mechanisms that ensure electronic markets behave in a stable manner or fulfil other desirable criteria. Drawing upon a diverse range of scientific disciplines, including computer science, economics, artificial intelligence, operations research and game theory, researchers have started to address some of these challenges, and the papers collected in this volume represent a cross-section of this work. They are revised and extended versions of papers first presented in 2012 at the Joint Workshop on Trading Agent Design and Analysis (TADA) and Agent-Mediated Electronic Commerce (AMEC), which was co-located with the AAMAS 2012 conference held in Valencia, Spain.

Specifically, the papers collected here cover a broad range of topics within the field of electronic markets, ranging from designing strategies for individual trading agents, to the design of markets and interaction protocols between agents, as well as a variety of applications.

The first paper, by Chapman et al., investigates the impact that social networks have on the performance of market traders and shows that communities of traders that share advice with each other can perform better, and indeed improve the overall market performance. The next two papers deal with the design of efficient trading strategies for single agents. Chatzidimitriou et al. use machine learning algorithms to design efficient trading strategies for an agent operating in an automated supply chain, and show that these allow the agent to respond to prevailing market conditions. Diamantopoulos et al. also consider trading agents, but in the energy domain, an emerging application area for autonomous agents. They consider the problem of designing broker agents within power markets, and discuss the advantages and disadvantages of various price formation policies.

Goff et al. describe a framework that allows the simulation of complex market settings, where not only multiple types of agents compete with each other, but also where several market mechanisms co-exist. In the context of energy markets, Haghpanah et al. focus on how consumers can exchange their experiences with different brokers and merge this with their personal preferences and observations to choose the best broker. While most work so far in this volume has focused on traditional electronic commerce settings, Jumadinova and Dasgupta consider the problem of fusing information within sensor networks. Here, they show that work on prediction markets can be applied to incentivize truthful reporting when sensors may be self-interested.

As many markets contain human participants, Kim et al. study settings where market participants do not behave rationally, and where an agent needs to conform to certain norms in order to perform well. For these settings, they design a software agent that performs better than human participants. In contrast, Papakonstantinou and Bogetoft take a more traditional view of rationality, and extend existing auction mechanisms to a multi-dimensional setting, where a seller of goods is incentivized to truthfully report both the cost of production as well as the quality of the goods.

Finally, several papers discuss applications within the topical domain of ad auctions. Schain et al. investigate how a simple model-free agent can be built that requires little domain-specific knowledge to achieve a high performance comparable to agents that use more specialized and tailored models. To encourage further research on the complexities of ad auctions, Schain and Mansour propose a new competition specifically for tackling the challenges faced by ad networks that have multiple contracts with advertisers and bid on their behalf on ad exchanges. Stavrogiannis et al. also consider ad networks, but focus on the problem arising when an advertiser needs to decide what ad network to participate in, and they characterize the equilibria that arise in these settings.

We hope that these papers offer readers a comprehensive summary of the state of the art in research on electronic markets. We would like to thank everyone who contributed to this volume, including the paper authors, the members of the Program Committee, who provided comprehensive reviews to ensure a high standard of quality for the selected papers, and the workshop participants, who engaged in lively discussions during the workshop.

April 2013

Esther David
Christopher Kiekintveld
Valentin Robu
Onn Shehory
Sebastian Stein

Organization

TADA&AMEC Workshop Organizers

Esther David   Ashkelon Academic College, Israel
Christopher Kiekintveld   University of Texas at El Paso, USA
Valentin Robu   University of Southampton, UK
Onn Shehory   IBM Haifa Research Lab, Israel
Sebastian Stein   University of Southampton, UK

Program Committee

Bo An   University of Southern California, USA
Sofia Ceppi   Politecnico di Milano, Italy
Michal Chalamish   Ashkelon Academic College, Israel
Maria Chli   Aston University, UK
John Collins   University of Minnesota, USA
Shaheen Fatima   Loughborough University, UK
Enrico Gerding   University of Southampton, UK
Maria Gini   University of Minnesota, USA
Amy Greenwald   Brown University, USA
Minghua He   Aston University, UK
Patrick Jordan   University of Michigan, USA
Radu Jurca   Google Inc., Switzerland
Wolfgang Ketter   Erasmus University, The Netherlands
Jérôme Lang   LAMSADE, France
Kate Larson   University of Waterloo, Canada
Peter McBurney   King's College London, UK
Pericles Mitkas   Aristotle University of Thessaloniki, Greece
Jinzhong Niu   CUNY, USA
David Pardoe   University of Texas, USA
Zinovi Rabinovich   Bar-Ilan University, Israel
Juan Antonio Rodriguez
  Aguilar   IIIA-CSIC, Spain
Harry Rose   University of Southampton, UK
Jeffrey Rosenschein   The Hebrew University of Jerusalem, Israel
Alberto Sardinha   Instituto Superior Técnico, Portugal
David Sarne   Bar-Ilan University, Israel
Lampros C. Stavrogiannis   University of Southampton, UK
Andreas Symeonidis   Aristotle University of Thessaloniki, Greece
Ioannis Vetsikas   NCSR Demokritos, Greece
Michael Wellman   University of Michigan, USA
Dongmo Zhang   University of Western Sydney, Australia

Table of Contents

Social Networking and Information Diffusion in Automated Markets

Martin Chapman[1], Gareth Tyson[1], Katie Atkinson[2],
Michael Luck[1], and Peter McBurney[1]

[1] Department of Informatics, King's College London, Strand, London, UK
{martin.chapman,gareth.tyson,michael.luck,peter.mcburney}@kcl.ac.uk
[2] Department of Computer Science, University of Liverpool, UK
katie@liverpool.ac.uk

Abstract. To what extent do networks of influence between market traders impact upon their individual performance and the performance of the specialists in which they operate? Such a question underpins the content of this study, as an investigation is conducted using the JCAT double auction market simulation platform, developed as a part of the CAT Market Design Tournament. Modifications to the JCAT platform allow for influential networks to be established between traders, across which they transmit information about their trading experiences to their connected peers. Receiving traders then use this information (which is the product of an n-armed bandit selection algorithm) to guide their own selection of market specialist and trading strategy. These modifications give rise to a sequence of experimental tests, the documented results of which provide an answer to the question phrased above. Analysis of the results shows the benefits of taking advice as a collective and demonstrates the properties of the communities which emerge as a result of engaging in widespread social contact.

Keywords: JCAT, CAT, agent-based trading, social networking, agent-based simulation, automated trading.

1 Introduction

Empirical ethnographies of financial trading firms and hedge funds have shown that traders are typically influenced by other people when making trading decisions or deciding strategies, e.g. [1,6]. These others may be fellow employees or superiors of the same company, or outsiders, including direct competitors, passing on tips or advice. If such interactions only happened once, one could imagine that they would be subject to manipulation by the advice-giver, for example, talking up the value of a company stock in which the advice giver has an undisclosed stake. But most participants in financial markets interact with one another repeatedly, and known manipulators risk being shunned in future interactions, and thus losing opportunities to receive future information. From an evolutionary game theory perspective, then, it makes sense even for

E. David et al. (Eds.): AMEC/TADA 2012, LNBIP 136, pp. 1–15, 2013.

self-interested utility-maximizing participants to be honest in these interactions, even with the provision of information to competitors.

While there has been considerable attention paid in recent years to modelling social influences on trading behaviours, dating back at least to [10], few researchers have considered trader interactions in a context where traders may choose between competing marketplaces. The only work we know is by Dumesny et. al [3], which considers how traders may detect deceptive information received from others in their social networks by means of a trust model. Our focus is different. We are concerned here with two key research questions:

- To what extent, if any, does reliance on a social network improve trader performance?
- To what extent, if any, does trader performance depend on the topology of the social network of traders?

The answers to these questions are not necessarily obvious or straightforward. For example, although it may seem that the network topology would be important for trader performance, a simulation study of adoption decisions for new information technology found that business network topologies had little influence on overall adoption patterns in some circumstances [12].

To explore these two questions, we modified the JCAT platform, a simulation platform for agent-based trading in competing markets[1], to allow for social networking between traders. Specifically, we integrated a set of algorithms that allow autonomous software traders to dynamically receive, reconcile, and judge advice from each other before deciding where to trade and what to quote. Through these modifications, we explored the impact of sharing historical information regarding strategies on trader performance. Following the modifications, we then performed a comprehensive set of computer simulations, looking at several metrics relevant to our research questions.

This paper is structured as follows. Section 2 first presents some background information on the operation of the CAT Market Design Tournament, the platform of which our study is based. Following this, in Section 3, we present the core algorithms used to integrate social awareness into our traders. Section 4 then describes the design of the simulation experiments undertaken using the modified platform, with the key results arising from these simulations being presented in Section 5. Finally, Section 6 concludes the paper with a brief discussion of possible future work.

2   The CAT Tournament

The CAT Market Design Tournament is an international competition established to promote research into automated and adaptive market mechanism design. JCAT was created in 2006 by a team from the Universities of Liverpool and Southampton, UK, and Brooklyn College, USA, to support the Tournament,

---

[1] See http://jcat.sourceforge.net/

which has been held annually since 2007.[2] Entrants to the competition design and implement software entities, called *specialists*, which operate as matchmakers between automated software traders. Specialists are competing marketplaces, in the same way that, say, the New York Stock Exchange, NASDAQ, the Paris Bourse, etc, are all competing markets. The traders are adaptive software agents provided by the Tournament organisers, which buy or sell a single generic commodity. Each trading day, each trader first selects a specialist to trade through on that day, and then decides what level of shout to bid or ask in that specialist. For the shout decision, each trader is endowed with one of four standard automated trading strategies.[3] For the research reported in this paper, only one trading strategy was used, namely an implementation of the Gjerstad and Dickhaut algorithm [5], choosing an offer based on an estimation of utility.

Each trading day in the CAT Tournament begins with specialists deciding on and posting their fee levels for all traders to see. The fee structure and fee levels inform the traders' decisions as to which specialist to select that day. Entrants to the Tournament are scored on three equally-weighted criteria each trading day: share of all profits earnt by specialists that day; share of traders attracted to their marketplace that day; and the specialist's transaction success rate, which is the percentage of traders that were successfully matched with counter-parties by the specialist. These daily scores are summed over the Tournament, with the winner being that specialist having the highest cumulative score across all scored days. There is a growing literature on the strategies of specialists, for example, [14,16,18], and on how traders may best choose between competing markets, e.g., [4,13].

3   Enabling Social Interaction between Autonomous Entities

3.1   Overview

In accordance with the apparent benefits of social connection presented above, this section presents several novel approaches to communication in a multi-agent system such as the JCAT platform.

Although conceptually social interaction can simply be understood by means of point to point connection, in practice, achieving worthwhile cross-entity communication is a multi-tiered process. First, traders must obtain the information to share; in the context of competing marketplaces, one would imagine the most sought after information to be the relative benefits of trading within each environment itself. With this in mind, our social entities exchange opinions on their historical strategies; that is, how well, in retrospect, their previous day's strategy caused them to perform with their last specialist. This includes their specialist choice and the exchange of a finer granularity of information, namely trading techniques themselves or the precise formation of market shouts.

---

[2] See www.marketbasedcontrol.com

[3] See [2] for details of these strategies.

Our social networks are established as restricted static subsets of the trading body, defined under the syntax of an adjacency matrix. This static nature is representative of a typical trading social network in which information will only be exchanged between previously known trusted parties. Once each trader is aware of their connected peers, a specific algorithm is employed to assess any potentially conflicting advice, the product of which is a recommendation for the invoking trader based on the opinions of the peer most likely to produce success via imitation.

As a final step to the information exchange process — employing advice — traders choose whether to use the experience of their peers with a given probability T, their own strategy at GD, or make a random selection at R. These probabilities are defined according to a given mentality or *profile*; credulous, sceptical or non-bias. The fact that traders therefore do not simply take advice verbatim, produces a secondary logical topology within which edges represent the transfer of advice.

Once advice is taken and a profit (or otherwise) made as a result of using it, our approach attributes this gain back to the original purveyor of the advice as (a surrogate for) utility in order to establish a subset of agents providing the strongest advice. Hence the intention is to develop a system which facilitates the comparison of conflicting advice and attempts to establish those traders with whom others are most likely to *correlate*. That is, those traders whose advice is most generalisable to an individual agent.

3.2   Trader Experiences as the Precursor to Giving Advice

Before traders can actively direct one another towards particular specialists they first need to be endowed with the ability to gauge their own historical performance. In order to capture this notion of personal experience, traders are given a specific success metric; that of trading above a proportion of their given trade entitlement within a particular specialist. If traders are able to transact above specifically half of their trade entitlement, they deem their experiences positive; if they can only attain a level below this threshold, their experiences are negative. The code below specifies the operation of such a procedure:

```
program traderExperience (TransactionExecutedEvent)
var
   seller = SellerObject
   buyer = BuyerObject
begin
   numBuyerMatches = numBuyerMatches + 1
   numSellerMatches = numSellerMatches + 1

   if numTraderMatches(buyer) >
```

```
          buyer.tradeEntitlements() / 2 then
            buyer.setExperience(true)
          else if numTraderMatches(seller) >
          seller.tradeEntitlements() / 2 then
            seller.setExperience(true)
        end if
      end
```

Based on an event-driven architecture, this code stores the details of the buyer and seller traders involved in this transaction and sets their *rating* of the specialist in which they are transacting according to how many overall matches they obtain. This rating is based upon a buyer or seller being able to match half of its entitled trade units.

With this system in place, the potential to exchange such information becomes apparent. Using a variant upon existing mechanisms, the code below seeks to select a fellow trader who, itself, holds an informed historical opinion on how beneficial its previous actions have been. Alongside this, the set of available traders is limited to a fixed social subset using the information contained in an adjacency matrix, thus restricting the body of entities from whom advice is available. Such a state of affairs is analogous to real world scenarios, in which individuals tend to hold core social groups.

```
program giveAdvice (traderId)
var
   row[] = AdjacencyMatrix(traderId)
   {Store this trader's row from the adjacency matrix.}
   linkedTraders<integer> = a new array of integers
begin
   for i = 0 to row.length
     if ValueInCell = 1
       linkedTraders += i
       {If the value in the matrix is a 1 (they are linked),
       store the trader at that position as a potential
       trader to receive advice from.}
     end if
   end for

recommendedTraderId = adviceTaken(linkedTraders)
{Taking a list of linkedTraders, store one of these traders
as the trader to take advice from.}

referrer = recommendedTraderId
referee = traderId
referee.setReferrer(referrer)
```

```
if adviceTaken = null
  return Error
else
  return recommendation = History.get(formalTraderIds
  .get(recommendedTraderId)), experience.
  {Return the historical record of the linked trader
  recommended and an opinion on the merit of this
  choice, to the invoking trader.}
endif
end
```

In practice, this algorithm consists of two key parts. The first establishes those traders with whom the invoking agent is linked. Note that the social channels provided by these links are static. The second selects a trader from whom to take information and returns this information as a *recommendation* after storing a record of the exchange. This second algorithm contributes to a dynamic 'logical' topology, which represents the flow of good advice between agents taking place over the underlying static social topology. The content of a recommendation is either a <market, advice> pair or a <shout, advice> pair; where to trade and how to trade respectively.

3.3   Correlation System and *n*-Armed Bandit

Expanding upon this notion of trader selection mentioned above, the next stage in achieving social interaction involves solving the conflicts apparent in the resolution of the recommendedTraderId. Although the presented code abstractly selects an advising trader, with a trader being open to an *n*ary number of connections, the potential for conflicting experiences is high. This presents the need for a specific selection technique. Whilst the possibility of majority voting could be a device considered, a mechanism which weights traders according to a given metric would provide a more accurate choice. The statistical *n*-armed bandit approach provides an efficient solution in this case [17]. Using existing platform mechanisms, we employ a technique which attributes to each possibility (each 'advisor') utility gain estimates based on previous results, and approaches a decision amongst these utilities in a greedy manner; that is to say, a *greedy* strategy is employed which consistently *exploits* the highest estimate as opposed to *exploring*. We express the pure greedy strategy as follows:

$$Q_t(a^*) = max_q Q_t(a) \tag{1}$$

whereby $Q_t(a)$ is any given play (choice) and $a*$ is the chosen greedy action.

Despite the classification of this strategy as greedy, it does introduce a factor *epsilon* (ϵ) by which a random option may be explored thus classifying it as ϵ-*greedy*. In this way, at times, such an algorithm may make an explorative decision based upon an unexpected *play*.

In addition to this, we also establish the notion of *potential correlation* as an input into the n-armed decision process. Extracting profit from the previously self-contained records of each trader, we attribute it back to the advising trader upon whose advice this trader is currently acting. The success of others using an advising trader's advice is therefore attributed back to that specific advising agent and seen to be indicative of how transferable one trader's actions are to the rest of its social subset.

4   Experimental Setup

To study the effects of the above techniques on an agent populous, we implemented them into the JCAT platform and ran of series of full, local CAT game simulations. To vary our experimental state, for each network topology and trader type, we ran 5 of these simulations, creating 80 in total.

4.1   Traders

For the purposes of our experiments, we chose a sample size of 20 trading agents with *types* applied uniformly across the population. This size we felt was justifiable in relation to the standard number of traders in a normal JCAT simulation. Types we define to be of three specific categories, each denoting how a trader approaches social interaction. **Credulous** traders are susceptible to the advice of others and almost always willing to act on it; **sceptical** traders are unlikely to take the advice of others and more trusting of their inherent strategies, and **non-bias** traders are equally as likely to take advice as to ignore it. Theoretically, we define these through the variable probability $P[T \cup GD \cup R\,]$; taking advice, using an inherent strategy and using a random strategy respectively. Table 1 formalises this probability distribution whilst the code below presents an implementation:

```
program marketChoice (P[T], P[GD], P[R])
var
   rand = (Distribution.nextRandom())
   courseOfAction = null
begin
   if rand <= P[R] then
     courseOfAction = R
   else if P[R] > rand <= P[GD] then
     courseOfAction = GD
   else if P[GD] > random <= 1.0 then
     courseOfAction = T
   else
     Error
   end if
end
```

Table 1. Trader profiles

Action / Profile	Non-bias	Sceptical	Credulous
Use networked trader advice	49%	4%	94%
Use underlying strategy	49%	94%	4%
Select a random specialist	2%	2%	2%

4.2   Social Networks

In addition to the above, we implemented five standard static network structures within which our traders operate: random, fully connected, small-world [9], ring and hierarchical, whilst holding the use of no social network as a control benchmark. As discussed, these networks were simulated under the formation of adjacency matrix files and varied in co-ordination with the trader types above to provide more insightful analysis into the impact of social structures.

4.3   Specialists

Our trader population was provided with access to four specialists within our simulations, three of which were successful entrants to previous real games, namely jackaroo (Winner 2009), PersianCAT (Winner 2008), and PoleCAT (Standard entrant, 2010)[4]. The final specialist, MetroCAT, we describe as experimental as it was engineered for research based on an intimate knowledge of the game structure.

4.4   Measures

Although a large number of response variables were recorded from our simulations those most pertinent to the subsequent analysis are listed in Table 2.

Table 2. Recorded variables

Metric	Description
Trader Profit	The difference between a trader's valuation and the amount centrally paid or received.
Specialist Profit	Profit from all fees charged that trading day.
Advice taken and from whom	A record, for each trader, of who they are taking advice from across a given period.

Notably, variables were to be recorded on average per trader (or specialist), per day and then per game using the following metric:

---

[4] Retrieved from http://www.sics.se/tac/showagents.php

$$\sum_{t=1}^{d} \frac{(\sum_{i=1}^{n} (\sum_{j=1}^{k} m_t^i(j)))}{n} \tag{2}$$

in which we record a moving average for a group of traders t, for our simulations, over a particular metric m, across the 30 trading days, d, of a simulation.

5   Results

5.1   Trader and Market Performance

The histograms in Figures 1 and 2 demonstrate the differences in aggregate trader and aggregate market profit that arose between the configured simulation environment with its realised social extensions and the environment without. Here, profit is used as the dominant indicator of both trader and specialist performance.

Figure 1 shows the comparative profits of traders who communicate and are able to use each other's advice, against the profits of those traders who work independently. Similarly, Figure 2 depicts the ability of specialists to make a profit, again, when traders work together and when they work alone. Depicted on the far right of both graphs are the profits made when no networking strategy is used (traders are independent). Immediately, one can observe that a much lower profit level is obtained for both the traders and the markets in which they trade when advice is not available.

Using this information and returning to the focus of our original research questions, it can be stated that, indeed, social influence has an impact on both the performance of the autonomous traders within the platform and the markets in which they transact. The extent of this impact is so positive that it creates a marked statistical difference in the financial performance of both these entities within the simulation environment (c.f. Table 3).

Table 3. Statistical Test of Difference of mean values over the metric given in (2)

Measure	Informed Social Strategy	No Social Network
Mean	29.60	21.96
Variance	90.25	44.80
Standard Deviation	9.50	6.69
Mean Difference	7.64	
Standard Error of Difference	1.34	
Degrees of Freedom	148	
t-statistic	5.70	
p-value	< 0.001	

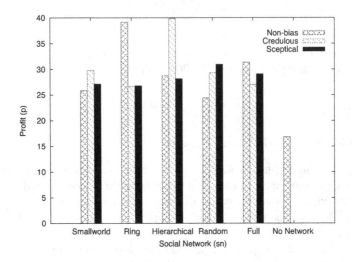

Fig. 1. How aggregate trader profits are affected by the introduction of social networking. Social traders are displayed by type, grouped by network and compared to traders who operate with no social network.

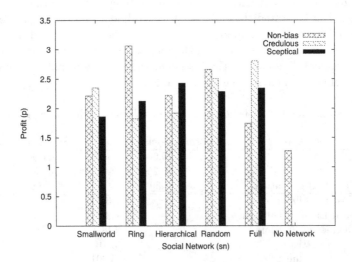

Fig. 2. How aggregate market profits are affected by the introduction of social networking

Intuitively, given the *giveAdvice* code in Section 3.2, this state of affairs makes sense. If trader T has access to $max\{T'_0 \ldots T'_n\}$ whereby each member of this set is a trader from T's network marked with a utility value representing their correlation to the rest of their social circles, then (assuming advice is taken) one would expect T's strategy to be optimal. In other words, having access to the experiences of others clearly allows traders to combine more informed market and shout choices, and thus potentially make a higher profit. In turn, due to the fee setup of a CAT game [2], the by-product of this is that specialists may also make a higher profit as they attain a greater portion of higher transaction levels.

However, we do make further comment on the differences in profit between traders and specialists, particularly under the hierarchical network. This seems to suggest some conflict of interest in both the gain and retention of profit within the market paradigm; when traders succeed, the level of profit made by specialists is reduced dramatically. By framing specialists and traders as conflicting agents, such a state of affairs makes sense. This is a beneficial result in context, as the focus of a CAT tournament is to increase the complexity of automated markets and the challenges they face in becoming successful entities. Therefore, by increasing the capabilities of agents, we change the dynamics of the market place, and so increase this challenge by forcing specialists to adapt.

5.2   Clustering, Hubs and Minority Powers

By focussing on our agents as a group of intelligent social entities, we can make some comment on their patterns of behaviour as a collective. Although the initial network structures used in our platform are static and thus the communication channels open to individual traders fixed, due to the utilisation of our correlation system, the formation of virtual network clusters around certain trader individuals can be noted. In other words, if one imagines the utilisation of an advice channel as the formation of a secondary network edge superimposed onto an existing one, the clustering coefficients of some of the individual agents become orthogonal to the others. An exemplary logical topology can be seen in Figure 3.

We describe these very 'popular' individuals (e.g. buyerGD7 in Figure 3) as *opinion leaders* [11] or power nodes, as their high level of connectivity makes a significant and, by the notion of preferential attachment, growing subset of the trader population, highly susceptible to their recommendations. Whether this almost reputation-like by-product of introducing utility as a measure of correlation is positive or not, is obviously therefore dependent on whether entities quote their historical results truthfully. Although, in our model the danger of traders purporting their poor performance as copyable (effectively lying) is not a possibility[5], injecting this potential into the network could be an interesting focus of future work. Such work is likely to be grounded in the trust and reputation literature, e.g. [7].

---

[5] Hence using static trusted social networks.

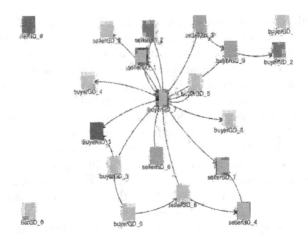

Fig. 3. The typical attraction of traders to specific local hubs. Here, *buyerGD7* has been weighted significantly by our matching algorithm and thus is highly connected in the logical topology. Traders are coloured according to market selection.

Despite the apparent influence of a small number of nodes in a network, Figure 4 tells us that in fact this dominant position does bring with it a large amount of volatility. Plotting each trader against the number of socially linked colleagues taking their advice, we can observe the fluctuations in the most reputable trader to be huge, as the consensus as to whom it is best to take advice from continuously shifts. Whilst traders seem to be easily admitted into their social hubs, the length of time they spend in such a role is notably limited.

We attribute the changeability of leadership in our networks to the minority power phenomenon [8] whereby opinions of a few eventually have a large effect on the majority. The behaviour of these outliers [19] is usually tangential to the performance of the opinion leaders and thus we observe a constant contest for influence in the network. The performance of these outliers and their influence is therefore not necessarily negligible as we observe consistently high profit levels throughout our simulations. It would appear therefore that, in fact, exploring away from the consensus of the collective is altruistically beneficial.

5.3   Initial Insights on the Importance of Topology

Our second research question brings us into a discussion about the relative importance of the underlying topology employed to facilitate social interaction. Interestingly, it can be observed that, in our simulations, topology actually has little effect on the ability for traders to disseminate advice (c.f. Figure 5). On the one hand, it is possible to attribute this to the limited size of the simulations.[6] However, we believe these results allow us to tentatively state that, in accordance with [12], topology is not a critical factor in the transfer of advice.

---

[6] With simulations of 20 nodes, in practice, information dissemination can occur quickly over any topology.

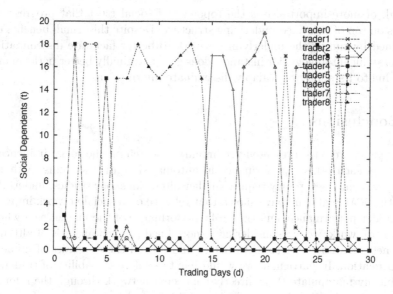

Fig. 4. A graphical representation of the tumultuous 'reign' of (a subset of) individual traders. Interestingly the choice of whom to take advice from seems to be restricted to an individual reputable group. *Game State: fully-connected, credulous.*

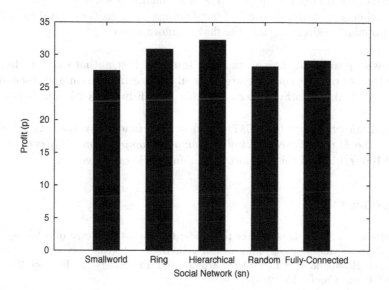

Fig. 5. The varying profit levels of traders exhibited between different **network topologies**

Instead, of more importance is the topology of social trust that progressively evolves on top of this fixed underlying structure. Despite this, small benefits can be gained by tuning the underlying network to better facilitate dissemination; the hierarchical topology, for instance, does gain marginally better performance, likely due to its ability to scalably disseminate information.

6   Conclusions

In this paper we have presented preliminary research on the social influence of traders on each other's performance in automated trading systems. Although our experimental setup may require further alterations, our studies, undertaken using the JCAT platform, have shown that reliance on a social network improves both trader performance, and the profit performance of the market as a whole.

In future work, we are considering a more fined grained analysis of alternate social network topologies so as to better understand the dynamics of influence and correlation. In particular, we would like to explore the ability of traders to dynamically manipulate their directly-connected network through the information passed to it (thereby, introducing the potential for receiving information through new non-trusted agents). A related topic of interest is the extent to which social networks of traders facilitate or inhibit the co-evolution of segmentation that we have observed in CAT games and elsewhere, as traders and specialists co-self-organise into clusters or segments, discussed, for example, in [15]. Further, to expand on some of our findings, we consider it vital to look at larger population sizes to study the flow of information.

Acknowledgements. This work arose from the first author's dissertation at the University of Liverpool. We are grateful for assistance from and discussions with Guan Gui, Timothy Miller, Jinzhong Niu, Edward Robinson and Rahul Savani.

The development of the JCAT platform was funded by the UK EPSRC, through the *Market Based Control of Complex Computational Systems* project (GR/T10657/01) and this support is gratefully acknowledged.

References

1. Beunza, D., Stark, D.: Tools of the trade: the socio-technology of arbitrage in a Wall Street trading room. In: Pinch, T., Swedborg, R. (eds.) Living in a Material World: Economic Sociology Meets Science and Technology Studies, pp. 253–290. MIT Press, Cambridge (2008)
2. Cai, K., Gerding, E., McBurney, P., Niu, J., Parsons, S., Phelps, S.: Overview of CAT: A market design competition (version 2.0), Technical Report ULCS-09-005, Department of Computer Science, University of Liverpool, Liverpool, UK (2009)
3. Dumesny, J., Miller, T., Kirley, M., Sonenberg, L.: TATM: A trust mechanism for social traders in double auctions. In: Wang, D., Reynolds, M. (eds.) AI 2011. LNCS (LNAI), vol. 7106, pp. 402–411. Springer, Heidelberg (2011)

4. Ganchev, K., Nevmyvaka, Y., Kearns, M., Wortman Vaughan, J.: Censored exploration and the Dark Pool Problem. Communications of the ACM 53(5), 99–107 (2010)

5. Gjerstad, S., Dickhaut, J.: Price formation in double auctions. Games and Econic Behaviour 22, 1–29 (1998)

6. Hardie, I., MacKenzie, D.: Assembling an economic actor: the agencement of a Hedge Fund. The Sociological Review 55(1), 57–80 (2007)

7. Huynh, T.D., Jennings, N.R., Shadbolt, N.R.: Fire: An integrated trust and reputation model for open multi-agent systems. In: ECAI, vol. 16, pp. 18–22 (2004)

8. Kearns, M., Judd, S., Tan, J., Wortman, J.: Behavioral experiments on biased voting in networks. Proceedings of the National Academy of Sciences of the United States of America 106(5), 1347–1352 (2009)

9. Kleinberg, J.M.: Navigation in a small world. Nature 406(2), 845 (2000)

10. Lux, T.: Herd behaviour, bubbles and crashes. The Economic Journal 105(431), 881–896 (1995)

11. Mahdi, K., Torabi, S., Safar, M.: Diffusion and Reverse Diffusion Processes in Social Networks: Analysis using the Degree of Diffusion alpha. In: Proceedings of the 3rd IEEE International Conference on Ubi-media Computing, U-Media (US) (May 2010)

12. McKean, J., Shorter, H., Luck, M., McBurney, P., Willmott, S.: Technology diffusion: the case of agent technologies. AAMAS 17(3), 372–396 (2008)

13. Miller, T., Niu, J.: An assessment of strategies for choosing between competitive marketplaces. Electronic-Commerce Research and Applications 11(1), 14–23 (2012)

14. Niu, J., Cai, K., Parsons, S., McBurney, P., Gerding, E.: What the 2007 TAC Market Design Game tells us about effective auction mechanisms. AAMAS 21(2), 172–203 (2010)

15. Robinson, E., McBurney, P., Yao, X.: Market niching in multi-attribute computational resource allocation systems. In: Kettler, W., Lang, K.R., Lee, K.J. (eds.) Proceedings of the 13th International Conference on Electronic Commerce (ICEC 2011), Liverpool (August 2011)

16. Shi, B., Gerding, E., Vytelingum, P., Jennings, N.: An equilibrium analysis of market selection strategies and fee strategies in competing double auction marketplaces. Journal of Autonomous Agents and Multi-Agent Systems 26(2), 245–287 (2013)

17. Sutton, R.S., Barto, A.G.: An n-armed bandit problem. In: Reinforcement Learning: An Introduction (Bradford, ed.), pp. 2.1–2.2. The MIT Press, Cambridge (2005)

18. Vytelingum, P., Vetsikas, I.A., Shi, B., Jennings, N.R.: IAMwildCAT: The winning strategy for the TAC Market Design Competition. In: Proceedings of 18th European Conference on Artificial Intelligence, Patras, Greece, pp. 428–434 (2008)

19. Zhou, J., Zhou, C., Wang, J., Qi, L., Huang, W.: Detection of clusters and outlying nodes in spatial networks. In: Geoinfomatics 2008 and Joint Conference on GIS Built Environment, vol. 7147(1), pp. 1–8 (2008)

Policy Search through Adaptive Function Approximation for Bidding in TAC SCM

Kyriakos C. Chatzidimitriou[1,2],
Andreas L. Symeonidis[1,2], and Pericles A. Mitkas[1,2]

[1] Department of Electrical and Computer Engineering,
Aristotle University of Thessaloniki, Greece
[2] Informatics and Telematics Institute,
Centre for Research and Technology Hellas, Greece
mertacor@olympus.ee.auth.gr

Abstract. Agent autonomy is strongly related to learning and adaptation. Machine learning models generated through the use of historical data or current environmental signals, provide agents with the necessary decision-making and generalization capabilities in competitive, dynamic, partially observable and stochastic environments. In this work, we discuss learning and adaptation in the context of the TAC SCM game. We apply a variety of machine learning and computational intelligence methods for generating the most efficient sales component of the agent, dealing with customer orders and production throughput. Along with utility maximization and bid acceptance probability estimation methods, we evaluate regression trees, particle swarm optimization, heuristic control and policy search via adaptive function approximation in order to build an efficient, near-real time, bidding mechanism. Results indicate that a suitable reinforcement learning setup coupled with the power of adaptive function approximation techniques is a good candidate for enabling high performance strategies.

Keywords: adaptive function approximation, trading agent competition, supply chain management, echo state networks, neuroevolution of augmented reservoirs.

1 Introduction

An agent in the trading agent competition (TAC) supply chain management (SCM) game should follow the rule: *"An agent should sell as high as possible and buy as low as possible, while maintaining the highest possible throughput in both factory and inventory (and by throughput we mean to have a high factory utilization, but also sell the produced personal computers and not just store them) and not default on deliveries"* [1]. Based on this context, we focus on the selling and throughput aspects of the agent, in order to improve performance. We thoroughly investigate the daily task of selecting the requests-for-quote to respond to and the prices to offer, given the limited amount of time (near real-time) and bounded resources, and try to provide an optimal decision making solution.

E. David et al. (Eds.): AMEC/TADA 2012, LNBIP 136, pp. 16–29, 2013.
© Springer-Verlag Berlin Heidelberg 2013

Additionally, within the context of our work we perform adaptive function approximation methodology through neuroevolution of augmented reservoirs (NEAR), in order to adapt the architecture and the parameters of the function approximator to the problem at hand, with little or no human input [2]. We form the selling problem as a standard reinforcement learning [3] control problem and let NEAR find an appropriate policy in the form of an echo-state network (ESN). For evaluation purposes, we benchmark RL approach against machine learning, particle swarm optimization and heuristic control techniques.

The paper is structured as follows: Section 2 provides a rough introduction into TAC SCM game and NEAR. Section 3 discusses the different methods used to approach the problem along with related work for each method. Section 4 presents the experimental setup and the results obtained, along with a brief discussion. Finally, Section 5 summarizes findings and concludes the paper.

2   Background

2.1   TAC SCM

Within the scenario of the TAC SCM game [4,5], each agent participating represents a personal computer manufacturer with limited production capacity. Six such agents compete in selling 16 different types of PCs to potential customers. The agents' tasks are to negotiate on supply contracts, bid for customer orders, manage daily assembly activities and ship completed orders to customers. Every day, customers send Request-For-Quote (RFQ) messages and agents bid on them, depending on their ability to satisfy delivery dates and prices. Bid should not exceed the reserve price the customer requires. The next day, the customer orders from the agent that made the winning offer. The agent must deliver the products on time, otherwise it is charged with a penalty. Winner is declared the agent with the greater bank balance at the end of the game. Game length is 220 simulated days, with each day lasting 15 seconds.

2.2   Echo State Networks

The idea behind *reservoir computing* (RC) and in particular ESNs [6] is that a random *recurrent neural network* (RNN), created under certain algebraic constraints, could be driven by an input signal to create a rich set of dynamics in its reservoir of neurons, forming non-linear response signals. These signals, along with the input signals, could be combined to form the so-called *read-out function*, $y = \mathbf{w}^T \cdot \phi(\mathbf{x})$, which is a linear combination of features and constitutes the prediction of the desired output signal, given that the weights, w, are trained accordingly.

A basic form of an ESN is presented in Figure 1. The reservoir consists of a layer of K input units, connected to N reservoir units through an $N \times K$ weighted connection matrix W^{in}. The connection matrix of the reservoir, W, is an $N \times N$ matrix. Optionally, an $N \times L$ backprojection matrix W^{back} could be employed, where L is the number of output units, connecting the outputs back to the reservoir neurons. Input units' (linear features) and reservoir units' (non-linear features) weights are defined in an $L \times (K + N)$ matrix, W^{out}.

Based on existing literature, the following rules should hold when creating ESNs and the respective matrices W^{in}, W and W^{back}. Briefly, these are: (i) W should be sparse, (ii) the mean value of weights should be around zero, (iii) N should be large enough to introduce more features for better prediction performance, (iv) the spectral radius, ρ, of W should be ≤ 1 to practically (and not theoretically) ensure that the network will be able to function as an ESN. Finally, a weak uniform white noise term can be added to the features for stability reasons. A detailed discussion on ESNs best practices can be found in [6].

In this work, we consider discrete time models and ESNs without backprojection connections. In addition, for the current implementation, the reservoir units employ $f(x) = tanh(x)$ as an activation function, while the output units employ the sigmoid function $g(x) = \frac{1}{1+e^{a \cdot x}}$. We scale and shift the input signal, $\mathbf{u} \in \mathbb{R}^K$, depending on whether we want the network to work in the linear or the non-linear part of the sigmoid function. The reservoir feature vector, $\mathbf{x} \in \mathbb{R}^N$, is given by Equation 1:

$$\mathbf{x}(t+1) = \mathbf{f}(\mathbf{W}^{in}\mathbf{u}(t+1) + \mathbf{W}\mathbf{x}(t) + \mathbf{v}(t+1)) \qquad (1)$$

where $\mathbf{f}$ is the element-wise application of the reservoir activation function and $\mathbf{v}$ is a uniform white noise vector. The output, $\mathbf{y} \in \mathbb{R}^L$, is then given by Equation 2:

$$\mathbf{y}(t+1) = \mathbf{g}(\mathbf{W}^{out}[\mathbf{u}(t+1)|\mathbf{x}(t+1)]) \qquad (2)$$

where $\mathbf{g}$ is the element-wise application of the output activation function and $|$, the aggregation of vectors.

For RL tasks with K continuous states and L discrete actions, we can use an ESN to model a Q-value function, where each network output unit l, can be mapped to an action $a_l, l = 1 \ldots L$, with the network output value y_l denoting the long-term discounted value, $Q(\mathbf{s}, a_l)$ of performing action a_l, when the agent is at state $\mathbf{s}$. Given $g(x) = x$, this Q-value can be represented by an ESN as:

$$y_l = Q(\mathbf{s}, a_l) = \sum_{i=1}^{K} w_{li}^{out} s_i + \sum_{i=K+1}^{K+N} w_{li}^{out} x_{i-K}, l = 1, \ldots, L \qquad (3)$$

while actions can be chosen under the ϵ-greedy policy [3]. Linear Gradient Descent (GD) SARSA TD-learning can be used to adapt weights [3,7] but in this work the weights will be perturbed through evolutionary computation as a form of policy search.

2.3   NeuroEvolution of Augmented Reservoirs

NeuroEvolution of Augmented Topologies (NEAT) [8] is a topology and weight evolution algorithm for artificial neural networks, founded on four principles.

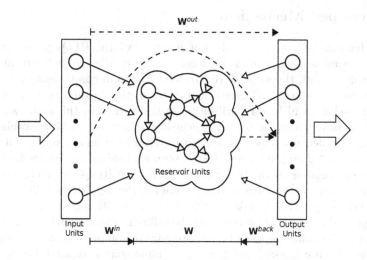

Fig. 1. A basic form of an ESN. Solid arrows represent fixed weights and dashed arrows adaptable weights.

First, the network, i.e. the phenotype, is encoded as a linear genome (genotype), making it memory efficient with respect to algorithms that work with full weight connection matrices. Secondly, NEAT employs the notion of *historical markings*, in order to annotate with innovation numbers, newly created connections. During crossover, NEAT aligns parent genomes by matching the innovation numbers and performs crossover on these matching genes (connections). The third principle is to protect innovation through *speciation*. Organisms are clustered into species in order to have time to optimize by competing only in their own niche. Last but not least, NEAT starts with minimal networks (networks with no hidden units), in order start with a minimal search space and to justify every complexification made in terms of fitness. NEAT complexifies networks through the application of structural mutations (adding nodes and connections), and further adapts the networks through weight mutation (perturbing or restarting weight values). These primitives can be employed in other NE settings also, in the form of a meta-search evolutionary procedure. In our case, we consider them to achieve efficient search in the space of ESNs.

NeuroEvolution of Augmented Reservoirs (NEAR) [9] further utilizes NEAT as a meta-search algorithm and adapts its four principles to the ESN model of neural networks. NEAR adapts the NEAT search algorithm mainly with respect to gene representation, crossover with historical markings, clustering and including some additional evolutionary operators related to ESNs. An important difference from NEAT is that both evolution and classic learning algorithms (least squares, temporal difference learning) can be employed in order to adapt networks to the problem at hand.

3   Developed Mechanism

The mechanism built aims to help the agent select the RFQs to bid on and the offers to make. Apart from the reserve price of the RFQs (more in TAC SCM specifications), the agent is constrained also from component availability and daily factory capacity. Nevertheless, focus of the current work is on optimizing the selling and factory utilization of the agent. To this end, two basic assumptions have been made: a) the agent has an infinite, on-time, availability of components, decoupling any procurement modules from our study and b) all algorithms will bid on the current RFQs, without holding any cycles for future orders. In competition mode, by generating predicted RFQs for future days [10] and adding them to the current RFQ portfolio, the algorithms will implicitly save the cycles by including fake, but more profitable RFQs.

The agent's bidding portfolio employs the utility maximization approach [10,1], due to the uncertainty imposed by the presence of competitors. Since, procurement strategies are ignored and thus costs minimization is not taken into account, utility is calculated based on revenue, rather than profit, without making any comparison between bidding mechanisms unfair. The RFQs are sorted based on the estimated utility, normalized over the product's required manufacturing cycles [11]:

$$Utility = \frac{P(offer = accepted|bid) \cdot BidPrice}{Cycles(Product)}. \tag{4}$$

In the developed mechanism, we have adopted the *partial order approach*, where we assume that we win a part of the order, proportional to the probability of acceptance at the given bid price [10]:

$$PartialCycles = P(offer = accepted|bid) \cdot Quantity \cdot Cycles(Product). \tag{5}$$

Even if one cannot win partial orders, the idea is that in the end, the total quantity of cycles won would be close to the total quantity of cycles won, if partial orders were available in the game.

The selected RFQs are the set:

$$SelectedRFQs = \{x \in RFQBundle| \sum PartialCycles(x) \leq 2000; \text{ and}$$
$$Utility(x) > Utility(y), y \notin SelectedRFQs\}. \tag{6}$$

Algorithm 1 summarizes the above methodology.

3.1   Probability Estimation

On the problem of estimating the probability of acceptance of an offer given a price a lot of work has been done. Other works have approached the same problem using linear regression [11,12], particle filters [10], heuristics [13], sigmoid curves [14] or even more elaborate schemes with a combination of radial basis

---

Algorithm 1. Utility maximization given bidding prices. These bidding prices can be winning prices predicted from past games, or prices derived by some optimization procedure.

For each RFQ select a price to bid on
For each RFQ bid calculate the probability of acceptance
For each RFQ calculate its estimated utility
Sort RFQ Bundle based on utility
$CyclesRemaining \leftarrow 2000$
while $CyclesRemaining > 0$ **do**
   $RFQ \leftarrow$ RFQBundle.next()
   $CyclesRemaining- = RFQ.quantity \cdot RFQ.prob \cdot RFQ.cycles$
   OfferBundle.add(RFQ)
end while
Send offers

---

function networks, economic regimes and on-line correction mechanisms [15]. In our case, we used the logistic regression learning algorithm, whose parametric nature provides us with the mechanism of adjusting a derived sigmoid curve to match current RFQ properties and market conditions in the form of features. The probability of acceptance is given by the equation:

$$f(z) = \frac{1}{1 + exp^{-z}}, \tag{7}$$

where

$$z = w_0 + w_1 x_1 + w_2 x_2 + \ldots + w_n x_n, \tag{8}$$

and x_i denotes the corresponding feature. Optimal weights are found through optimization routines. If gradient descent is used, the logistic regression model has the advantage of handling vast amounts of data or even adapting on-line through iterative weight updates.

Nine features are utilized for parameterizing the logistic regression curve. Features can either be properties of the RFQ or properties of the market conditions. The RFQ related features are: 1) *current date* (CD) 2) *due date* (DD) 3) *reserve price* (RP) 4) *quantity* (QNT) and 5) *product base price* (BP). On the other hand, market related features are: 6) *5-day average maximum selling product price* (AMAX) 7) *5-day average minimum selling product price* (AMIN) and 8) *total quantity of customer requested products* (TQNT). Finally we have, 9) *offer price* (OP). The target variable is whether the offer at the specific price, denoted by the ninth feature, was accepted (1) or not (0). Each feature was normalized according to Equation 9. When available, the minimum and maximum prices are taken from the game specifications, otherwise the values are derived from the training data, where due to the vast amount of available samples, the range includes any test sample presented to the model.

$$x' = \frac{x - \bar{x}}{range(x)} = \frac{x - \bar{x}}{max(x) - min(x)} \tag{9}$$

The final probability is given by:

$$Pr(accepted|bid) = \begin{cases} f & \text{if } bid <= \text{reserve price,} \\ 0 & \text{if } bid > \text{reserve price.} \end{cases} \tag{10}$$

3.2 Price Estimation

The second component of the developed mechanism is responsible for estimating the best price to offer. This problem can be approached either by using stochastic optimization [16] or greedy search [12]. In both cases the idea is that given an acceptance probability estimation, we search for the prices that will optimize the offering bundle under the given constraints. The former approach requires specialized software and large computational power for deriving near real-time solutions, so we turn out focus on the latter approach.

Winning Price Prediction. The first approach is to employ data mining on historical data in order to predict winning prices; classification and regression trees (CART) [17] or M5' [18] are typical algorithms for doing so. Using as predictor variables the features 1 through 8 described in Section 3.1, our goal is to predict the price that will convert our offer into an order. Previous work following this approach can be found in [1] using M5' and in [19] using k-Nearest Neighbors. The major problem with this approach is that the models are fitted on log files from games with other agents than those in operational mode. And, even though features related to market conditions are informative, the non-stationarity of the process leads to a decrease in prediction performance. For this reason the predictions are often corrected on-line [19,15].

Particle Swarm Optimization. Particle swarm optimization (PSO) [20] has also been applied. Our PSO approach was designed so that each individual represents a solution, i.e. contains a vector of prices for every RFQ in the RFQ bundle. Initial values are sampled randomly over the space $[0.9p, 1.1p]$, where p is the price predicted by M5' implementation (Section 3.2). Associated with each particle, besides the vector of prices $\tilde{x}$, is a velocity vector $\tilde{v}$ and a fitness value f. Each individual has a memory storing the highest fitness solution it has experienced since the beginning of the algorithm, denoted as P_{bst}. In addition, each particle, is also aware of the fittest individual in its neighborhood, G_{bst} (in this variant of PSO, the neighborhood is defined as the entire population).

In every iteration the particles update their "positions", $\tilde{x}$, based on their "velocities", whereas the velocities of each particle are based on its P_{bst} and the G_{bst} vectors. Under this policy, the particles steer towards the fittest particle in the population and the fittest region of the space each has visited so far. The state transition equation is thus:

$$\tilde{v}_t = \chi(\tilde{v}_{t-1} + r_1\phi_1(P_{bst} - \tilde{x}_{t-1}) + r_2\phi_2(G_{bst} - \tilde{x}_{t-1})) \tag{11}$$

$$\tilde{x}_t = \tilde{x}_{t-1} + \tilde{v}_t \tag{12}$$

where χ is the inertial coefficient, ϕ_1 and ϕ_2 are acceleration constants and r_1, r_2 are sampled randomly from $U(0, 1)$. The inertial coefficient defines how reactive a particle is to velocity changes, the acceleration constants define the factor by which particles tend to fly toward their P_{bst} and G_{bst} positions, and the random variables are used to introduce stochasticity into the transition. Stochasticity is necessary to jostle particles out of an equilibrium that occurs at points between P_{bst} and G_{bst} which are not necessarily optimal [20]. PSO has an advantage over genetic algorithms with respect to its relative finesse with real values.

Bidding via Control. An alternative approach is to view the problem as a control problem. The goal is to adjust prices offered, in order keep a metric near its optimal value. For example this metric could be related to having 100% factory utilization without any late or canceled orders. If the prices proposed by the agent are high, then the factory utilization will drop as a consequence of not winning any orders. The opposite holds for high factory utilization and missed or delayed orders. Previous approaches in the TAC SCM domain include distributed feedback control, fuzzy logic control or heuristic control, respectively [21,22,13].

In our proposed mechanism, we have employed the heuristic control method introduced by PhantAgent [13], winner of the 2007 competition, and posed it as a reinforcement learning problem. Our goal is to find an appropriate policy that will optimize the agent's selling and manufacturing performance through adaptive function approximation. PhantAgent's control strategy is presented in Algorithm 2. Based on how many orders the agent wins, the utilization of its factory and the orders queued for production, PhantAgent manipulates a factor f that adjusts the 3-day maximum of the maximum selling price for the specific product in the RFQ. We conjecture that its limitation is the adaptation strategy of factor f, which is not optimized and thus performance gains can be achieved.

Algorithm 2, slightly modified, could be posed as a reinforcement learning (RL) control problem. The Markov decision process is formed as follows:

$$S = \{won\ cycles/capacity, queued\ cycles/capacity, total\ quantity/3500\} \quad (13)$$
$$A = \{0.9, 0.91, 0.92, ..., 1.04, 1.05\}, |A| = 16 \quad (14)$$
$$r = -\left|\frac{won - capacity}{capacity}\right| - \left|\frac{queue - capacity}{capacity}\right| \quad (15)$$

The engineering of the reward function was made in order to punish a bidding strategy that would diverge from winning 2000 cycles a day and have 2000 cycles queued each day in the factory, waiting to be manufactured. The state variable *total quantity* was normalized between 0 and 1 using an upper bound of 3500 PCs requested over one day by the customers. The bound can be estimated both from the game specifications and from the training data.

4   Experiments and Results

Experiments were conducted using log files from the TAC SCM 2011 finals (16 games) and semi-finals (20 games). All the models (logistic regression, CART,

Algorithm 2. PhantAgent's heuristic control algorithm. The algorithm keeps track of several variables: factor f with initial value 1, variable won, which holds the total number of cycles needed to assemble all the bids won in the last day, cap, the factory capacity for one day, $price$, the offer price, $high$, the highest of the last 3 days highest winning prices and $pqueue$, the total number of cycles needed to assemble all the computers that still have to be delivered

---

$f = f + \frac{(won - cap)}{(cap*5)}$
if $pqueue > (2 * cap)$ **then**
    $f \leftarrow f + 0.01$
end if
if $pqueue < cap$ **then**
    $f \leftarrow f - 0.005$
end if
if $f < 0.9$ **then**
    $f \leftarrow 0.9$
end if
if $f > 1.05$ **then**
    $f \leftarrow 1.05$
end if
$price \leftarrow high \cdot f$

M5' and NEAR) were trained on semi-finals data and tested with the finals logs. The supervised learning schemes were trained with 40% of the semi-finals data, corresponding to 952953 tuples for the logistic regression (includes both accepted and non-accepted offers) and 312891 tuples for the regression tree methods (includes only accepted, won, offers). The R package `rpart` [23,24] and the WEKA library [25] were employed for the CART implementation and the M5' implementation respectively. Simulations were performed on the finals games. We have kept only RFQs for which at least one offer was made, in order for the final results to be in accordance with competition mode.

First we tested the logistic regression fit. Feature weights are provided in Table 1. Figure 2 illustrates the fitted logistic curves for a specific RFQ over the range of possible offer price values $[0, 1.25 \cdot basePrice]$, for different values for reserve price (Figure 2a) and due date (Figure 2b). One may easily identify their effect on the curve. A quantitative metric of the logistic regression performance is to predict whether an order will be accepted ($Pr \geq 0.5$) or not ($Pr < 0.5$). CART predicts a bidding price for every unseen finals' RFQ and logistic regression predicts the probability of acceptance. The results provide a 72.6% classification accuracy.

Selling and throughput factory performance of the different approaches was performed on the adjusted total revenue (adj.tot.rev.) value, which follows the equation:

$$\text{adj.tot.rev.} = \text{tot.rev.} - max(\overline{\text{daily cycles}} - 2000, 0) \cdot \overline{\text{lost cycle cost}}. \quad (16)$$

Table 1. The weights of the logistic regression fit. The most important features are the offer price (**OP**) and the average maximum report price (**AMAX**), having negative and positive effect respectively on the probability of a successful bid the higher they are. Third in importance is the reserve price (RP). Importance is based on their contribution to the final outcome and is comparable due to normalization performed before fitting.

CD	BP	DD	QNT	AMAX	AMIN	TQNT	RP	OP
-0.19	-0.67	-1.26	0.80	17.96	1.61	0.52	2.39	-22.94

Equation 16 adjusts the total revenue (tot.rev.) to include costs incurred by the extra average daily cycles ($\overline{\text{daily cycles}}$) won above the 2000 capacity limit. In order to account for the extra cycles and make the results comparable, we identify how much an extra cycle costs to the agent on average ($\overline{\text{lost cycle cost}}$), in order to subtract it from the total revenue and compare the results again. The average RFQ has 10 items to deliver with 5.5 average manufacturing cycles per item, summing up to 55 cycles. The average price of 10 items is 10 times the average base price (2000), equal to 20000. The penalty incurred is on average 10%, thus the total price we subtract from the revenue is $20000 \cdot 1.1 = 22000$ for 55 cycles (that it 400 per cycle). If this is true for 216 days, then the amount to subtract for every extra average cycle is 86400. For example, if we have 100 extra average cycles, then $86400 \cdot 100 = 8640000$ must be subtracted in the end from the total revenue.

NEAR experiments were executed with a population of 100 networks, for 100 generations. The performance of the champion in terms of average total reward over all the finals games behavior is depicted in Figure 3 and is indicative of the evolutionary pressure applied by the algorithm to discover efficient networks.

PSO included 100 particles which were allowed to iterate 100 times. At a standard desktop, it took around $1''$ of processing time. Thus, this setup allows adequate time to add predicted RFQs in order to have a 10 day optimization plan when in competition. PSO parameters χ and $\phi_{1,2}$ were set to 0.1 and 0.5, respectively.

Table 2 summarizes the adjusted total revenue (ATR) and the average daily cycles (ADC) won for each one of the 2011 finals games, for all the techniques presented.

Based on the guidelines in [26] we employed the Wilcoxon signed-ranks test [27] for pairwise statistical significance comparison between the RL method and the rest. We calculate the statistic z and if $z < -1.96$ we can discard the null hypothesis that the two competitors have the same performance on average for $\alpha = 0.05$. The test gave values $z = -2.32$, $z = -2.53$, $z = -2.63$ and $z = -3.51$ when comparing RL versus CART, M5', PSO and heuristic control respectively, providing statistical confidence over the superiority of the RL/NEAR method in pairwise comparisons.

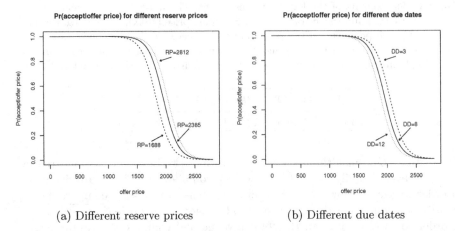

(a) Different reserve prices   (b) Different due dates

Fig. 2. Both figures display the probability of accepting an offer (y-axis) given the offer price (x-axis) for different values of other variables that affect the curves like due date and reserve price. The representation of the acceptance probability through a sigmoid function is close to the reality, since prices near the reserve price are unlikely to be accepted in a competitive environment, while low prices will be accepted almost certainly. The steep descent should be at the price the current market condition indicate.

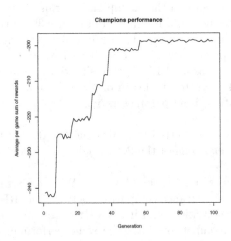

Fig. 3. The average per game (episode) sum of rewards gathered over the 216 days of the champion network per generation. We can observe how the evolutionary pressure drives the policy search towards more efficient networks.

Table 2. Adjusted total revenue (ATR) and average daily cycles (ADC) for all finals games. ATR is in millions.

Game ID	CART		M5'		Heuristic		PSO		RL	
	ATR	ADC	ATR	ADC	ATR	ADC	ATR	ADC	ATR	ADC
4584	119.9	2338	121.1	2256	124.9	1882	120.7	2287	**129.2**	1984
4585	**126.2**	2174	123.9	2157	121.5	1909	123.5	2181	125.6	1971
4586	123.0	2259	122.4	2130	121.8	1915	121.4	2134	**125.7**	1994
4587	**132.0**	2321	125.6	2294	125.4	1930	125.4	2322	128.9	1995
4588	123.4	2324	126.1	2252	125.0	1908	124.8	2302	**129.4**	1992
4589	123.6	2289	123.4	2251	124.0	1906	122.9	2258	**130.0**	1996
4590	108.2	2239	108.9	2089	104.5	1827	108.0	2141	**109.6**	1910
4591	**135.0**	2084	132.1	2003	124.5	1831	132.9	2059	128.3	1906
4360	137.6	2234	132.0	2206	141.4	1921	135.3	2181	**145.1**	1990
4361	120.8	2184	119.4	2116	119.4	1862	120.3	2113	**123.6**	1944
4362	112.7	2290	111.0	2088	112.9	1905	110.9	2130	**116.6**	1979
4363	97.8	2349	110.3	2054	109.5	1920	108.4	2107	**111.8**	1980
4364	116.0	2137	**119.1**	2100	107.8	1799	117.6	2143	113.1	1907
4365	120.4	2218	120.2	2120	124.8	1918	120.2	2125	**127.1**	1983
4366	118.9	2244	118.3	2049	118.9	1915	119.2	2098	**123.3**	1998
4367	97.1	2300	102.9	2102	105.9	1891	101.3	2155	**108.7**	1973
Average	119.5	2249	119.8	2141	119.5	1889	119.6	2171	**123.5**	1968

Besides heuristic control and RL, all the other methods continuously underestimate the winning price during simulations. As a consequence, they win more orders and have a factory utilization above the 2000 cycles limit. This behavior may seem strange at the beginning, since it is expected that the finals are more competitive and thus have lower market prices than the semi-finals (training data). The cause of this paradox is the specific mix of agents participating in the finals, which led to a less competitive set of games, evident by the range of the final bank accounts of 1st and 6th place, being $12M$ and $13M$ in 2009 and 2010 respectively, and $29M$ in 2011[1]. On the other hand, the control methods, and especially RL, are working only by receiving feedback from the current market conditions and agent state leading to better robustness and generalization behavior. Prior to experimentation. one could conjecture that the PSO appears to be a more efficient approach, since it tests a lot of solutions, picking the best one among many. The fact that it lags behind is probably due to the noisy premises induced by the probability estimation upon which the PSO method relies heavily on.

5   Conclusions and Future Work

In this work we have designed a bidding mechanism in the context of TAC SCM formed by three decoupled components: price selection, acceptance probability

---

[1] Results are taken from http://tac.cs.umn.edu/

estimation and offer selection. Under this scheme, performance boosts in any of the three components would increase profitability in the competition. In our case we have used logistic regression as our acceptance probability model, greedy utility maximization as our offer selection mechanism and experimented with five price selection mechanisms. Our adaptive function approximation methodology via policy search for controlling the bidding prices provided good generalization behavior on unseen market conditions and picked up as the best performing solution among the rest. In the future we plan to test the derived methodology of price control through policy search in this year's TAC SCM competition and continue to improve the logistic regression component by adding for example penalty terms on the weights during the optimization procedure.

References

1. Chatzidimitriou, K.C., Symeonidis, A.L., Kontogounis, I., Mitkas, P.A.: Agent mertacor: A robust design for dealing with uncertainty and variation in scm environments. Expert Systems with Applications 35(3), 591–603 (2008) (Cited by: Collins2008)
2. Stone, P.: Learning and multiagent reasoning for autonomous agents. In: Proceedings of the 20th International Joint Conference on Artificial Intelligence, pp. 13–30 (January 2007)
3. Sutton, R.S., Barto, A.G.: Reinforcement Learning: An Introduction. MIT Press, Cambridge (1998)
4. Arunachalam, R., Sadeh, N.M.: The supply chain trading agent competition. Electronic Commerce Research and Applications 4(1), 66–84 (2005)
5. Collins, J., Arunachalam, R., Sadeh, N., Eriksson, J., Finne, N., Janson, S.: The supply chain management game for the 2007 trading agent competition. Technical Report CMU-ISRI-07-100, Carnegie Mellon University (December 2006)
6. Jaeger, H.: Tutorial on training recurrent neural networks, covering BPTT, RTRL, EKF and the "echo state network" approach. Technical Report GMD Report 159, German National Research Center for Information Technology (2002)
7. Szita, I., Gyenes, V., Lőrincz, A.: Reinforcement learning with echo state networks. In: Kollias, S.D., Stafylopatis, A., Duch, W., Oja, E. (eds.) ICANN 2006. LNCS, vol. 4131, pp. 830–839. Springer, Heidelberg (2006)
8. Stanley, K.O., Miikkulainen, R.: Evolving neural networks through augmenting topologies. Evolutionary Computation 10(2), 99–127 (2002)
9. Chatzidimitriou, K.C., Mitkas, P.A.: A neat way for evolving echo state networks. In: European Conference on Artificial Intelligence. IOS Press (August 2010)
10. Pardoe, D., Stone, P.: An autonomous agent for supply chain management. In: Adomavicius, G., Gupta, A. (eds.) Handbooks in Information Systems Series: Business Computing, vol. 3, pp. 141–172. Emerald Group (2009)
11. Benisch, M., Greenwald, A., Grypari, I., Lederman, R., Naroditskiy, V., Tschantz, M.: Botticelli: A supply chain management agent designed to optimize under uncertainty. ACM Transactions on Computational Logic 4(3), 29–37 (2004)
12. Pardoe, D., Stone, P.: Bidding for customer orders in TAC SCM. In: Faratin, P., Rodríguez-Aguilar, J.-A. (eds.) AMEC 2004. LNCS (LNAI), vol. 3435, pp. 143–157. Springer, Heidelberg (2006)

13. Stan, M., Stan, B., Florea, A.M.: A dynamic strategy agent for supply chain management. In: Proceedings of the Eighth International Symposium on Symbolic and Numeric Algorithms for Scientific Computing, pp. 227–232 (2006)
14. Chatzidimitriou, K.C., Symeonidis, A.L.: Data-mining-enhanced agents in dynamic supply-chain-management environments. Intelligent Systems 24(3), 54–63 (2009); Special issue on Agents and Data Mining
15. Hogenboom, A., Ketter, W., van Dalen, J., Kaymak, U., Collins, J., Gupta, A.: Product pricing in TAC SCM using adaptive real-time probability of acceptance estimations based on economic regimes. In: Workshop: Trading Agent Design and Analysis (TADA) at Twenty-First International Joint Conference on Artificial Intelligence (IJCAI 2009), 15–24 (July 2009)
16. Benisch, M., Greenwald, A., Naroditskiy, V., Tschantz, M.C.: A stochastic programming approach to scheduling in TAC SCM. In: Proceedings of the 5th ACM Conference on Electronic Commerce, EC 2004, pp. 152–159. ACM, New York (2004)
17. Breiman, L., Friedman, J., Stone, C.J., Olshen, R.: Classification and Regression Trees. Chapman and Hall (1984)
18. Wang, Y., Witten, I.H.: Induction of model trees for predicting continuous classes. Poster Papers of the 9th European Conference on Machine Learning, pp. 128–137 (1997)
19. Kiekintveld, C., Miller, J., Jordan, P.R., Callender, L.F., Wellman, M.P.: Forecasting market prices in a supply chain game. Electronic Commerce Research and Applications 8, 63–77 (2009)
20. Kennedy, J., Eberhart, R.: Particle swarm optimization. In: Proceedings of the International Conference on Neural Networks, pp. 1942–1948 (1995)
21. Kiekintveld, C., Wellman, M.P., Singh, S., Estelle, J., Vorobeychik, Y., Soni, V., Rudary, M.: Distributed feedback control for decision making on supply chains. In: Fourteenth International Conference on Automated Planning and Scheduling (2004)
22. He, M., Rogers, A., Luo, X., Jennings, N.R.: Designing a successful trading agent for supply chain management. In: Fifth International Joint Conference on Autonomous Agents and Multiagent Systems, AAMAS 2006 (2006)
23. R Development Core Team: R: A Language and Environment for Statistical Computing. R Foundation for Statistical Computing, Vienna, Austria (2011) ISBN 3-900051-07-0
24. Therneau, T.M., port by Brian Ripley, B.A.R.: rpart: Recursive Partitioning, R package version 3.1-50 (2011)
25. Hall, M., Frank, E., Holmes, G., Pfahringer, B., Reutemann, P., Witten, I.H.: The weka data mining software: An update. SIGKDD Explorations 11(1), 10–18 (2009)
26. Demšar, J.: Statistical comparisons of classifiers over multiple data sets. Journal of Machine Learning Research 7, 1–30 (2006)
27. Wilcoxon, F.: Individual comparisons by ranking methods. Biometrics Bulletin 1(6), 80–83 (1945)

Designing Robust Strategies for Continuous Trading in Contemporary Power Markets

Themistoklis G. Diamantopoulos,
Andreas L. Symeonidis, and Anthony C. Chrysopoulos

Electrical and Computer Engineering Dept., Aristotle University of Thessaloniki,
Informatics and Telematics Institute, CERTH, Thessaloniki, Greece
{thdiaman,asymeon,achryso}@issel.ee.auth.gr

Abstract. In contemporary energy markets participants interact with each other via brokers that are responsible for the proper energy flow to and from their clients (usually in the form of long-term or short-term contracts). Power TAC is a realistic simulation of a real-life energy market, aiming towards providing a better understanding and modeling of modern energy markets, while boosting research on innovative trading strategies. Power TAC models brokers as software agents, competing against each other in Double Auction environments, in order to increase their client base and market share. Current work discusses such a broker agent architecture, striving to maximize his own profit. Within the context of our analysis, Double Auction markets are treated as microeconomic systems and, based on state-of-the-art price formation strategies, the following policies are designed: an adaptive price formation policy, a policy for forecasting energy consumption that employs Time Series Analysis primitives, and two shout update policies, a rule-based policy that acts rather hastily, and one based on Fuzzy Logic. The results are quite encouraging and will certainly call for future research.

Keywords: Double Auctions, Trading Agent Competition (TAC), Energy Market, Fuzzy Logic, Time Series Analysis.

1 Introduction

A *Double Auction (DA)* is an auction where multiple sellers and buyers participate, placing *asks/bids* on the product(s) they want to sell/buy, trying to maximize their profit. DAs are a particularly interesting case of dynamics for Computer and Economics scientists, since product prices and demand/response may fluctuate in an unpredictable manner, thus giving room for research.

Power TAC, initially launched in 2011 [8], provides a powerful competition benchmark of applying DAs' theory to real-life problems. It simulates a modern energy market, where producer, consumer and prosumer needs of electrical power are modeled. Competing agents act as brokers, procuring energy from producers and selling it to consumers in order to acquire the maximum possible profit. The profit, however, does not depend only on monetary units, but also on factors

E. David et al. (Eds.): AMEC/TADA 2012, LNBIP 136, pp. 30–44, 2013.

such as the agent's fees or its bias towards renewable energy sources [8]. In the highly dynamic environment of Power TAC agents face the following challenges:

- Create tariffs to attract customers and create a portfolio of producers and consumers of Electric Energy, according to the current state of the Market.
- Determine the amount of energy to be procured based on the prediction of customers' power load consumption, since any imbalance of the power load is penalized.
- Maximize their profit either by attracting new customers, or improving terms of the existing contracts.

Thus, broker agents have to be equipped with innovative trading and decision making strategies, in order to optimize agent performance. To this end, we have designed agent `Mertacor`. The rest of the paper is organized as follows: Section 2 provides a state-of-the-art review on price formation strategies through the prism of DAs, whereas Section 3 discusses the key modeling elements of Power TAC. The `Mertacor` architecture is presented in Section 4, while Section 5 presents the experiments conducted. Section 6 provides useful conclusive remarks, directions for future research and concludes the paper.

2 Double Auctions

Double Auctions are thoroughly described using *microeconomics* theory, where a product's *price* and *quantity* are determined by the *supply* and *demand* for that product [9,6]. In a given *exchange*, each participant has a *limit price* (aka *private value*) denoting the maximum or minimum price one is willing to offer/accept, being a buyer/seller respectively. In DAs, product price is inversely proportional to the demand and proportional to product supply. The intersection point of the supply and demand curves is called *competitive equilibrium* and is a crucial factor dictating whether shouts are successful or not.

This process is identified as *market clearing* and its timing is actually one of the main criteria that differentiates DAs into various types. Although there are several types, they can typically be divided into two main lines of research: the *Continuous Double Auctions (CDAs)* and the *Clearing House Double Auctions (CH)*. The latter provide an interesting research framework, mainly due to their high market efficiency. Nevertheless, the complexity of CDAs attracts even more researchers interested not only in designing such markets, but also in developing antagonistic price formation policies.

2.1 A Taxonomy of Strategies

Although properly designing a market is an interesting challenge, no market is complete without traders. A trading strategy may have several features depending on the type of the market it is designed for. Strategies may be designed to converge to some equilibrium, mimic human behavior or simply gain profit.

In any case though, the core feature of a strategy is its price formation technique, which is yet an open issue in DAs. This section discusses a taxonomy of price formation techniques, while commenting on the benefits of each approach.

Despite extensive research has been realized on this field, no concrete taxonomy has been established yet, mainly due to the complexity of the techniques involved. The classification proposed within the context of this paper is inspired by the model of Rust et al. [11] and is formed along two axes: *adaptiveness* and *predictivity*.

A strategy is considered *adaptive* if it employs data from previous auction rounds in order to formulate the next shout price. By contrast, a *non-adaptive* strategy is based only on current information, thus achieving simplicity. Strategies employing Reinforcement Learning primitives cannot be classified to either of the above categories, since they usually base decisions upon considering only their own past. Thus, they may be abusively named *self-adaptive*.

An agent may be either *predictive* or *non-predictive*. A non-predictive agent exploits only present and/or past data to form its next shout. In contrast, a predictive agent tries to construct a future state of the market in order to transact in an intelligent manner. To achieve this, it also requires past data, thus predictive strategies are usually adaptive. Finally, non-adaptive and self-adaptive strategies can be regarded as non-predictive, since the former don't make use of past data, while the latter may only construct a model of their own future state, ignoring future states of other agents. Based on the above analysis, the following section discusses the most popular price formation strategies.

2.2   Discussion on State-of-the-Art Price Formation Strategies

Non-adaptive Strategies. The main representative of this category is the Zero *Intelligence (ZI)* strategy, authored by Gode and Sunder [6]. A ZI agent actually submits offers randomly, either freely (*ZI Unconstrained – ZI-U*) or within limit values (*ZI Constrained – ZI-C*). Though ZI may seem as a deprecated strategy, its contribution is substantial in the design of more advanced strategies, since it provides a benchmark against random guessing.

The *KAPLAN* strategy [10], is a "sniping" strategy, in the sense that the agent makes a move towards the end of the current trading period. Although such a simple strategy has had success in the Santa Fe DAs tournament[4], the KAPLAN strategy cannot be applied to competitions like Power TAC, which do not reveal the duration of the rounds.

Adaptive Strategies. Most state-of-the-art strategies are adaptive. Predictive strategies, like *Zero Intelligence Plus (ZIP)*, also model future states [2]. A ZIP agent uses a *learning rule (delta rule)* to update its *profit margin*. It decides whether the latter is increased or decreased based on the type (bid or ask), as well as the success (or not) of the last shout.

An interesting line of research is the one followed by Vytelingum et al. [12], resulting in the *Adaptive Aggressiveness (AA)* strategy. An AA agent initially makes a prediction of the market's equilibrium based on previous shouts, and then computes the price which it should pursue (*target price*). The agent uses a ZIP-like algorithm to determine the trend of its *degree of aggressiveness*, which is used to update the price of the next shout.

On the other hand, non-predictive strategies seem to have a rather straightforward policy on deciding their next move. However, this does not mean that they are less efficient or complex. Strategies like *Gjerstad-Dickhaut (GD)* achieve good results [5]. A GD agent tries to maximize its *expected surplus*, which is defined by the agent's *belief function*. This function is updated according to the success rate of a number of past shouts, i.e. the memory of the agent.

Additionally, He et al. suggest a *Fuzzy Logic based (FL)* strategy [7]. A FL agent computes the *reference price*, i.e. the mean price of the last κ transactions (since the agent has memory), and bases its accepting offer strategy on a comparison to current outstanding shouts. The proximity of the reference price to the shouts is dissolved using fuzzy sets. The agent also has a *learning rate*, which is updated using fuzzy rules, in order to adjust its will to transact according to the frequency of its transactions.

Self-adaptive Strategies. The main advantage of Reinforcement Learning strategies is their utter independence from the other agents' actions, and sometimes even from the market. Although this may seem ineffective, techniques such as *Roth-Erev (RE)* achieve significant performance, especially in sealed DAs, where the amount of information that is given to the agents is limited [3]. The RE agent has been designed to mimic human behavior. The agent's *propensity* of making a move is updated at each round through an *experience function*, which is a reflection of the agent's satisfaction (or disappointment) concerning the considered move. The optimum move is selected using a *choice probability function*.

Finally, the Q strategy is an interesting expansion of the Q-learning technique that employs an *e-greedy* policy [1]. This way, the Q agent either explores the environment or decides using its knowledge up to that point. The agent updates its pricing policy based on which action has been the most profitable in its recent history.

3   The Power TAC Environment

The broker agents' main challenge is the *Tariff Market*. It contains all households, low energy consumers, and small producers. Agents submit their tariffs (asks or bids) to the market, trying to acquire as large market share as possible, while keeping their prices within an affordable level. As far as the customers' contract choices are concerned, they are based on the concept of *tariff utility*. A customer's tariff utility for a given tariff i is given in equation (1):

$$u_i = -(c_u + c_f) \cdot a_{cost} - e_i \cdot a_{energy} - r_i \cdot a_{risk} - I_i \cdot a_{inertia} \qquad (1)$$

where the parameters a_{cost}, a_{energy}, a_{risk} and $a_{inertia}$ define the weights given by the customer to costs (either variable (c_u) or fixed (c_f)), energy sources e_i

(e.g. renewable sources), any risks r_i (e.g. dynamic contracts), and the customer's will to remain idle I_i. This way the customer computes the tariff utility of a subset of tariffs offered. Instead of choosing the tariff with the highest utility, the customer selects a tariff in a probabilistic way (see [8]). Agents may also trade energy amongst each other in the *Wholesale Market*, or with large-scale consumers directly, through *requests for quotes (RFQ)*, in order to balance their *portfolio*.

Other entities of Power TAC include the *Distribution Utility (DU)*, which imposes penalty fees when there is an imbalance between broker procured and consumed energy, the *Weather Service*, which provides weather forecast data to brokers, and the *Accounting Service*, which keeps track of all agents' transactions and provides them with portfolio information.

According to Power TAC specifications, all customers are initially bound to a contract with a *default agent*, which is not meant to be competent. Upon initialization, the number of timeslots is determined but not reported to the agents. Brokers can submit tariffs during each timeslot, nevertheless there is a *tariff publication fee* and a maximum number of shouts per agent to avoid market "spamming".

Given that focus of the current work is on the price policy, only variable rate tariffs are taken into account. Thus, (1) is dealt with as (2):

$$u_i = -c_u \cdot a_{cost} \tag{2}$$

given c_u is computed as the mean energy cost for the consumption during k randomly selected past days and a_{cost} is a parameter defining the weight given to that cost.

Thereby, a comprehensive DA environment is created, in the sense that brokers have to buy energy from the producers and sell it to the consumers, aiming to make profit. However, the environment is still too complex to be treated as a simple price formation problem. With respect to the Power TAC challenges discussed, our broker's objectives in the Tariff Market are to:

- Form the price of the next bid (or ask)
- Update (or not) its current shouts or decide to submit new shouts
- Determine the amount of energy to be requested by its producers.

4   Agent Mertacor Design

In accordance with the above mentioned objectives, *Mertacor*, our agent-broker comprises of three modules defining three policies: a price formation policy, a tariff update policy, and an energy prediction policy. These policies provide the necessary input to the core agent mechanism that integrates decisions and defines the final agent strategy, communicated to the Power TAC server.

4.1   Price Formation Policy

Vast amount of information is shared to the agents participating in the Tariff market, thus adaptive strategies should typically be advantageous compared to non-adaptive and self-adaptive ones. The policy developed aspires to exploit any available information as optimally as possible.

Initially, the agent uses data from the last transactions to calculate the *successful price*, which is defined as the mean of all successful transactions of the market and is computed using a *moving average* method. Considering that the agent's memory holds the latest N transactions, the successful price is given by equation (3):

$$SP = \frac{\sum_{i=T-N+1}^{T} w_i s_i p_i}{\sum_{i=T-N+1}^{T} w_i s_i} \tag{3}$$

where w_i is the weight of shout i with price p_i, and s_i denotes whether the offer was successful ($s_i = 1$) or not ($s_i = 0$). Considering transaction T is the most recent, then $w_T = 1$ and all other weights are updated based on equation (4):

$$w_{i-1} = r \cdot w_i \qquad r \in [0,1] \tag{4}$$

where r determines the importance given to former shouts by the agent. Equations (3) and (4) are valid for both bids and asks.

Mertacor also behaves in a predictive manner. A *risk factor* R determines the agent's eagerness to take risks in order to pursue greater profit. R values range in the interval $[-c, c]$, where c defines the maximum deviation of the final shout price from the successful price. The success rate of the agent's M latest shouts is computed as follows:

$$k = \frac{\sum_{i=1}^{M} acceptedShouts(i)}{M} \tag{5}$$

where $acceptedShouts(i)$ returns 1 or 0 if the shout was successful or not respectively. Equation (5) is then normalized to the interval $[-c, c]$:

$$\hat{k} = c \cdot (2k - 1) \tag{6}$$

Note that the risk factor could be assigned the value of $\hat{k}$. For example, if the success rate of the agent's latest M asks is higher than 50%, then the normalized $\hat{k}$ is positive, meaning that the agent should probably take risks by increasing its shout pricing policy. However, for the sake of experimentation, Mertacor's risk factor follows a Gaussian distribution.

In order to avoid extreme adjustments to the final shout price, the distribution is restricted between intervals, thus it is given by equation (7):

$$g(x) = \frac{1}{\sqrt{2\pi\sigma^2}} \cdot e^{\frac{-(x - \mu^2)}{2\sigma^2}} \qquad g(x) \in [-l, l] \tag{7}$$

where the distribution limit l is defined as follows:

$$l = \min \left\{ |\hat{k} - c|, |\hat{k} + c| \right\} \tag{8}$$

The distribution's mean is $\hat{k}$ and its standard deviation is given by equation (9):

$$\sigma = \frac{e - l}{3} \qquad e \in (0, \infty) \tag{9}$$

where e is an experimentation parameter, defining the relationship between σ and l. Figure 1 illustrates the influence of e to the height of the distribution as well as its limits. The risk factor is given randomly from the distribution part denoted from the shaded area of Figure 1. The smaller the parameter e, the more likely the agent chooses a value closer to the mean of the distribution, while as the parameter increases, the agent may choose a more risky value.

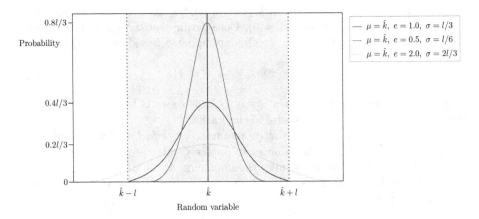

Fig. 1. Experimentation function of the agent

Finally, if s_{ask} is defined to be the agent's ask limit price, the next ask is given by equation (10):

$$ask = \max \left\{ SP \cdot (1 + R), s_{ask} \right\} \tag{10}$$

In accordance, let s_{bid} be the agent's bid limit price, the next bid is calculated using equation (11):

$$bid = \min \left\{ SP \cdot (1 - R), s_{bid} \right\} \tag{11}$$

The agent's limit values may be considered fixed. In fact, they only change barely to avoid stiff situations, where all agents stick to their limit values.

4.2   Tariff Update Policy

A tariff update policy should deal successfully with submitting tariffs to the Tariff Market, as well as updating already existing ones. Two policies are proposed, both considering the balance of the broker's portfolio and the maximum number of offers permitted.

Basic Update Policy. Striving for an aggressive policy, the agent submits at first a new tariff each round it is given the right to. Thus, it could quickly conquer the market, since the more the tariffs the better the chance of more customers accepting them. However, the policy's spontaneity may lead to ineffective tariffs, since during the first rounds the agent's price formation policy is not likely to have converged to optimal shout values.

Determining whether to update an already existing tariff or not is a matter of the agent's portfolio. Mertacor compares its portfolio balance with what is called the *balance limit*. If Mertacor's portfolio balance surpasses this limit, then it is penalized by the DU. Taking the absolute balance limit into account, the Mertacor's main strategy for asks is depicted in Figure 2a and for bids in Figure 2b. *PBalance* and *BLimit* stand for portfolio balance and balance limit, respectively.

```
if (PBalance > BLimit)
    if (unsuccessful asks exist)
        Update min unsuccessful ask
    else
        Update min ask
else_if (PBalance < - BLimit)
    if (unsuccessful asks exist)
        Update max unsuccessful ask
    else
        Update max ask
```

```
if (PBalance > BLimit)
    if (unsuccessful bids exist)
        Update min unsuccessful bid
    else
        Update min bid
else_if (PBalance < - BLimit)
    if (unsuccessful bids exist)
        Update max unsuccessful bid
    else
        Update max bids
```

(a)   (b)

Fig. 2. Basic update policy update algorithms for (a) asks and (b) bids

This way Mertacor adapts and actually understands any imbalances between the number of producers and the number of consumers contracted to it. For example, when the portfolio balance is greater than the positive balance limit, the agent has an energy deficit, thus alters its minimum shouts to reduce the assigned consumers' and increase the respective producers' market share.

Changing minimum or maximum shouts provides a neat way to adjust Mertacor's contracts to producers and consumers and, as a result, its portfolio balance. However, since the Tariff Market is highly competitive, breaking a contract is rather risky. Thus, Mertacor first attempts to modify any unsuccessful shouts and, if all offers are accepted, only then does it decide to break successful contracts (the less profitable ones).

Fuzzy Logic Update Policy. In order to provide a more comprehensible way of defining the values of the metrics that affect the agent's state, Fuzzy logic primitives have been employed. In fact, two fuzzy sets are defined: one with respect to the number of consumers (producers) under contract and one with respect to the agent's portfolio balance.

The first fuzzy set is defined as the number of consumers (producers) who have a contract with Mertacor. Let B be the number of brokers and C the number of the current consumers (producers) of the agent, the fuzzy set is shown in Figure 3.

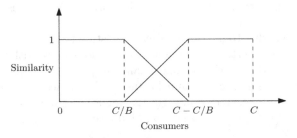

Fig. 3. Fuzzy set for the consumers of the agent. Producers set is defined in an analogous manner.

Dividing the number of brokers by the number of e.g. the agent's consumers provides the number of consumers that the agent should have if they were shared equally among brokers.

The second fuzzy set, describing the agent's portfolio balance, is depicted in Figure 4, where L is the balance limit.

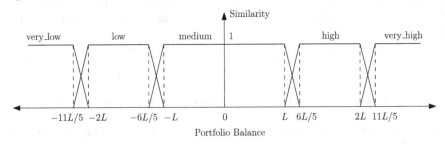

Fig. 4. Fuzzy set for the portfolio balance of the agent

Observing Figure 3 and Figure 4, both fuzzy sets' values are summed to 1 regardless of the independent variable. Thus, the fuzzy sets are regarded in a probabilistic manner, using a uniform random distribution from 0 to 1. For example, as far as the fuzzy set of Figure 3 is concerned, if Mertacor's customers are $C/2B$, they are considered too few. However, if they are $C/2$ then Mertacor has a 50% probability for considering them few and the same probability for believing they are many.

Upon defining the fuzzy sets as well as their use, the policy is analyzed along two main decisions: submitting new tariffs, and updating existing ones. Considering the former, Mertacor submits new offers if customers are few, as long as current offers don't exceed the maximum allowed number of offers for each agent. If consumers are few, Mertacor submits a new ask and if producers are few, Mertacor submits a new bid. The agent submits new shouts only if its market share is not satisfactory, in order to avoid any loss due to tariff submission fees.

As far as tariff updates are concerned, Mertacor updates its maximum ask if the balance is low or very low or if consumers are few. If Mertacor's balance is high or very high, or if producers are few, then Mertacor updates the minimum bid. So far, the policy seems rational, yet not optimal. In order to optimize it, Mertacor also updates the minimum ask if its portfolio balance is very high and it also updates the maximum bid if it is very low. Figures 5a and 5b depict Mertacor's strategy with respect to asks and bids update policy.

```
if ((PBalance is low or very_low)
      or (consumers are few))
   if (unsuccessful asks exist)
      Update max unsuccessful ask
   else
      Update max ask
else_if (PBalance is very_high)
   if (unsuccessful asks exist)
      Update min unsuccessful ask
   else
      Update min ask
```

```
if ((PBalance is high or very_high)
      or (producers are few))
   if (unsuccessful bids exist)
      Update min unsuccessful bid
   else
      Update min bid
else_if (PBalance is very_low)
   if (unsuccessful bids exist)
      Update max unsuccessful bid
   else
      Update max bid
```

(a)   (b)

Fig. 5. Fuzzy Logic update policy update algorithms for (a) asks and (b) bids

Interpreting Metacor's update strategy leads to identifying the relation between the agent's market share and its respective portfolio balance. When that balance is low, Mertacor needs to balance the energy deficit by updating the maximum ask. Thus, Mertacor decreases ask prices in order to increase his consumers' market share. Mertacor acts in a similar manner when consumers are few. However, if the portfolio balance is very low then Mertacor not only considers increasing consumers (Figure 5a) but also decreasing producers (Figure 5b), in order to fix the portfolio imbalance more efficiently. When Mertacor's portfolio balance is high or very high, respective decisions are made.

4.3 Energy Prediction Policy

Through the energy prediction policy Mertacor estimates the amount of energy needed to cover contracted consumers' needs during the forthcoming timeslot. Mertacor receives energy consumption measurements for each timeslot and constructs a time series $\{x_1, x_2, \ldots, x_n\}$, where x_i is the total energy consumption in the market for timeslot i and n is the number of previous timeslots. This way the problem is transformed to predicting the future value of the series. The latter is found using *exponential smoothing*, according to equation (12):

$$\hat{x}_{n+1} = a \cdot x_n + (1 - a) \cdot \hat{x}_n \qquad (12)$$

where a defines the importance given to every previous value. Equation (12) is initialized as $\hat{x}_1 = x_1$.

The total energy that the agent is going to need for the next timeslot is computed using equation (13):

$$E_{n+1} = \frac{C_{agent}}{C} \cdot \hat{x}_{n+1} \qquad (13)$$

given C_{agent} is the number of the agent's consumers and C is the number of all consumers of the market. Upon checking its portfolio, Mertacor asks for the following amount of energy from every one of its contracted producers:

$$e_{n+1} = \frac{E_{n+1}}{P_{agent}} \qquad (14)$$

where P_{agent} is the number of producers in the portfolio.

5   Experiments

Three sets of experiments were conducted in order to identify the parameters that would lead to the most profitable policies for Mertacor. Policies were evaluated against their mean market share of producers/consumers, and the total profit of the agents participating. Each of the experiments was conducted for different configurations of producers and consumers (discussed below) and each experiment was conducted ten times, so the mean values of the derived metrics are presented.

It should also be denoted that all agents tested were assigned the same energy prediction policy. Results are quite intriguing and discussed later on.

5.1   Price Formation Parameters Experiments

From the various parameters of the price formation policy proposed in 4.1, the experimentation parameter is by far the most interesting, since it is crucial for the agent's competing tactics. Other parameters may be given some determined pseudo-optimal values as their impact is not optimum for a certain value. Take agent memory for instance: the moving average method utilized ensures proper weights as long as the memory is not too small. To this end, variables c and r are assigned the values 0.20 and 0.95 respectively.

Several experimentation parameter values were tested (omitted due to space limitations). Table 1 discusses market share and total profit for three different consumer/producer compilations, for experimentation parameter values 0.5, 1.0, and 2.0.

Referring to Table 1, deviations are small, something expected since the other policies encapsulated in the agent are identical, resulting in partial absorption of the influence of the experimentation parameter. However, when the latter is set to 0.5, one may notice that Mertacor makes more total profit than its

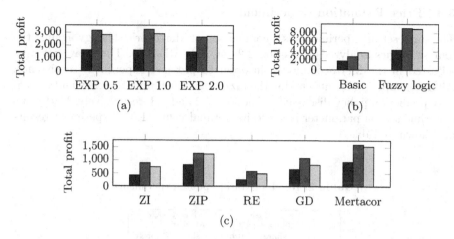

Fig. 6. Graphs showing the total profits for experiments competing (a) different values of the experimentation parameter (b) the two tariff update policies and (c) different price formation policies. The experiments are shown for different settings of producers and consumers, 4 producers & 8 consumers (■■), 4 producers & 16 consumers (■■), 8 producers & 16 consumers (▯▯).

competitors for small numbers of customers (4 consumers and 8 producers). On the contrary, setting the parameter to 2.0 is more effective with respect to market share, something expected since the agent is more willing to explore its space (see Section 4.1). Taking the golden rule, the value 1.0 is selected as the optimal one for Mertacor, in order to perform well for both profit and market share.

Table 1. Results of price formation parameters experiments

	EXP 0.5		EXP 1.0		EXP 2.0	
	Market share	Total profit	Market share	Total profit	Market share	Total profit
4 cons 8 prod	31,11	32,25	1621,9	31,19	32,65	1614,6	36,89	31,95	1490,7
4 cons 16 prod	29,88	32,32	3164,4	31,98	30,02	3249,8	37,33	34,70	2671,4
8 cons 16 prod	29,31	26,29	2830,3	31,42	31,91	2917,1	37,69	36,26	2728,1

5.2   Tariff Update Experiments

The two tariff update policies introduced in Section 4.2 were tested against each other. Mertacor's experimentation parameter was set to 1.0. The results are depicted in Table 2, where it is evident that the fuzzy logic tariff update policy clearly outperforms the basic scheme, both with respect to profit, as well as market share.

5.3   Price Formation Experiments

The third set of experiments is a comparison of Mertacor's strategy against the four strategies analyzed in Section 2.2: ZI, ZIP, RE, GD. The strategies were adjusted in the Mertacor model, in order to preserve experiment consistency. All five competing agents employ the fuzzy logic tariff update policy and the energy prediction policy discussed in Sections 4.2 and 4.3, respectively. Mertacor's experimentation parameter is set to its optimal value (1.0). Experiment results are shown in Table 3.

Table 2. Results of tariff update experiments

| | Basic | | Fuzzy logic | |
	Market share	Total profit	Market share	Total profit
4 cons 8 prod	25,25	33,95	1926,9	72,94 57,40 4310,1
4 cons 16 prod	19,36	31,55	2880,5	76,79 58,33 9065,0
8 cons 16 prod	23,96	39,6	3734,3	72,88 41,79 8917,2

Table 3. Results of price formation experiments

| | ZI | | ZIP | | RE | | GD | | Mertacor | |
	Market share	Total profit	Market share	Total profit	Market share	Total profit	Market share	Total profit	Market share	Total profit
4 cons 8 prod	11,58	8,60	416,4 20,61	20,15	822,7	4,13 5,85	254,1	18,36 10,55	652,7	44,66 51,35 940,1
4 cons 16 prod	14,39	5,80	890,1 19,36	19,50	1259,0	6,46 7,20	575,1	18,00 11,94	1080,9	41,55 51,23 1604,7
8 cons 16 prod	10,28	12,96	741,0 20,56	19,39	1237,5	6,11 11,11	485,0	15,26 16,15	824,4	46,91 34,15 1528,5

Results are quite encouraging for the Mertacor approach. Additionally, useful conclusions are drawn for the potential of the various approaches on Power TAC in general: ZIP outperforms all other agents, GD outperforms ZI and RE, and RE has disappointing results since its total profit is comparable to the random ZI agent. Thus, one may argue that adaptive strategies (ZIP, GD, Mertacor) seem to achieve better results than non-adaptive (ZI) or self-adaptive (RE) ones. In addition, predictive agents (ZIP, Mertacor) perform better than all others. These conclusions are rather expected since Power TAC's tariff market is an open auction market that provides agents with vast amount of exploitable information.

6   Conclusion

The research challenges provided by competitions such as Power TAC are manyfold. Even when the problem of a free decentralized market is delimited within such a competition, the field is certainly productive when it comes down to designing DA strategies. To do so, one has to explore various research areas, such as Fuzzy Logic or Time Series Analysis.

Based on the experiments conducted, adaptive predictive price formation policies prove efficient in such open-type markets. Learning techniques perform worse, since their sealed-type advantage is depressed. In general, strategies that exploit optimally information seem to be advantageous, like in the case of the fuzzy logic tariff update strategy. In addition, the agent's ability to explore is crucial. This is proven not only by the optimization of the experimentation parameter, but also by the success of predictive strategies.

Further research is encouraged along several aspects of the agent's strategy. As far as the price formation policy is concerned, it would be possible to design different experimentation procedures (e.g. use another probability density function). The strategy could prove even more effective if certain values, such as the experimentation parameter or the limits of the fuzzy logic update policy, were dynamically adjusted to the market, instead of being pre-specified. Finally, with respect to the energy prediction policy, exponential smoothing could be replaced by several time series forecasting models (e.g. an ARMA model), in order to further explore for the optimal production scheme.

References

1. Borissov, N., Wirström, N.: Q-Strategy: A Bidding Strategy for Market-Based Allocation of Grid Services. In: Meersman, R., Tari, Z. (eds.) OTM 2008, Part I. LNCS, vol. 5331, pp. 744–761. Springer, Heidelberg (2008)
2. Cliff, D.: Minimal-intelligence agents for bargaining behaviors in market-based environments (1997)
3. Erev, I., Roth, A.E.: Predicting How People Play Games: Reinforcement Learning in Experimental Games with Unique, Mixed Strategy Equilibria. The American Economic Review 88(4), 848–881 (1998)
4. Friedman, D.: The Double Auction Market: Institutions, Theories and Evidence (Santa Fe Institute Studies in the Sciences of Complexity Proceedings). Westview Press (March 1993)
5. Gjerstad, S., Dickhaut, J.: Price Formation in Double Auctions. Games and Economic Behavior 22(1), 1–29 (1998)
6. Gode, D.K., Sunder, S.: Allocative Efficiency of Markets with Zero-Intelligence Traders: Market as a Partial Substitute for Individual Rationality. The Journal of Political Economy 101(1), 119–137 (1993)
7. He, M., Leung, H.F., Jennings, N.R.: A Fuzzy-Logic Based Bidding Strategy for Autonomous Agents in Continuous Double Auctions. IEEE Transactions on Knowledge and Data Engineering 15(6), 1345–1363 (2003)
8. Ketter, W., Collins, J., Reddy, P.P., Flath, C.M.: The Power Trading Agent Competition. Report Series ERS-2011-011-LIS, Erasmus Research Institute of Management (2011)
9. Mas-Colell, A., Whinston, M.D., Green, J.R.: Microeconomic Theory. Oxford University Press, USA (1995)

10. Rust, J., Miller, J.H., Palmer, R.: Behavior of trading automata in a computerized double auction market. In: The Double Auction Market: Institutions, Theories, and Evidence (Santa Fe Institute Studies in the Sciences of Complexity Proceedings), pp. 155–198 (March 1993)
11. Rust, J., Miller, J.H., Palmer, R.: Characterizing effective trading strategies: Insights from a computerized double auction tournament. Journal of Economic Dynamics and Control 18(1), 61–96 (1994)
12. Vytelingum, P., Cliff, D., Jennings, N.R.: Strategic bidding in continuous double auctions. Artificial Intelligence 172(14), 1700–1729 (2008)

JACK: A Java Auction Configuration Kit

Thomas Goff[1], Amy Greenwald[1], Elizabeth Hilliard[1], Wolfgang Ketter[2],
Andrew Loomis[1], and Eric Sodomka[1]

[1] Department of Computer Science, Brown University
[2] Rotterdam School of Management, Erasmus University

Abstract. A key step in the evaluation of an intelligent agent (either
autonomous or human) is determining the agent's success as compared
to other agents designed to participate in the same environment. Such
comparisons are the basis for the Trading Agent Competition (TAC),
in which autonomous trading agents compete in simulated market scenarios. TAC servers and agents alike are highly specialized, and typically require teams of developers as TAC simulations tend to be rather
complex. In this work, we present a client-server infrastructure that is
capable of simulating not just one complex market and its corresponding
set of agents, but a wide space of markets and potentially more robust
agents. Supported market mechanisms include both user-designed auctions and a configurable set of auctions whose basic building blocks are
commonly-studied (e.g., first-price, second-price, simultaneous, sequential auctions). Our so-called Java Auction Configuration Kit (JACK) is
intended to facilitate research on the interplay between a variety of auction mechanisms and a variety of agent strategies (both autonomous and
human) by simplifying the orchestration of auction simulation.

Keywords: trading agents, auctions, simulation.

1 Introduction

In many real-world economic markets, goods and services are sold through simultaneous and/or sequential auctions to bidders with complex valuation functions
and incomplete information about competing bidders. Such domains include online ad auctions, spectrum auctions, eBay, the Dutch flower auctions, the New
York Stock Exchange, and entertainment spaces like Fantasy Football. While
auction theory can sometimes provide equilibrium solutions, this theory does
not always map directly into practice. First, in most complex auctions, computing equilibria is intractable, making it difficult to predict agent strategies. Second, even if an equilibrium can be computed, bidders may not conform to that
or any other equilibrium strategy. In such auctions, it is often best to support
theoretical analyses (to the extent they are even possible) with corresponding
experimental and empirical studies.

Experimental economists often perform user studies in simulated auction
games to determine whether bidders play equilibrium strategies [1, 2, 3]. Researchers in autonomous agents often develop bidding strategies for simulated

E. David et al. (Eds.): AMEC/TADA 2012, LNBIP 136, pp. 45–60, 2013.
© Springer-Verlag Berlin Heidelberg 2013

auction games [4, 5] and then search for equilibria in the space of those strategies [6]. In this paper, we introduce the Java Auction Configuration Kit (JACK), an auction simulator that allows researchers to customize auctions and collect empirical data from participating bidders (whether human or autonomous).

We envision the uses of JACK to include:

1. In trading agent design and analysis, JACK can facilitate the simulation of autonomous agents in a specific auction domain by providing auction simulation infrastructure and not restricting the developer's language choice.
2. In experimental economics, JACK can facilitate user studies (either in the lab or online via Mechanical Turk [7]) by allowing researchers to test human behavior in a variety of different auction domains, including environments with some autonomous and some human agents.
3. In artificial intelligence, JACK can be used to develop mixed-initiative bidding agents, in which human bidders receive recommended bids from an underlying autonomous bidding agent and are free to accept or reject those recommendations as they see fit.
4. In mechanism design, JACK can be employed in empirical game-theoretic analysis [6] to ascertain the equilibrium strategies of the auction mechanisms it supports. Then, employing empirical mechanism design [8], researchers can evaluate the quality of those mechanisms.
5. JACK can also be used for educational purposes. We have used it in the classroom to run competitions among autonomous agents developed by students to bid in simultaneous and sequential sealed-bid auctions.

The rest of this paper proceeds as follows. Section 2 explores related work. Section 3 describes JACK's client-server architecture, including communication between the server and its clients. Sections 4 and 5 discuss the auction types and valuation structures that are built in to JACK. Sections 6 and 7 demonstrate the usefulness of JACK through a classroom case study and an implementation of the Dutch Flower Auctions, a complex, real-world auction domain. Section 8 concludes and discusses directions for future work.

2   Related Work

There exist a multitude of frameworks in the experimental economics literature and trading agent design community for running auctions and other games. Most work in experimental economics has been focused on whether equilibrium strategies are borne out by humans in practice, so naturally the types of auctions studied in that field are typically simpler auctions that are amenable to theoretical analysis [3]. One of the most prominently used frameworks in the experimental economics literature is z-Tree [9], a client-server programming environment that is used for auctions and other economic experiments. Because it is capable of expressing a variety of games, z-Tree is programming intensive beyond a set of built-in experiments. With our focus being only on auctions, we may be able to express games more succinctly, thereby making it easier for the researcher to initiate his experiments.

At the other end of the spectrum, VeconLab Pre-Programmed Experiments [10] and EconPort [11] are less programming intensive but can express fewer games. VeconLab allows for numerous pre-programmed economic games to be played, such as simple auctions, bargaining games, and public goods games, but they are limited because the agents' valuations for bundles of goods are often decomposable into values for individual goods; that is, even simple complements and substitutes are not immediately expressible. The degree of expressivity achieved by VeconLab does align well with much of the literature on economic theory, but to model more complex, real-world settings, a richer game representation is required.

Arguably more complex auctions have been studied in the autonomous trading agent community. Wurman et. al. [12] created the Michigan Internet Auction-Bot, a server for hosting various types of online auctions, where bidders can be either agents or humans. The Swedish Institute of Computer Science developed a client-server architecture from which several complex trading agent games have been built [13]. Indeed, the annual trading agent competitions (TAC) have been run using these two servers. TAC Classic [13], where agents act as travel agents assembling travel packages for their individual sets of clients, involves three different auction mechanisms (continuous one-sided, continuous double, and ascending multi-unit auctions) and goods that exhibit complementarity and substitutability. In TAC Supply Chain Management [14], agents act as manufacturers in a supply chain and must bid in reverse auctions to sell their finished goods to customers. TAC Ad Auctions [15] is a game in which agents act as online advertisers on a search engine. Agents bid for items exhibiting imperfect substitutability and uncertain payoffs in a parameterized model of the generalized second price auction used in real-world sponsored search.

As seen in these examples from experimental economics and the trading agent research community, there are auctions spanning a wide range of complexity under investigation. Wurman et. al. [16] decomposed the vast auction design space into several key features such as bidding rules, closing conditions, and information revelation. The authors proposed a parameterization of each of these features. JACK represents only a subset of Wurman's auction design space by defining a simpler (albeit more restrictive) set of auction parameters but additionally parameterizes part of the valuation space.

3   Client-Server Framework

We now describe the architecture of our auction framework. JACK is set in the client-server model and consists of three modules: server, client, and user interface. A schematic diagram of JACK, decomposed into these modules, is shown in Figure 1.

The server module contains functionality for creating socket connections and sending and receiving messages from clients. It handles all multi-threading necessary for simultaneous communication with multiple clients. The messages it sends are strings, where the start of message is a substring stating what type

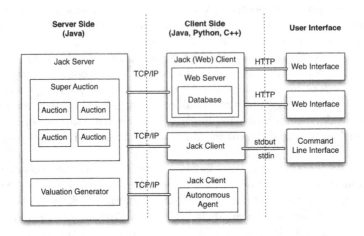

Fig. 1. Client-server architecture of JACK

of message is being passed (e.g., "Status"). Similarly, it receives messages with instructive starting substrings sent by clients (e.g., "Bid").

The client module contains the functionality for handling messages from the server and sending messages containing bids and other pertinent information to the server. Clients may be implemented in any language that supports socket communication, and currently we provide example clients in Java, Python, and C++. We show in Figure 1 how the JACK client can be extended to communicate either an autonomous agent or human bidders' decisions to the JACK server. A client could be extended to provide some autonomous way of making bidding decisions, or it could communicate with human bidders through a user interface. In the user interface module, we have developed two user interfaces: the first is a command line interface, which allows a human to send and receive server messages directly using standard IO, and the second is a web interface, which allows multiple users to participate in an auction by interacting with a dynamic web page. A screenshot of one of the JACK web client interfaces is shown in Figure 2. It shows a user participating against other users in sequential ascending auctions within the context of a fantasy football auction draft.

The JACK web client is implemented using Python's Django framework. It receives messages from the server and stores them in a sqlite database. The web interface (implemented in HTML and Javascript) is a web application that constantly updates itself to reflect the current state of the database. When auction participants place bids using this interface, the bids are transmitted as HTTP posts to the JACK web client. The client then forwards these posts back to the server, where they are processed.

Note that while each JACK client could represent a single bidder, our architecture and messaging protocol are robust enough to allow multiple bidders to

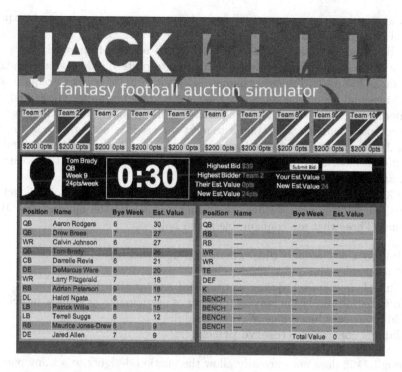

Fig. 2. Example JACK web interface. Here, bidders compete in sequential ascending common-value auctions. Their goal is to assemble the best virtual football team without exceeding a fixed salary cap. The current player up for auction is in the center of the screen, the schedule of players going up for auction is shown in the left pane, and the bidder's current team is shown in the right pane.

commuicate with the server through a single client. As seen in Figure 1, the JACK web client is responsible for passing messages from multiple web bidders to the server, where they are handled independently.

Within the server module there are two packages. The auction package, which interprets a set of configuration files, specifies the auction rules (i.e., payment and allocation), creates the auction schedule, and writes log files. The valuation package specifies parameters that determine priors over bidder valuations and draws valuations from those priors. These packages are discussed in detail in the following two sections, respectively.

4 Auctions Overview

When designing a multi-purpose auction simulator, one must consider the trade-off between expressiveness—the ability to model a large set of auctions—and the compactness and simplicity that can be achieved by modeling any one particular auction. When considering this trade-off, one should consider the goals of potential users and what types of auctions they might be interested in simulating.

We assume our primary users will be autonomous agents researchers, experimental economists, and educators.

While these users may all have a need for an auction framework, the complexity of their desired application domains are quite different. Experimental economists interested in testing human behavior in auctions likely require simpler games and have a higher cost for lower-level programming. Those studying autonomous agents require, and are perhaps more willing to explicitly program, more complex domains. We attempt to meet the needs of both groups by including in JACK some commonly-studied auctions that are easily configurable and by providing a basic auction infrastructure on top of which it is relatively easy to build any auction game.

JACK allows users to configure parameters across five dimensions of the auction space. The following list outlines these dimensions and the options that JACK provides. Those that are configurable are in bold.

1. Bidding rules (**sealed bid, ascending, descending**)
2. Pricing rules (**1st price, 2nd price**)
3. Multiple auction scheduling (**sequential** and/or **simultaneous**)
4. Information revelation policies (number of participants, past bids, individual bidder actions, upcoming auction schedule)
5. Bidding constraints (**reserve prices**)

Although JACK does not currently allow the auction designer to set any parameters to control what information is revealed to agents, some basic information is sent from the server to the agents before, during and after the auction. The reserve price for each good as well as the entire auction schedule is announced before the auctions begin, for all auction types. Only the ascending auction setup allows for information revelation during an auction. In this case, we chose not to reveal all agents' bids; instead JACK reveals only the agent ID and the current bid of the current highest bidder after each round. The minimum acceptable bid is also sent to the agents. For all auction types, after an auction closes, the winning agent's ID and closing price, not its bid, are announced to all agents. This means that in second price auctions agents are not told the winning bid, but instead only the second highest bid.

Figure 3(a) and 3(b) depict a GUI that is used for auction configuration. After specifying the number of simultaneous and sequential auctions on the Basic Setup tab, the JACK user can click on the Auction Schedule tab to see a grid-based layout of these auctions. The user can then highlight any of these auction boxes and click the add button to assign these auctions to one of several default auction types. Figure 3(b) shows the Good Schedule which allows for similar functionality when a user is deciding what goods will be sold in what auction slots. When the user is done, the GUI writes the user's selections to a set of configuration files which provide an auction game definition to the server.

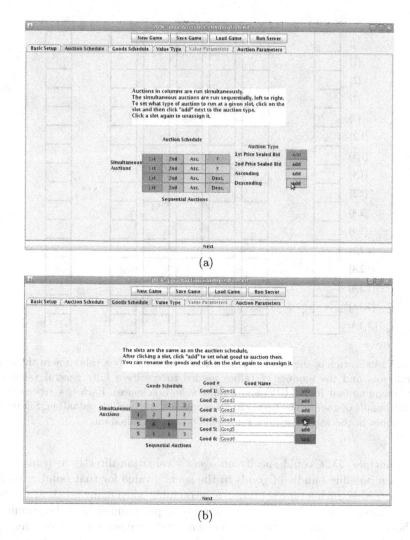

Fig. 3. (a)GUI for specifying the auction configuration. (b) GUI for specifying goods schedule.

5   Valuation Expression

We now turn to the problem of expressing valuations in general auction games. Assume there are N distinct types of goods, and let $\mathcal{X} = \langle X_1, \ldots, X_N \rangle$ denote a multiset set of goods of these types, where each X_i, for $i \in \{1, \ldots, N\}$, denotes a set of homogeneous goods. We denote by the N-vector g be a *bundle*, where $g_i \in \{0, \ldots, |X_i|\}$ is the number of copies of good i in g. A bidder's *value* of a bundle is a measure of that bundle's worth to the bidder. A bidder's *valuation* V is a mapping from bundles to values.

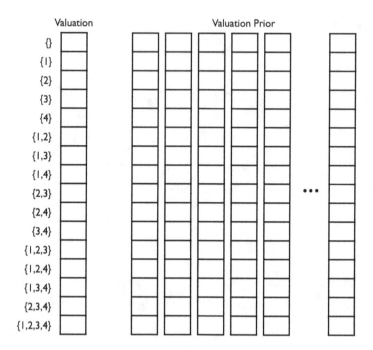

Fig. 4. Visualization of the number of values needed to specify a valuation in the most general case, and the number of values needed to specify a fully general valuation prior (assuming four items, IPV, and a finite valuation space). Each row represents a possible bundle of goods. The first column represents one possible valuation. Similarly, each column in the valuation prior represents a possible valuation.

In principle, JACK could specify an agent's valuation directly as a mapping from each possible bundle of goods to the agent's value for that bundle. While fully expressive, such a representation is intractable when many goods are up for auction. Even if $\mathcal{X} = \langle 1, \ldots, 1 \rangle$, 2^N values (one per bundle) must be specified. Furthermore, most auction theory relies on agents having some prior over the distribution of other agents' valuations [17]. A JACK user thus needs to express more than individual valuations—he must express a *prior* over these valuations.

Figure 4 shows the JACK user's problem of specifying general priors over valuations, assuming $\mathcal{X} = \langle 1, \ldots, 1 \rangle$ (i.e.,. 2^N possible bundles). If each bundle can independently take on V possible discrete values, then in total V^{2^N} valuations can be realized. Since each valuation consists of 2^N values (one per possible bundle), representing the entire prior over valuations as a map from valuations to probabilities requires $V^{2^N} 2^N$ values and V^{2^N} probabilities.

Providing full expressiveness over valuation priors may be feasible for toy problems but quickly becomes burdensome. We instead try to express priors over valuations in such a way as to make them compact and easily configurable. But if the priors we provide are too restrictive, users can always implement their own specialized valuation priors on top of JACK's basic infrastructure.

Currently, JACK allows its users to define a prior over valuations in terms of five basic structures. These include constant, increasing, and decreasing marginal values; scheduling valuations; and contract valuations. These valuations are by no means exhaustive, but they do represent a range of interesting and commonly studied possibilities.

Homogenous Additive Valuations. Three of these types—constant, increasing, and decreasing marginal values—share a base structure, which we refer to as *homogenous additive* valuations. This structure is governed by two parameters, α and β, that are used to express a bidder's precise valuation. A value V for a given bundle g is given by $V(g, \alpha, \beta) = \alpha_1 g_1^{\beta_1} + \alpha_2 g_2^{\beta_2} + \ldots + \alpha_N g_N^{\beta_N}$, where α_i and β_i are parameters specifying the shape of the valuation for good type i. Using this structure, we can express increasing marginal values whenever $\beta > 1$, decreasing marginal values whenever $0 < \beta < 1$, and constant marginal values whenever $\beta = 1$.

Figure 5 depicts several different homogeneous additive valuations, each over bundles of two good types. The axes indicate the number of each good type in the bundle, and the color at each point represents the valuation associated with achieving that bundle (with lighter colors representing higher valuations). In 5(a), the goods both exhibit decreasing marginal values ($\alpha_1 \in [1, 2], \beta_1 = 0.3, \alpha_2 \in [1, 2], \beta_2 = 0.6$). In 5(b) the goods both exhibit increasing marginal values ($\alpha_1 \in [1, 3], \beta_1 = 1.3, \alpha_2 \in [1, 3], \beta_2 = 1.3$). Figure 5(c) shows constant marginal values ($\alpha_1 = 6, \beta_1 = 1, \alpha_2 = 4, \beta_2 = 1$). The increasing, decreasing, and constant marginal values are visualized by the increasing, decreasing, and constant rate of change in heatmap color as the number of goods increases.

To specify priors over valuations with homogenous additive structure, the user specifies ranges $[\alpha_i^{min}, \alpha_i^{max}]$ and $[\beta_i^{min}, \beta_i^{max}]$ from which α_i and β_i are uniformly drawn. Assuming N good types, the user only has to specify $4N$ parameters to fully define this prior over valuations.

Homogeneous additive valuations cannot express a "threshold," in which a bidder ascribes a value of 0 to a bundle unless a specific quantity of some good type is obtained. Valuations are also restricted to being additive across good types. To address these limitations, we turn to contract valuations.

Contract Valuations. Contract valuations ascribe bidders value when they fulfill contracts. A contract c is a vector over goods, where $c_i \leq |X_i|$ indicates the number of copies of good i needed to fulfill the contract. If $v \in \mathbb{R}^N$ is a vector of values, then the value of fulfilling contract c is $V(c, v) = c \cdot v$.

Each bidder is assigned a set $\mathcal{C} = \{c^1, \ldots, c^M\}$ of contracts, each of which it may or may not fulfill. Given a bundle of goods, to calculate a bidder's value one must solve the following multi-dimensional knapsack problem:

$$V(g, \mathcal{C}) = \max_x x^j (c^j \cdot v)$$

$$s.t. \quad c_i \cdot x \leq g_i \quad \forall i \in \{1, \ldots, N\}$$

$$x^j \in \{0, 1\}$$

Here, each binary variable x^j indicates whether the contract c^j is fulfilled.

To allow for a compact representation of priors over contract valuations, the space of possible contracts is parametrized as follows. For each good type i, let $[c_i^{min}, c_i^{max}]$ represent the range of contract fulfillment quantities, and let $[v_i^{min}, v_i^{max}]$ represent a per-good range of values. For every contract, the necessary values of c_i and v_i are sampled uniformly from these user-specified intervals. Representing these valuation priors requires only $4N + 1$ parameters (the additional one is M, the number of contracts).

As an example, suppose the user configured the contract valuation space for a single agent as follows:

$$[c_1^{min}, c_1^{max}] = [2,4], \ [c_2^{min}, c_2^{max}] = [0,1], \ [c_3^{min}, c_3^{max}] = [0,6].$$

$$[v_1^{min}, v_1^{max}] = [2,6] \ [v_2^{min}, v_2^{max}] = [5,9] \ [v_3^{min}, v_3^{max}] = [3,8]$$

A sample contract $\boldsymbol{c} = \langle 3,1,4 \rangle$ and per-good values $\boldsymbol{v} = \langle 5,8,3 \rangle$ give rise to a total value of $V(\boldsymbol{c}, \boldsymbol{v}) = \langle 3,1,4 \rangle \cdot \langle 5,8,3 \rangle = 35$ if the contract is fulfilled.

Figure 5(d) shows a visualization of contract valuations when there are two different good types. The valuation parameters are $M = 10$ contracts,

$$[c_1^{min}, c_1^{max}] = [0,10], \ [c_2^{min}, c_2^{max}] = [0,10],$$

$$[v_1^{min}, v_1^{max}] = [2,7], \text{ and } [v_2^{min}, v_2^{max}] = [10,11].$$

This visualization shows complementarity between the two goods. In order for an agent to increase the value it receives it is not enough to obtain more of a single good (i.e., increase along the vertical or horizontal axis only). The agent must, instead, obtain more of both goods (i.e., increase along both the horizontal and vertical axes).

Contract valuations do not allow an auction designer to create perfect substitutes. On the other hand, they do require that agents acquire a minimum number of goods before receiving any value; therefore, they can be used to model complementarities.

Scheduling Valuations. The above valuations are applicable to homogenous good settings. Reeves et. al. [18], and later Yoon and Wellman [19], study a valuation for non-homogenous goods, among which there are both complements and substitutes, in an auction-based scheduling problem. The goods are time slots, of which there are N in total: i.e., $|X_i| = 1$, for all $i \in \{1, \dots, N\}$. These time slots can be thought of as scheduled time that can be purchased on a supercomputer.

Each bidder has a task to perform, which requires λ time slots. The bidder's value depends on how early its task will complete: If the bidder's λth time slot occurs at time i, it receives value is v_i. Bidders do not have to purchase contiguous time slots to complete their task; value is based only on the *time* in which the bidder's task is completed.

As above, let $\boldsymbol{g}$ be bundle of goods, but note that here $g_i \in \{0,1\}$ is a binary variable indicating whether or not time slot i is in bundle $\boldsymbol{g}$. Define the completion time T to be the earliest time by which λ time slots can be obtained:

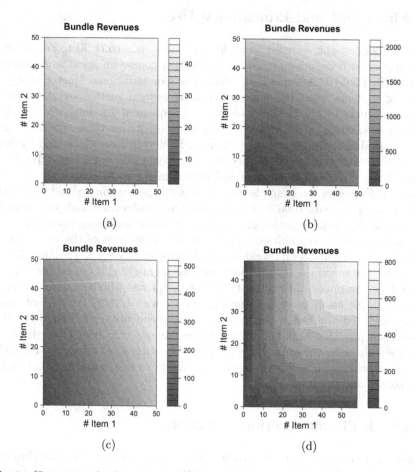

Fig. 5. Heatmaps of valuations for finishing the auction with different item bundles, given the following valuations: (a) additive valuations with decreasing marginal values for both items; (b) additive valuations with increasing marginal values for both items; (c) additive valuations with constant marginal values for both items; and (d) contract valuations

$T(\boldsymbol{g}, \lambda) = \min\left(\{t \text{ s.t. } |\{g_i = 1 \mid i \leq t\}| \geq \lambda\} \cup \{\infty\}\right)$. Using this notation, a bidder's value for bundle $\boldsymbol{g}$ is: $V(\boldsymbol{g}, \boldsymbol{v}, \lambda) = v_{T(\boldsymbol{g}, \lambda)}$.

To express priors over these valuations, the user specifies a range $[\lambda^{min}, \lambda^{max}]$ from which λ is drawn uniformly. Additionally, the user specifies a range $[v^{min}, v^{max}]$ from which N task completion values are drawn uniformly. Those N task completion values can then be either sorted or ironed so that earlier completion times demand higher values: i.e., $v_i \geq v_{i+1}$. In total, a JACK user need only specify 4 parameters to define priors over these scheduling valuations.

6   Alpha Test and Educational Use

As a proof of concept, we used an alpha version of JACK (αJACK) to run several auction competitions amongst students taking a course on agent and auction design (CSCI 2951-C Autonomous Agents and Computational Market Design). Teams of students spent the semester creating general auction simulators and designing agents to bid in simultaneous and sequential auctions with market scheduling valuations [18]. After they designed agents for these settings, they were provided with sample code for "dummy" bidders in Java, C++, and Python that could interface with αJACK. These dummy clients were not competitive; they merely demonstrated how to parse and format messages to communicate with the server. Following the example dummy agents, the students edited their own agents to interface with αJACK, and competed in simultaneous 2nd-price sealed-bid, sequential 2nd-price sealed-bid, and simultaneous ascending auctions.

Running student competitions on αJACK was a dry run of the system and highlighted its strengths and weaknesses. The inconvenience of running all the agents and the server on a single host machine highlighted the need for remote connections. An important test of the JACK concept was whether or not existing agents could be easily modified to communicate with αJACK. As students had already designed and tested their agents in independently coded auctions, the competition provided confidence that existing agents can indeed be edited to interface with JACK. Given the large number of existing agents designed for TAC games and other specific environments, the ability to adapt agents to interface with JACK is an important quality.

7   Dutch Flower Auctions Example

We now turn to a more complex domain which cannot be created in JACK through simple configuration but is nevertheless relatively easily to implement on top of the JACK infrastructure. We focus on the real-world domain of the *Dutch Flower Auctions (DFA)*, which accounts for nearly two-thirds of the global flower trade. The DFA are an information-rich, time-critical market in which it is not obvious how to bid effectively. Accurate simulation could facilitate the development of effective bidding strategies.

The DFA halls, an example of which can be seen in Figure 6 [20], run multiple auctions simultaneously, sequentially, and asynchronously. Each one is a multi-unit auction—meaning multiple goods exchange hands with each auction clearing—implemented using a single-handed clock that initially points to a high price and rapidly decreases. As the price falls, each buyer can bid by pressing a button indicating the portion of the lot being auctioned he is willing to accept at the current price. The first buyer to bid wins. If the winning bidder does not select the entire remaining quantity, the process repeats. The clock restarts at a new high price and the auction reruns until the entire lot is sold, or until the price falls below the seller's reserve price, in which case any unsold goods remaining in that lot are destroyed. Our DFA simulation mimics this design.

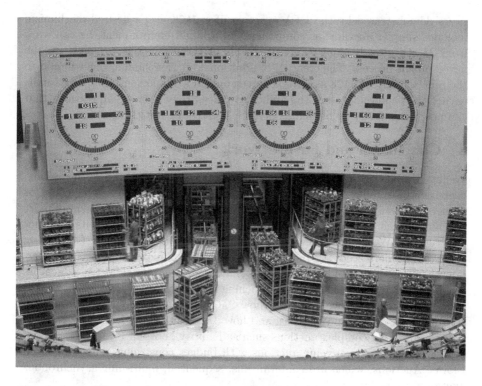

Fig. 6. A set of four simultaneous, multi-unit Dutch auctions. In addition to the current asking price, each clock also contains information about the current seller, the winning buyer, the type of flowers being sold, the minimum purchase quantity, the reserve price, and flower quality.

In a live DFA, bidders must buzz in exactly when the clock reaches the point at which they would like to bid. In contrast, clients in our simulation enter proxy bids and quantities, which can be updated at any time. Before the auction clock decrements, it checks whether any bidders have entered a proxy bid at that price. If so, a winner is declared. (If multiple bidders have placed proxy bids at that price, a winner is chosen randomly.) This eliminates race conditions that occur in the true DFA, allowing clients to focus more on their bidding strategy than on their timing. Furthermore, in practice proxy bidding minimizes concerns of delayed bids caused by network latency.

There are some properties of the DFA that prevent it from being expressible through simple configuration in the current version of JACK. First, JACK does not currently handle multi-unit auctions. Second, the auction clocks in the DFA are running asynchronously, meaning that an auction can begin on one clock while an auction on another clock is still running. While we eventually intend to make options such as these configurable, we use these current shortcomings in the configuration space to demonstrate how JACK can run any non-configurable auction on top of its existing infrastructure.

As demonstrated by the DFA example, if a JACK user's desired mechanism includes simpler auctions as components in a larger environment, he can work from JACK's already implemented versions of these auctions to speed up the development process. The creation of additional auction simulations will add to the functionality of JACK as a whole: given our DFA implementation, multi-unit, asynchronous auctions, and the ability to place proxy bids are all features that can now more easily be offered as default JACK configuration options.

8   Conclusion and Future Work

We introduced the Java Auction Configuration Framework (JACK), an in-the-box, user-friendly simulator of general auction games. JACK is easily configurable for numerous auction mechanisms and valuations, and enables development of more specific auction domains and othe interesting valuations on top of its basic infrastructure. We expect three groups will benefit from using JACK: (1) trading agent researchers studying bidding strategies in complex domains, (2) experimental economists studying human behavior in auctions, and (3) educators looking for hands-on exercises for teaching auction theory or artificial intelligence. In this paper, we described how JACK was used in our own course on trading agent design and analysis, and how JACK can be specialized to simulate real-world highly complex auctions such as Fantasy Football, which are sequential ascending common-value auctions with budget constraints, and the Dutch Flower Auctions, which are simultaneous, sequential, multi-unit asynchronous auctions.

There are many future directions we could pursue to make JACK more useful to researchers. Our main focus will be on improving both the expressiveness and simplicity of designing auctions and valuations. We intend to add additional built-in auction types such as combinatorial auctions and continuous double auctions, as well as control over parameter settings like information revelation policies, number of units sold per auction, and budget constraints. With time, these and other more obscure parameters such as all-pay settings will hopefully become part of JACK's configurable functionality. Additionally, we would like to improve the expressiveness of JACK's valuations. While allowing a fully expressive prior over combinatorial valuations is infeasible, previous literature on experimental economics and autonomous agents (specifically, TAC games) provides some direction as to what types of valuations should be easily expressible. With a more expressible auction and valuation space, we could implement previous and/or future TAC games.

Our second focus will be on simplifying the process of autonomous bidding agent design. We plan to incorporate baseline bidding strategies from the auction literature into JACK. Users can compete against and use as starting points for developing their own agents. These baseline bidding strategies, especially if written in several languages, will allow for more flexibility for educators using JACK in the classroom.

In complex auctions, as the number of auctions increases or the allowed time between bids decreases, humans may find the task of manually placing bids and assessing the outcomes of past auctions overwhelming. A mixed-initiative system could aggregate auction data, present summary statistics to humans to better inform about upcoming decisions, provide bid recommendations, or to take control of low-level tasks. One useful addition to JACK would be to create a set of mixed-initiative agents for some of the standard auction domains. Such agents would lower the startup costs for researchers studying mixed-initiative auction systems, much like dummy bidders provide a low barrier-to-entry for researchers building autonomous bidding agents.

JACK's modular and flexible design allows users to simulate many different auction designs. Further, the JACK web client facilitates running experiments with human participants dispersed over large geographic areas, without requiring them to download any software. Experimental economists can thus leverage the large numbers of people on sites like Amazon Mechanical Turk to not only enhance our understanding of human bidding behavior, but also to allow human bidders to compete directly against autonomous agents. For particular auction designs of interest, we plan to incorporate GUIs, like the one designed for Fantasy Football, that will facilitate human participation. But it will be challenging to design any one GUI that is general enough to be useful as a default GUI for multiple auction designs.

A third area of focus will be on simplifying the process of experimentation. For trading agent researchers, this would include adding an agent repository and an experiment manager that can schedule games for tournaments or perform empirical game-theoretic analyses [6], and improving logging capabilities.

We have released JACK as an open-source project at http://jack.cs.brown.edu. We expect the functionality of JACK to grow as researchers use and extend the software to meet their own auction simulation needs. We hope the availability of JACK will enable the TAC community, experimental economists, educators, and others to more sharply focus on their core interests in autonomous agent and auction design.

Acknowledgments. This research was supported in part by Grant CCF-0905139 from the U.S. National Science Foundation. This research was also supported by a grant from the Dutch Organization for Scientific Research (NWO).

References

[1] Dorsey, R., Razzolini, L.: Explaining overbidding in first price auctions using controlled lotteries. Experimental Economics 6(2), 123–140 (2003)

[2] Isaac, R.M.: Just who are you calling risk averse? Journal of Risk and Uncertainty 20(2), 177–187 (2000)

[3] Kagel, J.H., Levin, D., Hall, A.: Auctions: A survey of experimental research, 1995-2008. In: Handbook of Experimental Economics, vol. 2 (2008)

[4] Greenwald, A.: The 2002 trading agent competition: An overview of agent strategies. AI Magazine (April 2003)

[5] Wellman, M.P., Greenwald, A., Stone, P.: Autonomous Bidding Agents: Strategies and Lessons from the Trading Agent Competition. MIT Press (2007)

[6] Jordan, P.R., Kiekintveld, C., Wellman, M.P.: Empirical game-theoretic analysis of the tac supply chain game. In: AAMAS 2007: Proceedings of the 6th International Joint Conference on Autonomous Agents and Multiagent Systems, pp. 1–8. ACM, New York (2007)

[7] Mason, W., Suri, S.: Conducting behavioral research on Amazons Mechanical Turk. Behavior Research Methods 44(1), 1–23 (2011)

[8] Vorobeychik, Y., Kiekintveld, C., Wellman, M.P.: Empirical mechanism design: Methods, with application to a supply-chain scenario. In: Seventh ACM Conference on Electronic Commerce, pp. 306–315 (2006)

[9] Fischbacher, U.: z-Tree: Zurich toolbox for ready-made economic experiments. Experimental Economics 10(2), 171–178 (2007)

[10] Larson, N., Elmaghraby, W.: Procurement auctions with avoidable fixed costs: An experimental approach (2011)

[11] Cox, J.C., Swarthout, J.T.: EconPort: Creating and maintaining a knowledge commons. Technical report, Experimental Economics Center, Andrew Young School of Policy Studies, Georgia State University (2005)

[12] Wurman, P.R., Wellman, M.P., Walsh, W.E.: The Michigan Internet AuctionBot: A configurable auction server for human and software agents. In: Second International Conference on Autonomous Agents, pp. 301–308 (1998)

[13] Eriksson, J., Finne, N., Janson, S.: Evolution of a supply chain management game for the trading agent competition. AI Communications (2000)

[14] Collins, J., Arunachalam, R., Sadeh, N., Eriksson, J., Finne, N., Janson, S.: The Supply Chain Management Game for the 2007 Trading Agent Competition. Technical report, Carnegie Mellon University (2006)

[15] Jordan, P.R., Wellman, M.P.: Designing an ad auctions game for the trading agent competition. In: David, E., Gerding, E., Sarne, D., Shehory, O. (eds.) AMEC 2009. LNBIP, vol. 59, pp. 147–162. Springer, Heidelberg (2010)

[16] Wurman, P.R., Wellman, M.P., Walsh, W.E.: A parametrization of the auction design space. Games and Economic Behavior 35, 304–338 (2001)

[17] Krishna, V.: Auction Theory, 2nd edn. Academic Press (2010)

[18] Reeves, D.M., Wellman, M.P., MacKie-Mason, J.K., Osepayshvili, A.: Exploring bidding strategies for market-based scheduling. Decision Support Systems 39(1), 67–85 (2005)

[19] Yoon, D.Y., Wellman, M.P.: Self-confirming price prediction for bidding in simultaneous second-price sealed-bid auctions. In: IJCAI 2011 Workshop on Trading Agent Design and Analysis (2011)

[20] van Heck, E., Ketter, W.: Software Agents Supporting Decision-Makers in Complex Flower Business Networks. Liber Amicorum In Memoriam of Prof. Dr. Ir. Jo van Nunen (2010)

A Decision Framework
for Broker Selection in Smart Grids

Yasaman Haghpanah[1], Wolfgang Ketter[2], Marie desJardins[1], and Jan van Dalen[2]

[1] University of Maryland, Baltimore County
[2] RSM, Erasmus University

Abstract. Trust and reputation are critical factors for successful cooperative relationships between broker agents and producers/consumers in "SmartGrids" electricity markets. In this paper, we present SmartRate, a trust and reputation-based decision framework for Smart Grids, based on the available ratings provided by other customers. This model considers multiple trust factors associated with the broker and the preferences of customers for each of these factors. Our previous work has shown the importance of learning the behavior of the agent who is providing reports or rates in selecting trustworthy partners. SmartRate uses direct interactions with brokers to learn the rating behavior of customers. We define a multi-attribute utility function for broker selection and show how learning customers' rating behaviors helps to increase a decision maker's utility, which leads to an increase in customer satisfaction. We evaluate this framework by simulating a market based on real-world data. Our results show that learning the characteristics of a rating population helps to interpret and personalize the rates, which results in better decision making and an increase in customer satisfaction.

Keywords: Behavioral modeling, trust and reputation, agents, decision framework.

1 Introduction

The increase in population size and the subsequent increase in energy demand have amplified the effects of power outages and have stressed power grids [2]. Smart Grid-enabled technologies can be used to manage this increased demand for electricity. Smart Grid extends and modernizes the existing power grid using digital communication technologies. Smart Grid consists of consumers and producers, similar to the existing power grid, but it is also equipped with digital controls and sensors along the transmission lines, enabling two-way communication between producers and customers. In this way, Smart Grid enhances and facilitates the ability of small-scale producers, such as households with solar panels and windmills, to sell their production to the power grid, creating a two-way flow of electricity. As a result, it improves efficiency and reliability, increases renewable power production, and balances demand and supply [4].

One downside of adding small-scale producers is that they are unpredictable, which creates complexity in the supply-demand balance of the system. Accordingly, there is a need for new control mechanisms. One approach to address this technical challenge

E. David et al. (Eds.): AMEC/TADA 2012, LNBIP 136, pp. 61–74, 2013.
© Springer-Verlag Berlin Heidelberg 2013

in Smart Grids is by introducing *Broker Agents*, who buy electricity from producers and sell it to consumers using a market mechanism, the *Tariff Market*, in which agents publish their bid and ask prices [12]. Tariff Markets control balance by incentivizing broker agents. Broker agents who are able to simultaneously gain profit and maintain the balance between supply and demand, contribute to the stability of the grid.

As in many other multi-agent systems, finding trustworthy broker agents will help customers and producers to increase their profit and/or satisfaction. However, there is no solution in the literature that defines or uses a trust and reputation model for broker agents in Smart Grids. In this paper, we propose a trust and reputation-based decision framework, *SmartRate*, for Smart Grid applications. In our model, customers work with brokers and provide ratings for each aspect, or *factor*, of the service they receive (e.g., price, customer service, etc.). We define Broker's *reputation* as the average rating given by the customers. These ratings depend on the customers' behavior and expectations as well as the Brokers' performance. Therefore, customers who want to use these ratings to find the best broker who is fit to their preferences, must first learn the population's *rating behavior*, and then customize and adjust the ratings to reflect their own thresholds and preferences. We demonstrate how this model helps customers to select the best broker that will increase their satisfaction in the received service.

In our previous work [6], the PRep model, we showed the importance of learning the behavior of the agent who is providing reports or rates. This learned information helped agents to gain more payoffs and to find their trustworthy partners more accurately in the Iterated Prisoner's Dilemma context where we had biased reporters or raters. Our model outperformed other state-of-the-art trust and reputation models, in terms of speed, accuracy and overall payoffs. In Smart Grids rating websites, the population or customers who are providing rates and reports about the providers' performance can have different preferences and view points for service factors, (e.g., price, customer service, etc.). For example, a customer could be very picky about the customer service while the population's (who have provided ratings) main concern might be price.

We incorporate the lessons from PRep model form our previous framework, SmartRate, by defining a *rating interpretation* procedure that takes into account the behavior of raters. Moreover, we add the following contributions:

- We propose a novel approach that uses the average ratings of all raters instead of individual ratings, since individual ratings of each factor are not readily available on many websites or are hard to collect.
- We model preferences and satisfaction thresholds of customers, and multiple service factors of brokers (or, in general, service providers).

We define the *trust* of a customer in a broker using these adjusted rates. Our trust-based decision framework considers ratings provided by other customers, along with direct interactions with a small group of brokers, to decide whether to accept a given tariff from a new broker. The outcome of this study will help individuals to use rating data more effectively and to make better decisions based on this information. We define a multi-attribute utility function and claim that this proposed model for Smart Grid increases a customer's utility, which yields an increase in customer satisfaction. We simulate a Smart Grid using real-world data to evaluate our proposed decision framework.

2 The SmartRate Model

In this section, we present our trust and reputation model, SmartRate, which is a decision framework based on the provided ratings of broker agents in Smart Grids. We propose a rating interpretation and utility-based approach that takes into account the behavior of agents who have provided rates. In SmartRate, we define the customized rates as the *trust* of a customer to a broker. Our framework considers multiple factors of a service (received from a broker) that are essential in the decision making. It also considers preferences of each customer, ratings provided by other customers, and direct interaction with brokers to decide whether to accept a tariff from a broker.

2.1 Utility Calculation and Preferences

The aim of our model is to increase customer's satisfaction, therefore, we first start by defining our utility function to quantify the satisfaction. In decision theory, utility is a measure of the desirability of outcomes of actions, which applies to decision making under uncertainty [20]. In economics, utility of one customer has been defined as a measure of his satisfaction for a received service or good. In our model, we define the utility of a customer by his satisfaction of the service he has received from a broker. So, we first model each broker's performance on each factor of the service that it is providing to the customers. We denote a broker, B_l, and its performance on the factors of the service that it provides by $\beta_l = \{\beta_{l1}, ..., \beta_{lM}\}$, where M is the number of factors of the service, and β_{li} represents how well factor i is provided, on a scale from 0 to 1. Note that β_{li} is objective (i.e., independent from a customer's viewpoint or preferences).

Now, we define the utility of a single service factor i of broker B_l, by the performance the broker has on that factor:

$$u_{li} = \beta_{li}, \tag{1}$$

where β_{li} is the performance of the broker on factor i. Note that u_{li} has the same range as β_{li}, i.e., from 0 to 1.

Customers may have different view points and preferences for various factors of a service. For example, a customer (e.g., a factory) may want to have a service that is reliable in terms of minimizing power outages, but the price is less important than for another customer (e.g., a household). Therefore, in our SmartRate model, to compute the overall utility of a broker we have to consider all factors and this requires a multi-attribute utility function or MAU function. In utility theory, a MAU function incorporates customer's preferences by defining a set of scaling factors that are proportional with the customer's preferences. These scaling factor are multiplied by attributes' utilities (broker's performance in a factor of service in our case) and combined to obtain the overall utility. In SmartRate, we define the preferences of a customer, k, for each factor (e.g., price, quality, and customer service) of a service as $Pref_k = (Pref_{k1}, ..., Pref_{kM})$, where M is the number of factors. These preferences' weights are defined such that:

$$\sum_{i=1}^{M} Pref_{ki} = 1, \tag{2}$$

where $Pref_{ki}$ is the customer k's preference for factor i. [11] showed that a MAU function has an additive form when the sum of the scaling factors equals to 1. Therefore, we define an additive utility function for the customer k to show his satisfaction of broker B_l, by multiplying the utility of the broker for each factor u_{li} by the customer k's preference for that factor and then summing these values for all the factors of the service. The overall utility can be computed as:

$$U(k, l) = \sum_{i=1}^{M} Pref_{ki} \times u_{li}, \tag{3}$$

where $Pref_{ki}$ is the preference of customer k for factor i. Note that u_{li} satisfies the basic assumptions of additive utility function, which are the preferential independence and utility independence, as explained in [11].

2.2   The Rating Model

In our rating model, customers receive service from brokers (and interact with brokers) by accepting their tariffs. Then, customers rate brokers based on the experience that they have had with those brokers, for each of their service factors. In most of the rating websites, a common approach is for rates to assign numerical values to the ordered categories (e.g., 1 = poor, 2 = fair, 3 = good, 4 = very good, 5 = excellent). In our model, each customer k is modeled as computing its satisfaction in broker B_l for a factor i as $y_{kli} = \beta_{li} x_{kl}$, where y_{kli} is the satisfaction of customer k, x_{ki} is the factor multiplier of this customer for factor i, and β_{li} is the provided service performance for factor i. In essence, x_{ki} reflects how much a customer cares about a specific factor or how "hard to please" he is about that factor. To model the ratings in this work, a customer maps this satisfaction level to a scale-based rating, R, using a defined set of thresholds α, where $\alpha_0 < \alpha_1 < ... < \alpha_r$, and each threshold corresponds to a rating from 1 to r. These α thresholds are constants that are the same among the customers of a rating population. The actual satisfaction y and thresholds α are not directly observable, but we show how they can be inferred indirectly through the posted ratings, R.

As we discussed in the Section 2.1, each customer has different preferences for each factors of the provided service ($Pref_{ki}$). In our model, we assume an inverse relation between $Pref_{ki}$ and rating factors x_{ki}. This assumption comes from the fact that a lower factor multiplier x_{ki} means that the customer will be harder to please in that specific factor and is expecting a high performance from the broker in order to give a good rating. This implies that this factor has high preference for the customer, which results in the inverse relation. Therefore:

$$x_{ki} = \frac{1}{Pref_{ki}} \tag{4}$$

Since $Pref_{ki}$ is less than 1, x_{ki} will be a real number greater than 1. The ratings of all customers in a population are reported to a centralized system (see Figure 1), and this rate is not visible to other customers. In the centralized system, the available rates for each factor and each broker are accumulated and are averaged by the number of ratings provided for that factor:

$$R_{li} = \frac{\sum_{k=1}^{N_{li}} R_{kli}}{N_{li}}, \tag{5}$$

where R_{kli} is the rating reported by customer k for broker l on factor i to the centralized system. N_{li} is the number of customers who have rated factor i of broker l. The average result R_{li} is the rating posted for broker l on factor i. We define R_{li} as *reputation* of the broker l on factor i, and this rating is visible to all customers. Note that some customers may opt not to give rates to all the factors of a service, in this case, the final rate will not reflect their rating i.e., R_{kli}. However, in our model we are considering large populations (when N_{li} is large), and this will not affect the average rate.

2.3   The Learning Process

Now, we explain how a new customer estimates the rating characteristics of a population, i.e., factor multipliers x and thresholds α, by comparing his personal experience to the population's rates for a service provider.

Figure 1 explains the learning process of our model using a scenario involving brokers and customers. In the following scenario, C stands for a new customer, who is looking to find a reputable broker, given a population of customers, who have rated broker (or service provider) B_l. C is presumed to have accepted tariffs from a few brokers (e.g., $B1$ and $B2$) previously and to have observed the performance of different aspects of their service (e.g., reliability, price). That is, C has experienced and learned $B1$ and $B2$'s service factors (β_{B1} and β_{B2}) through direct interactions with them. Now, C needs a new service and wants to switch to another broker, such as $B3$. C wants to use the ratings posted on the central system in order to see if it is better to switch to $B3$, or continue using $B1$ or $B2$. Therefore, it needs to predict $B3$'s performance on the service factors, for which it needs to learn the population's rating characteristics.

C examines the population's ratings for various factors of $B1$ and $B2$. Using already learned β_{B1} and β_{B2}, C computes the population's rating (or satisfaction) threshold and its factor multipliers for each of the service factors using an ordered probit model, as explained in the next subsection.

Ordered Probit Model. The ordered probit model is a formal specification of the relationship between an ordinal dependent variable and various explanatory variables. Let us assume that a population rates their satisfaction with a particular service factor by means of an ordered categorical variable R with r possible outcomes, $j = 1, ..., r$. The ratings are based on an underlying latent variable (satisfaction), which is denoted by y. As we explained, the satisfaction may differ from one population to another, or even from one service to another, depending on the factor multipliers $x = (x_1, ..., x_K)$. So, for any factor i:

$$y_i = \beta_i x_i + p_i, \tag{6}$$

where p_i is an independent disturbance term. In the case of a probit model, these disturbances are assumed to be normally distributed with mean zero and variance one,

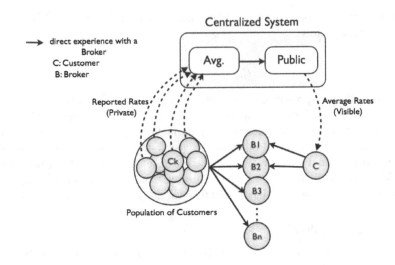

Fig. 1. Basic scenario

$p_i \sim n(0,1)$. This normally distributed noise, p_i, is the estimation error associated with the linearity assumption in Equation 6. To simplify the analysis, we have removed the index l from β_{li} of broker B_l, as the equation is valid for any broker. The latent satisfaction y_i is not directly observed, but indirectly via the ratings, R_i. Let $\alpha_0 < \alpha_1 < ... < \alpha_r$ be a set of threshold constants such that:

$$R_i = \begin{cases} 1 & if \quad \alpha_0 < y_i < \alpha_1 \\ 2 & if \quad \alpha_1 < y_i < \alpha_2 \\ ... & \\ r & if \; \alpha_{r-1} < y_i < \alpha_r \end{cases} \tag{7}$$

where $\alpha_0 = -\infty$ and $\alpha_r = +\infty$.

Estimation of the Model. For the purpose of estimation, it is helpful to introduce an indicator variable z_{ji} for each of the possible outcomes of the provided ratings, R, as follows: $z_{ji} = 1$, if $R_i = j$, and 0 otherwise. For each respondent i, the probability of a particular rating j is obtained as by:

$$\begin{aligned} P(z_{ji} = 1) &= P(\alpha_{j-1} < y_i < \alpha_j) \\ &= P(\alpha_{j-1} < \beta_i x_i + u_i < \alpha_j) \\ &= P(\alpha_{j-1} - \beta_i x_i < u_i < \alpha_j - \beta_i x_i) \\ &= \Phi(\alpha_j - \beta_i x_i) - \Phi(\alpha_{j-1} - \beta_i x_i), \end{aligned} \tag{8}$$

with $\Phi()$ representing the cumulative normal distribution. The parameters x_i and $\alpha_1, ..., \alpha_{r-1}$ can be estimated by maximum likelihood. The likelihood function is specified as:

$$\iota(\beta, \alpha_1, ..., \alpha r - 1) = \prod_{i=1}^{n} \prod_{j=1}^{r} [\Phi(\alpha_j - \beta_i x_i) - \Phi(\alpha_{j-1} - \beta_i x_i)]^{z_{ji}}, \qquad (9)$$

and the log-likelihood function as:

$$L(\beta, \alpha_1, ..., \alpha r - 1) = \sum_{i=1}^{n} \sum_{j=1}^{r} z_{ji} ln[\Phi(\alpha_j - \beta_i x_i) - \Phi(\alpha_{j-1} - \beta_i x_i)]. \qquad (10)$$

Although the first and second-order conditions for a maximum can be straightforwardly obtained, solving these conditions requires an iterative procedure. We optimize these functions in order to obtain estimates of the unknown parameters $x_i = (x_1, ..., x_M)$ and $\alpha_1, ..., \alpha_{r-1}$.

2.4   Learning Service Factors and Decision Making

In the previous subsection, C estimated the population's rating behavior i.e., x and α. Now, C needs to estimate a new service provider's factors, β, using this learned information.

In the scenario shown in Figure 1, C now looks for B3's ratings given by the population to learn the service factors of a given service from B3, $\beta_{B3} = \{\beta_1, ..., \beta_M\}$. Using Equation 10, and knowing the learned population's rating behavior for different factors of a service $x = \{x_1, ..., x_M\}$ and the satisfaction threshold, $\alpha_1, ..., \alpha_{r-1}$, C can estimate the maximum likelihood of $\beta_{B3} = \{\beta_1, ..., \beta_M\}$.

Now, C uses this estimated value β_{B3} for the last step, which is decision making and tariff selection. In order to make a decision as to whether to switch to another broker or stay with the current one, C computes the expected utility of B3 using Equation 3, and compares it with the observed utility of his current broker. The broker who provides highest utility will satisfy C the most, and will therefore be selected as C's future broker (or service provider).

3   Market Simulation

Unfortunately, there are not many data sets available for Smart Grids, due to the relative recency of this technology. We have developed a market simulation using data from a rating website for Texas electricity retailers [9]. The Texas electricity retailers website [9] provides a customer satisfaction study for Texas residential electricity retailers using performance ratings for different factors of the service provided by each electricity retailer in 2011. Twenty different electricity retailer companies are rated based on four service factors: billing and payment, price, communications, and customer service. They are also rated based on overall satisfaction with their service. Customers rate each factor of the retailer company by a 1-to-5 rating scale. The average ratings are visible to all customers and retailers. This data set has some limitations: for example, the number of ratings is not provided by this website and the performance ratings are discretized

Table 1. Customer satisfaction study for Texas Residential Electricity Retailers provided by JD Power ratings website

	Overall	Bill	Price	Communication	Customer Service
Ambit Energy	4	4	4	5	4
Amigo Energy	4	4	4	4	4
Bounce Energy	4	3	4	3	2
Champion Energy	5	5	5	5	4
Cirro Energy	4	4	4	3	4
CPL Retail Energy	2	3	2	3	3
Direct Energy	4	4	4	4	3
Dynowatt	4	3	4	2	2
First Choice Power	3	3	3	3	3
Gexa Energy	4	4	4	4	4
Green Mountain Energy	4	4	4	5	4
Just Energy Texas	3	2	3	2	3
Other Retailer	4	3	4	4	3
Reliant Energy Retail	3	3	3	3	4
Southwest Power Light	3	2	3	2	3
Spark Energy	5	4	5	5	5
StarTex Power	5	5	4	5	5
Stream Energy	4	4	4	4	3
Texas Power	3	3	3	4	4
TXU Energy Company	2	3	2	2	2

(i.e., we do not have any decimal ratings even for the overall ratings). We take these limitations into account in our simulations. Table 1 shows the rated performances for the service factors of the retailers.

In our experiment, we show how customer C, who has been offered service from a new retailer, decides whether it will stay with his current electricity provider or will switch to the new retailer, whose performance has not yet been experienced. This decision will be made by comparing the utility from the new retailer to the utility of the current retailer. For that matter, C needs to learn the rating characteristics of the population, who has provided rates on the website. Then, by using the learned characteristics and the posted rated performance for the new retailer, it will estimate the factors performance of the new retailer on each factor. Finally, C will decide which retailer is the best, based on its preferences and all of the learned performance factors.

To evaluate our model, we introduce two baselines. First, we define a naive approach to select the best broker by summing up all the rates of one broker. This approach does not consider each customer's preference for factors, and it does not personalize the rates based on a customer's view point:

$$U^{N1}(k,l) = \sum_{i=1}^{M} R_{li} \qquad (11)$$

where M is the number of factors of the service provided by a retailer. The second baseline is similar to the first one, but it also considers customer's preferences:

$$U^{N2}(k,l) = \sum_{i=1}^{M} R_{li} \times Pref_{ki} \tag{12}$$

We assume that customer C in our main scenario, Figure 1, has had electricity from a few retailers (i.e., Ambit Energy, Amigo Energy, and Bounce Energy) in the past and has observed their performance for each factor of their provided service. Let us assume that the result of this observed performance are shown in Table 2 for each service factor, β, of each of the mentioned retailers.

Table 2. Service Factors Experienced by Customer C

	Bill	Price	Communication	Customer Service
Ambit Energy	0.5	0.65	1.0	0.5
Amigo Energy	0.45	0.6	0.7	0.5
Bounce Energy	0.3	0.7	0.6	0.15

Now, suppose that C is currently with retailer "Bounce Energy," but also has an offer from "Cirro Energy," and he wants to explore if it is worth switching to this new retailer. C needs to estimate the performance of each factor of the service given by Cirro to the population using the provided rated performances. First, C needs to learn the rating characteristics (i.e., the factor multipliers x and thresholds α) of the population, by comparing the population's performance rates and its personal experience with the three mentioned retailers, whose performance had been observed previously.

We assume that the actual factor multipliers and thresholds are the values shown in Tables 3 and 4. Using Equation 10, C learns the threshold and factor multipliers of the population, which are also shown in the same tables.

At this stage, C has learned the population's threshold and factor multipliers, and can estimate the performance of each factor of the service given by Cirro to the population using Equation 10. These results of learned factors performance of Cirro Energy is shown in Table 5.

Customer C also has its own preferences for each factor of the service, given in Table 6. We assume C's satisfaction threshold is the same as the population's that has been learned. Now that the customer C has learned the factors of service by a new retailer (i.e., β of Cirro), it computes the utility gaining from switching to this new retailer, i.e, Cirro and the current retailer, i.e., Bounce:

$$\begin{aligned}
U(C, Cirro) &= \beta_1 \times Pref_1 + \beta_2 \times Pref_2 + \beta_3 \times Pref_3 + \beta_4 \times Pref_4 \\
&= 0.52 \times 0.1 + 0.61 \times 0.4 + 0.44 \times 0.4 + 0.52 \times 0.1 \\
&= 0.524, \\
U(C, Bounce) &= \beta_1 \times Pref_1 + \beta_2 \times Pref_2 + \beta_3 \times Pref_3 + \beta_4 \times Pref_4 \\
&= 0.3 \times 0.1 + 0.7 \times 0.4 + 0.6 \times 0.4 + 0.15 \times 0.1 \\
&= 0.565.
\end{aligned} \tag{13}$$

Table 3. Actual factor multipliers of the population vs. learned values

	Bill	Price	Communication	Customer Service
Actual preferences	0.2	0.25	0.33	0.22
Learned preferences	0.22	0.25	0.31	0.22
Actual factor multipliers	5.0	4.0	3.0	4.5
Learned factor multipliers	4.62	3.95	3.19	4.62

Table 4. Actual threshold of the population vs. learned values

	α_1	α_2	α_3	α_4
Actual threshold	0	1.0	2.0	3.0
Learned threshold	0	1.01	1.77	3.04

Table 5. Learned Factors for Cirro Energy

	β_1	β_2	β_3	β_4
Learned performance for factors	0.52	0.61	0.44	0.52

Table 6. Customer C's factor multipliers and preferences for different factors of a service

	$Billing$	$Price$	$Communication$	$Customer Service$
C's preferences	0.1	0.4	0.4	0.1
C's factor multipliers	10.0	2.5	2.5	10.0

Therefore, customer C, as a rational agent, will stay with the current retailer instead of switching to Cirro. The main reason behind this decision is that customer C gives high preferences to the second and third service factors, and it both cases Bounce performs much better than Cirro. The ratings alone fail to catch this difference, as both retailers have received same rate from the population on the second and third factors. The naive utility functions show this shortcoming clearly. Without the SmartRate model, customer C can use one of the naive utility functions to compute the utility gained by switching to Cirro Energy. If he uses Equation (11):

$$
\begin{aligned}
U^{N1}(C, Cirro) &= R_1 + R_2 + R_3 + R_4 \\
&= 4 + 4 + 3 + 4 \\
&= 15, \\
U^{N1}(C, Bounce) &= R_1 + R_2 + R_3 + R_4 \\
&= 3 + 4 + 3 + 2 \\
&= 12.
\end{aligned}
\tag{14}
$$

So, the result is that customer C should switch to Cirro. If he uses Equation (12) to calculate the utilities:

$$
\begin{aligned}
U^{N2}(C, Cirro) &= R_1 \times Pref_1 + R_2 \times Pref_2 + R_3 \times Pref_3 + R_4 \times Pref_4 \\
&= 4 \times 0.1 + 4 \times 0.4 + 3 \times 0.4 + 4 \times 0.1 \\
&= 3.6, \\
U^{N2}(C, Bounce) &= R_1 \times Pref_1 + R_2 \times Pref_2 + R_3 \times Pref_3 + R_4 \times Pref_4 \\
&= 3 \times 0.1 + 4 \times 0.4 + 3 \times 0.4 + 2 \times 0.1 \\
&= 3.3.
\end{aligned}
\tag{15}
$$

This again means C should switch to Cirro. As we can see, looking only at people's ratings, even if they are detailed, may not lead to the best choice.

The results of our market simulation show the effectiveness of my approach and indicate that my approach can help customers to fine-tune their decision making in finding the most beneficial retailer.

4 Related Work

4.1 Smart Grids

Smart Grid has recently been gaining a lot of attention among researchers and government organizations, and are in use in almost every country in Europe. The Department of Energy (DOE) and National Institute of Science and Technology (NIST) have recently started research on Smart Grids in the United States [4,16].

Researchers have started addressing several challenges of Smart Grids. [3] surveyed research on bidding strategies in electricity markets. Much of this research uses reverse-auction markets with a single buyer and multiple suppliers, but the Tariff Market strategy can model the situations with multiple customers and suppliers. This characteristic of Tariff Markets presents new challenges in electricity market research. [12] describe a competition setting and address some of the challenges in this new market.

There has also been research on using reinforcement learning strategies in power electricity grids. [13] propose a reinforcement learning method to solve the optimal power system dispatch and power supply stability problems using a multi-objective optimization approach. Researchers also have focused on customer demand response and Advanced Metering Infrastructure (AMI). AMI is the deployment of a metering solution that tries to a optimize power grid's efficiency by enabling control over how much power customers draw from the grid [7].

4.2 Trust and Reputation

Trust and reputation has been widely studied [10,15,18,19,8]. [5] describe a trust decision strategy, including decision making based on both who to trust and how trustworthy to be in reputation exchange networks. [1] build a system of trust degrees, weightings, and trust operators to merge multiple recommendations. Their scheme assigns higher values to more trustworthy agents, but is not rooted in probabilistic modeling. [19] propose a multi-faceted reputation model; however, their model, REGRET, is not utility-based. Instead, it uses ad hoc thresholds and weights.

Several approaches have been proposed for adding trust models specifically into supply chain applications as well. [14] build a trust model based on experiences with suppliers; trust is measured in terms of product quality, order-cycle time, and price. They generalize these factors to the abstract concepts of ability, integrity, and benevolence. This model does not use decision theory. Other supply chain trust factors have been studied as well, although many of them are not generalized, instead they are focused on specific industries. For example, [17] studied twelve trust factors, identifying three factors that are critical to the horticulture supply chain: shared values, point-of-sale information, and honesty.

A few reputation models proposed mechanisms to personalize rates. [22] proposed a personalized approach to handle unfair ratings. They use private and public reputation information to evaluate the trustworthiness of advisors. They estimate the credibility of advisors using a time window to calculate the recency of ratings, and then estimate the trustworthiness of advisors based on the ratings. Their model need to have large number of advisors to be able to estimate the trustworthiness of advisors. Our model is capable of using the rating information just by having one ratings of one population (or advisor). [21] measure how much the advisor's rating deviates from the consumer's experience. Their model identifies accurate advisors, and discards deceptive advisors. Again, their model is based on a large number of advisors, whereas in real world applications, a population provide ratings and we do not have information of how the individuals (or advisors) in the populations provides rates. Our model is capable of using the rating information from a population (or an advisor), where we do not have information about the individuals in that population.

To our knowledge, a trust-based decision framework for broker agents in Smart Grid Tariff Markets has not been explored in the literature. Our model, SmartRate, is based on utility terms and is capable of finding the rating behavior of the population who has provided rates, without having information about the individuals in the population. It also considers multiple factors in calculating trust and reputation.

5   Conclusions and Future Work

In this paper, we proposed a trust and reputation-based decision framework for Smart Grids. The SmartRate models multiple trust factors and preferences of customers. It also considers ratings provided by other customers and direct interaction with the broker to decide whether to accept a tariff from a broker. We have defined a multi-attribute utility function for broker selection based on these criteria. We also showed how learning factor multipliers and satisfaction thresholds of a population help to increase the customers utility, which yields to increase in the customer satisfaction. We evaluated our decision framework by simulating a market based on real-world data from an electricity retailer website. The results demonstrate that learning the characteristic's of a rating population helps to interpret and personalize the rates. All the above result in better decision making and increase customers' satisfaction and utility.

This model provides guidance for the design of a trust and reputation model for Smart Grid in the real world. We plan to apply this reputation-based decision framework to the Power Trading Agent Competition (Power TAC is the latest in the TAC series), which simulates Smart Grid markets in a comprehensive environment and aims to address various challenges in this field [12].

Our experimental results are at a preliminary stage. We plan to elaborate more on the market simulation section. For example in the current experiments, we do not consider the "overall" rated performance data in our computations. We will add this factor to our simulation by studying the correlation between the rated performance of individual factors and the overall performance rate. Moreover, we plan to introduce other baselines for evaluating our model. In addition to the real-world data that we are using now, we will expand the results and evaluate them with synthetic data as well.

References

1. Abdul-Rahman, A., Hailes, S.: Supporting trust in virtual communities. In: Hawaii Int. Conference on System Sciences, Maui, Hawaii, vol. 33, p. 9 (January 2000)
2. Ballman, J.: The great blackout of 2003 Aug. 14 power outage largest in us history. Disaster Recovery Journal 16 (2003)
3. David, A., Wen, F.: Strategic bidding in competitive electricity markets: a literature survey. In: IEEE Power Engineering Society Summer Meeting, vol. 4, pp. 2168–2173. IEEE (2000)
4. DoE (2011), http://energy.gov/oe/
5. Fullam, K.K., Barber, K.S.: Learning trust strategies in reputation exchange networks. In: AAMAS 2006, pp. 1241–1248. ACM Press, New York (2006)
6. Haghpanah, Y., desJardins, M.: Core: A cognitive reputation model. In: AAMAS 2012 (2012) (to appear)
7. Hart, D.: Using ami to realize the smart grid. In: 2008 IEEE Power and Energy Society General Meeting-Conversion and Delivery of Electrical Energy in the 21st Century, pp. 1–2. IEEE (2008)
8. Huynh, T.D., Jennings, N.R., Shadbolt, N.R.: An integrated trust and reputation model for open multi-agent systems. In: AAMAS 2006, vol. 13, pp. 119–154 (2006)
9. JDPower (2011), http://www.jdpower.com/homes/ratings/texas-electric-retailer-ratings
10. Josang, A., Ismail, R., Boyd, C.: A survey of trust and reputation systems for online service provision. Decision Support Systems 43(2), 618–644 (2007)
11. Keeney, R.: Multiplicative utility functions. Operations Research, 22–34 (1974)
12. Ketter, W., Collins, J., Block, C.: Smart grid economics: Policy guidance through competitive simulation. Erasmus Research Institute of Management, Erasmus University (2010)
13. Liao, H., Wu, Q., Jiang, L.: Multi-objective optimization by reinforcement learning for power system dispatch and voltage stability. In: 2010 IEEE PES Innovative Smart Grid Technologies Conference Europe (ISGT Europe), pp. 1–8. IEEE (2010)
14. Lin, F., Sung, Y., Lo, Y.: Effects of trust mechanisms on supply-chain performance: A multi-agent simulation study. International Journal of Electronic Commerce 9(4), 9–112 (2003)
15. Mui, L., Mohtashemi, M., Halberstadt, A.: Notions of reputation in multi-agent systems: A review. In: AAMAS 2002, Bologna, Italy, pp. 280–287 (July 2002), http://portal.acm.org/citation.cfm?id=544807&dl=ACM&coll=portal
16. NIST (2012), http://www.nist.gov/smartgrid/

17. Paterson, I., Maguire, H., Al-Hakim, L.: Analysing trust as a means of improving the effectiveness of the virtual supply chain. International Journal of Networking and Virtual Organisations 5(3), 325–348 (2008)
18. Resnick, P., Kuwabara, K., Zeckhauser, R., Friedman, E.: Reputation systems. Communications of the ACM 43(12), 45–48 (2000)
19. Sabater, J., Sierra, C.: Review on computational trust and reputation models. JAIR 24(1), 33–60 (2005)
20. White, D.: Decision Theory. Aladine Pub. Co., Chicago (1969)
21. Yu, B., Singh, M.: Detecting deception in reputation management. In: AAMAS 2003, pp. 73–80 (2003)
22. Zhang, J., Cohen, R.: Evaluating the trustworthiness of advice about seller agents in e-marketplaces: A personalized approach. Electronic Commerce Research and Applications 7(3), 330–340 (2008)

Prediction Market-Based Information Aggregation for Multi-sensor Information Processing

Janyl Jumadinova and Prithviraj Dasgupta

University of Nebraska at Omaha, Omaha, NE, USA
{jjumadinova,pdasgupta}@unomaha.edu

Abstract. Prediction markets have been shown to be a useful tool in forecasting the outcome of future events by aggregating public opinion about the event's outcome. We consider an analogous problem of information fusion from multiple sensors of different types with the objective of improving the confidence of inference tasks, such as object classification. We develop a multi-agent prediction market-based technique to solve this information fusion problem. To monitor the improvement in the confidence of the object classification as well as to dis-incentivize agents from misreporting information, we have introduced a market maker that rewards the agents based on the quality of the submitted reports. We have implemented the market maker's reward calculation in the form of a *scoring rule* and have shown analytically that it incentivizes truthful revelation by each agent. We have experimentally verified our technique for multi-sensor information fusion for an automated landmine detection scenario. Our experimental results show that, for identical data distributions and settings, using our information aggregation technique increases the accuracy of object classification favorably as compared to two other commonly used techniques for information fusion for landmine detection.[1]

Keywords: Prediction market, information fusion, multi-sensor aggregation, landmine detection.

1 Introduction

A prediction market is a market-based aggregation mechanism that is used to combine the opinions on the outcome of a future, real-world event from different people and forecast the event's possible outcome based on their aggregated opinion [22]. Prediction markets have shown to be a very successful tool in forecasting the outcome of future events as is evidenced from the successful predictions of actual events done by prediction markets run by the Iowa Electronic Marketplace(IEM), Tradesports, Intrade, and by companies such as

---

[1] This research has been sponsored as part of the COMRADES project funded by the Office of Naval Research, grant number N000140911174.

E. David et al. (Eds.): AMEC/TADA 2012, LNBIP 136, pp. 75–89, 2013.
© Springer-Verlag Berlin Heidelberg 2013

Hewlett Packard, Google and Yahoo's Yootles. The main idea behind the prediction market paradigm is that the collective, aggregated beliefs of humans on a future event represents the probability of occurrence of the event more accurately than the corresponding surveys and opinion polls.

Multi-sensor fusion is concerned with the problem of fusing data from multiple sensors in order to make a more accurate estimation of the environment, and has been a central research topic in sensor-based systems [21]. Our work in this paper is based on the insight that the problem addressed by prediction markets of aggregating the beliefs of different humans to forecast the outcome of an initially unknown event is analogous to the problem in multi-sensor fusion of fusing information from multiple sources to predict the outcome of an initially unknown object. Recently several multi-agent techniques [20] have been proposed to address the multi-sensor fusion problem. Most of the solutions for multi-sensor information fusion and processing are based on Bayesian inference techniques [8,14,17]. While such techniques have been shown to be very effective, we investigate a complimentary problem where sensors can behave in a self-interested manner. Such self-interested behavior can be motivated by the sensors that deliberately misreport to save power, CPU cycles and memory (for example, to devote more resources to other tasks), and therefore always behave in a way that maximize their own benefits [10,16]. Moreover, these sensors may be programmed by different people and the assumption of full cooperation may not always hold [19]. To address this problem, we develop a prediction market for multi-sensor information fusion that includes a utility driven mechanism to motivate each sensor, through its associated agent, to reveal accurate reports.

To motivate our problem we describe a distributed automated landmine detection scenario used for humanitarian demining. An environment contains different buried objects, some of which could potentially be landmines. A set of robots, each equipped with one of three types of landmine detection sensor such as a metal detector (MD), or a ground penetrating radar (GPR) or an infra-red (IR) heat sensor, are deployed into this environment. Each robot is capable of perceiving certain features of a buried object through its sensor such as the object's metal content, area, burial depth, etc. However, the sensors give noisy readings for each perceived feature depending on the characteristics of the object as well as on the characteristics of the environment (e.g., moisture content, ambient temperature, sunlight, etc.). Consequently, a sensor that works well in one scenario, fails to detect landmines in a different scenario, and, instead of a single sensor, multiple sensors of different types, possibly with different detection accuracies can detect landmines with higher certainty [4]. Within this scenario, the central question that we intend to answer is: given an initial set of reports from *self-interested* sensors about the features of a buried object, what is a suitable set (number and type) of sensors to deploy over a certain time window to the object, so that, over this time window, the fused information from the different sensors successively reduces the uncertainty in determining the object's type.

Building on the previous models of prediction markets, in this paper, we describe a multi-agent prediction market for multi-sensor information fusion.

Besides being an efficient aggregation mechanism, using prediction markets gives us several useful features - a mathematical formulation called a *scoring rule* that deters self-interested sensors from misreporting information, a regression-based belief update mechanism for the sensor agents for incorporating the aggregated beliefs (or information estimates) of other sensors into their own calculation, and the ability to incorporate an autonomous decision maker that uses expert-level domain knowledge to make utility maximizing decisions to deploy additional sensors appropriately to improve the detection of an object. Our experimental results illustrated with a landmine detection scenario while using identical data distributions and settings, show that the information fusion performed using our technique reduces the root mean squared error by $5 - 13\%$ as compared to a previously studied technique for landmine data fusion using the Dempster-Shafer theory [11] and by $3 - 8\%$ using distributed data fusion technique [9].

2   Related Work

Multi-agent Information Fusion. Multi-agent systems have been used to solve various sensor network related problems and an excellent overview is given in [20]. In the direction of multi-sensor information processing, significant works include the use of particle filters[17], distributed data fusion (DDF) architecture along with its extension, the Bayesian DDF [8,9], Gaussian processes [14] and mobile agent-based information fusion [23]. For most of the application domains described in these works such as water-tide height measurement, wind speed measurement, robot tracking and localization, etc., self-interested behavior by the sensors is not considered a crucial problem. For our illustrated application domain of landmine detection, decision-level fusion techniques have been reported to be amenable for scenarios where the sensor types are different from each other, and, non-statistical decision-level fusion techniques, such as Dempster-Shafer theory [11], fuzzy logic [3], and rule-based fusion techniques [4] have been reported to generalize well. However, in contrast to our work, these techniques assume that sensors are fully cooperative and never behave self-interestedly by misreporting information. Most sensor-based information aggregation techniques either do not consider selfish behavior or use high-overhead, cryptographic techniques to combat it [13]. To deter false reports by sensor nodes in a data aggregation setting, researchers propose various lower overhead reputation and trust-based schemes [13,18]. Our prediction market-based information aggregation technique is complimentary to such reputation-based aggregation techniques.

Decision-Making Using Prediction Markets. A prediction market is a market-based aggregation mechanism that is used to combine the opinions on the outcome of a future, real-world event from different people, called the market's *traders* and forecast the event's possible outcome based on their aggregated opinion. Recently, multi-agent systems have been used [7,15] to analyze the operation of prediction markets, where the behaviors of the market's participants are implemented as automated software agents. The seminal work on prediction market analysis [22] has shown that the mean belief values of individual traders about the outcome of a future event corresponds to the event's market price. The basic operation rules of a prediction market are similar to those of a continuous double auction, with the role of the auctioneer being taken up by an entity called the *market maker* that runs the prediction market. Hanson [5] developed a mechanism, called a *scoring rule*, that can be used by market makers to reward traders for making and improving a prediction about the outcome of an event, and, showed that if a scoring rule is *proper* or incentive compatible, then it can serve as an automated market maker. Recently, authors in [2,15] have theoretically analyzed the properties of prediction markets used for decision making. In [15], the authors analyzed the problem of a decision maker manipulating a prediction market and proposed a family of scoring rules to address the problem. In [2], the authors extended this work by allowing randomized decision rules, considering multiple possible outcomes and providing a simple test to determine whether the scoring rule is proper for an arbitrary decision rule-scoring rule pair. In this paper, we use a prediction market for decision making, but in contrast to previous works we consider that the decision maker can make multiple, possibly improved decisions over an event's duration, and, the outcome of an event is decided independently, outside the market, and not influenced by the decision maker's decisions. Another contribution our paper makes is a new, proper scoring rule, called the *payment function*, that incentivizes agents to submit truthful reports.

3   Problem Formulation

Let L be a set of objects. Each object has certain features that determine its type. We assume that there are f different features and m different object types. Let $\Phi = \{\phi_1, \phi_2, ..., \phi_f\}$ denote the set of object features and $\Theta = \{\theta_1, \theta_2, ..., \theta_m\}$ denote the set of object types. The features of an object $l \in L$ is denoted by $l_\Phi \subseteq \Phi$ and its type is denoted by $l_\theta \in \Theta$. As illustrated in the example given in Section 1, l_Φ can be perceived, albeit with measurement errors, through sensors, and, our objective is to determine l_θ as accurately as possible from the perceived but noisy values of l_Φ. Let $\Delta(\Theta) = \{(\delta(\theta_1), \delta(\theta_2), ..., \delta(\theta_m)) : \delta(\theta_i) \in [0,1], \sum_{i=1}^{m} \delta(\theta_i) = 1\}$, denote the set of probability distributions over the different object types. For convenience of analysis, we assume that when the actual type of object l, $l_\theta = \theta_j$, its (scalar) type is expanded into a m-dimensional probability vector using the function $vec : \Theta \to [0,1]^m : vec_j = 1, vec_{i \neq j} = 0$, which has 1 as its j-th component corresponding to l's type θ_j and 0 for all other components.

Let A denote a set of agents (sensors) and $A_{rep}^{t,l} \subseteq A$ denote the subset of agents that are able to perceive the object l's features on their sensors at time t. Based on the perceived object features, agent $a \in A_{rep}^{t,l}$ at time t reports a belief as a probability distribution over the set of object types, which is denoted as $\mathbf{b}^{a,t,l} \in \Delta(\Theta)$. The beliefs of all the agents are combined into a composite belief, $\mathbf{B}^{t,l} = Agg_{a \in A_{rep}^{t,l}}(\mathbf{b}^{a,t,l})$, and let $\hat{\Theta}^{t,l} : \mathbf{B}^{t,l} \to \Delta(\Theta)$ denote a function that computes a probability distribution over object types based on the aggregated agent beliefs. Within this setting we formulate the object classification problem as a decision making problem in the following manner: given an object l and an initial aggregated belief $\mathbf{B}^{t,l}$ calculated from one or more agent reports for that object, determine a set of additional agents (sensors) that need to be deployed at object l such that the following constraint is satisfied:

$$\min RMSE\left(\hat{\Theta}^{t,l}, vec(l_\theta)\right), \quad \text{for} \quad t = 1, 2, ...T, \tag{1}$$

where T is the time window for classifying an object l and RMSE is the root mean square error given by $RMSE(\mathbf{x}, \mathbf{y}) = \frac{||x-y||}{\sqrt{m}}$. In other words, at every time step t, the decision maker tries to select a subset of agents such that the root mean square error (RMSE) between the estimated type of object l and its actual type is successively minimized.

The major components of the object classification problem described above consists of two parts: integrating the reports from the different sensors and making sensor deployment decisions based on those reports so that the objective function given in Equation 1 is satisfied. To address the first part, we have used distributed information aggregation with a multi-agent prediction market, while for the latter we have used an expected utility maximizing decision-making framework. A schematic showing the different components of our system and their interactions is shown in Figure 1 and explained in the following sections.

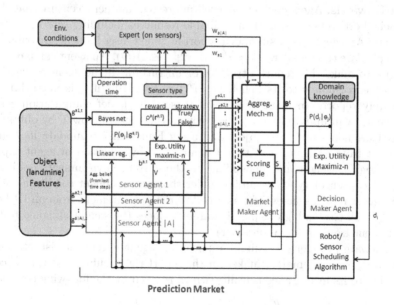

Fig. 1. The different components of the prediction market for decision making and the interactions between them

3.1 Sensor Agents

As mentioned in Section 1, there is a set of robots in the scenario and each robot has an on-board sensor for analyzing the objects in the scenario. Different robots can have different types of sensors and sensors of the same type can have different degrees of accuracy determined by their cost. Every sensor is associated with a software agent that runs on-board the robot and performs calculations related to the data sensed by the robot's sensor. In the rest of the paper, we have used the terms sensor and agent interchangeably. For the ease of notation, we drop the subscript l corresponding to an object for the rest of this section. When an object is within the sensing range of a sensor (agent) a at time t, the sensor observes the object's features and its agent receives this observation in the form of an information signal $g^{a,t} =< g_1, ..., g_f >$ that is drawn from the space of information signals $G \subseteq \Delta(\Theta)$. The conditional probability distribution of object type θ_j given an information signal $g \in G$, $P(\theta_j|g) : G \rightarrow [0,1]$, is constructed using domain knowledge [3,11,12] within a Bayesian network and is made available to each agent. Agent a then updates its belief distribution $\mathbf{b}^{a,t}$ using the following equation:

$$\mathbf{b}^{a,t} = w_{bel} \cdot \mathbf{P}(\Theta|g^{a,t}) + (1 - w_{bel}) \cdot \mathbf{B}^t, \qquad (2)$$

where $\mathbf{B}^t$ is the belief value vector aggregated from all sensor reports.

Agent Rewards. Agents behave in a self-interested manner to ensure that they give their 'best' report using their available resources including sensor, battery power, etc. An agent a that submits a report at time t, uses its belief distribution $\mathbf{b}^{a,t}$ to calculate the report $\mathbf{r}^{a,t} =< r_1^{a,t}, ..., r_m^{a,t} >\in \Delta(\Theta)$. An agent can have two strategies to make this report - truthful or untruthful. If the agent is truthful, its report corresponds to its belief, i.e., $\mathbf{r}^{a,t} = \mathbf{b}^{a,t}$. But if it is untruthful, it deliberately reports an inaccurate belief to save its belief computation costs. Each agent a can update its report $\mathbf{r}^{a,t}$ within the time window T by obtaining new measurements from the object and using Equation 2 to update its belief. The report from an agent a at time t is analyzed by a human or agent expert [11] to assign a weight $w^{a,t}$ depending on the current environment conditions and agent a's sensor type's accuracy under those environment conditions (e.g., rainy weather reduces the weight assigned to the measurement from an IR heat sensor, or, soil that is high in metal content reduces the weight assigned to the measurement from an metal detector).

To motivate an agent to submit reports, an agent a gets an instantaneous reward, $\rho^{a,t}$, from the market maker for the report $\mathbf{r}^{a,t}$ it submits at time t, corresponding to its instantaneous utility, which is given by the following equation:

$$\rho^{a,t} = V(n^{t'=1..t}) - C^a(\mathbf{r}^{a,t}), \qquad (3)$$

where $V(n^{t'=1..t})$ is the value for making a report with $n^{t'=1..t}$ being the number of times the agent a submitted a report up to time t, and, $C^a(\mathbf{r}^{a,t})$ is the cost of making report $\mathbf{r}^{a,t}$ for agent a. $C^a(\mathbf{r}^{a,t})$ is equal to the actual cost of resources used by the robot, such as expended time, battery power, etc. if the agent uses truthful strategy, and it is equal to some value $c_\epsilon \ll$ actual cost of resources if the agent uses untruthful strategy. We denote the agent's value for each report $V(n^{t'=1..t})$ as a constant-valued function up to a certain threshold and a linearly decreasing function thereafter, to de-incentivize agents from making a large number of reports. Agent a's value function is given by the following equation:

$$V(n^{t'=1..t}) = \begin{cases} \nu & ,n^{t'=1..t} \leq n^{threshold} \\ \frac{\nu(n^{t'=1..t}-n^{max})}{(n^{threshold}-n^{max})} & ,otherwise \end{cases}$$

where $\nu \in Z^+$, is a constant value that a gets by submitting reports up to a threshold, $n^{threshold}$ is the threshold corresponding to the number of reports a can submit before its report's value starts decreasing, and, n^{max} is the maximum number of reports agent a can submit before V becomes negative. Finally, to determine its strategy while submitting its report, an agent selects the strategy that maximizes its expected utility obtained from its cumulative reward given by Equation 3 plus an expected value of its final reward payment if it continues making similar reports up to the object's time window T.

3.2   Decision Maker Agent

The decision maker agent's task is to use the composite belief about an object's type, $\mathbf{B}^t$, given by the prediction market, and take actions to deploy additional robots(sensors) based on the value of the objective function given in Equation 1. Let AC denote a set of possible actions corresponding to deploying a certain number of robots, and $D = \{d_1, ...d_h\} : d_i \in Ac \subseteq AC$ denote the decision set of the decision maker, where h is the number of decisions the decision maker has. The decision function of the decision maker is given by $dec : \Delta(\Theta) \rightarrow D$. Let $\mathbf{u}_j^{dec} \in \mathbb{R}^m$ be the utility that the decision maker receives by determining an object to be of type θ_j and let $P(d_i|\theta_j)$ be the probability that the decision maker makes decision $d_i \in D$ given object type θ_j. $P(d_i|\theta_j)$ and $\mathbf{u}_j^{dec}$ are constructed using domain knowledge [3,11,12]. Given the aggregated belief distribution $\mathbf{B}^t$ at time t, the expected utility to the decision maker for taking decision d_i at time t is then $EU^{dec}(d_i, \mathbf{B}^t) = \sum_{j=1}^{m} P(d_i|\theta_j) \cdot \mathbf{u}_j^{dec} \cdot \mathbf{B}^t$. The decision that the decision maker takes at time t, also called its *decision rule*, is the one that maximizes its expected utility and is given by: $d^t = \arg\max_{d_i} EU^{dec}(d_i, \mathbf{B}^t)$.

3.3   Prediction Market

A conventional prediction market uses the aggregated beliefs of the market's participants or traders about the outcome of a future event, to predict the event's outcome. The outcome of an event is represented as a binary variable (event happens/does not happen). The traders observe information related to the event and report their beliefs, as probabilities about the event's outcome. The market maker aggregates the traders' beliefs and uses a scoring rule to determine a payment or payoff that will be received by each reporting trader. In our multi-agent prediction market, traders correspond to sensor agents, the market maker agent automates the calculations on behalf of the conventional market maker, and, an event in the conventional market corresponds to identifying the type of a detected object. The time window T over which an object is sensed is called the duration of the object in the market. This time window is divided into discrete time steps, $t = 1, 2, ..., T$. During each time step, each sensor agent observing the object submits a report about the object's type to the market maker agent. The market maker agent performs two functions with these reports. First, at each time step t, it aggregates the agent reports into an aggregated belief about the object, $\mathbf{B}^t \in \Delta(\Theta)$. Secondly, it calculates and distributes payments for the sensor agents. It pays an immediate but nominal reward to each agent for its report at time step t using Equation 3. Finally, at the end of the object's time window T, the market maker also gives a larger *payoff* to each agent that contributed towards classifying the object's type. The calculations and analysis related to these two functions of the market maker agent are described in the following sections.

Final Payoff Calculation. The payoff calculation for a sensor agent is performed by the market maker using a *decision scoring rule* at the end of the object's time window. A decision scoring rule [2] is defined as any real valued function that takes the agents' reported beliefs, the realized outcome and the decisions made by the decision maker as input, and produces a payoff for the agent for its reported beliefs, i.e. $S : \Delta(\Theta) \times \Theta \times D \longrightarrow R$. We design a scoring rule for decision making that is based on how much agent a's final report helped the decision maker to make the right decisions throughout the duration of the prediction market and by how close the agent a's final report is to actual object type. Our proposed scoring rule for decision making given that object's true type is θ_j is given in Equation 4:

$$S(r_j^{a,t}, d^{[1:t]}, \theta_j) = \varpi(d^{[1:t]}, \theta_j) log\left(r_j^{a,t}\right), \tag{4}$$

where, $r_j^{a,t}$ is the reported belief that agent a submitted at time t for object type θ_j, $d^{[1:t]}$ is the set consisting of all the decisions that the decision maker took related to the object up to the current time t, θ_j is the object's true type that was revealed at the end the object's time window, $log\left(r_j^{a,t}\right)$ measures the goodness of the report at time t relative to the true object type θ_j, and, $\varpi(d^{[1:t]}, \theta_j)$ is the weight, representing how good all the decisions the decision maker took up to time t were compared to the true object type θ_j. $\varpi(d^{[1:t]}, \theta_j)$ is determined by the decision maker and made available to the agents through the market maker. We assume that $\varpi(d^{[1:t]}, \theta_j) = \sum_{i=1}^t P(d_i \mid \theta_j) \cdot \mathbf{u}_j^{dec}$, which gives the expected utility of the decision maker agent for making decision i when the true type of the object is θ_j.

Aggregation. Since a sensor agent gets paid both through its immediate rewards for making reports during the object's time window and through the scoring rule function for decision making at the end of the object's time window, we define the total payment that the agent has received by the end of the object's time window as a *payment function*.

Definition 1. *A function* $\Psi(\mathbf{r}^{a,t}, d^{[1:t]}, \theta_j, n^{t'=1..t})$ *is called a* **payment function** *if each agent a's total received payment at the end of the object's time window (when $t = T$) is*

$$\Psi(\mathbf{r}^{a,t}, d^{[1:t]}, \theta_j, n^{t'=1..t}) = \sum_{k=1}^{t} \rho^{a,k} + S(r_j^{a,t}, d^{[1:t]}, \theta_j) \qquad (5)$$

where $\rho^{a,k}$, $S(r_j^{a,t}, d^{[1:t]}, \theta_j)$ *and their components are defined as in Equations 3 and 4.*

Let Ψ^{ave} denote a weighted average of the payment function in Equation 5 over all the reporting agents, using the report-weights assigned by the expert in Section 3.1, as given below:

$$\Psi^{ave}(\mathbf{r}^{A_{rep}^t,t}, d^{[1:t]}, \theta_j, n^{A_{rep}^t,t}) = \sum_{k=1}^{t} \sum_{a \in A_{rep}^t} w^{a,k} \rho^{a,k} + \varpi(d^{[1:t]}, \theta_j) \sum_{a \in A_{rep}^t} w^{a,t} log\left(r_j^{a,t}\right),$$

$$(6)$$

where A_{rep}^t is the subset of agents that are able to perceive object feature at time t and $w^{a,k}$ is the weight assigned to agent a at time k by the expert. To calculate an aggregated belief value in a prediction market, Hanson [5] used the generalized inverse function of the scoring rule. Likewise, we calculate the aggregated belief for our market maker agent by taking the generalized inverse of the average payment function given in Equation 6:

$$B_j^t = Agg_{a \in A_{rep}^t}(\mathbf{b}^{a,t}) = \frac{\frac{exp\left(\Psi^{ave} - \sum_{k=1}^{t} \sum_{a \in A_{rep}^t} w^{a,k} \rho^{a,k}\right)}{\varpi(d^{[1:t]}, \theta_j)}}{\sum_{\theta_j=\theta_1}^{\theta_m} \frac{exp\left(\Psi^{ave} - \sum_{k=1}^{t} \sum_{a \in A_{rep}^t} w^{a,k} \rho^{a,k}\right)}{\varpi(d^{[1:t]}, \theta_j)}} \qquad (7)$$

where $B_j^t \in \mathbf{B}^t$ is the j-th component of the aggregated belief for object type θ_j. The aggregated belief vector, $\mathbf{B}^t$, calculated by the market maker agent is sent to the decision maker agent so that it can calculate its expected utility given in Section 3.2, as well as, sent back to each sensor agent that reported the object's type till time step t, so that the agent can refine its future reports, if any, using this aggregate of the reports from other agents. We also note that the aggregation mechanism used by our market maker is similar to an LMSR technique which was shown to lead to Weak Perfect Bayesian Equilibrium when, like in our setting, the information signals of the traders are independent conditional on the state of the world [1].

4   Payment Function: Properties and Characteristics

In this section we first show that the payment function is proper, or incentive compatible. Then we show that when the market maker uses this payment function to reward each agent for its reported beliefs, reporting beliefs truthfully is the optimal strategy for each agent.

We can characterize a proper payment function similar to a proper scoring rule.

Definition 2. *A payment function* Ψ *is proper, or incentive compatible, if*

$$\Psi(\mathbf{b^{a,t}}, d^{[1:t]}, \theta_j, n^{t'=1..t}) \geq \Psi(\mathbf{r^{a,t}}, d^{[1:t]}, \theta_j, n^{t'=1..t}), \tag{8}$$

$\forall \mathbf{b^{a,t}}, \mathbf{r^{a,t}} \in \Delta(O)$. Ψ *is strictly proper if the inequality in Equation 8 strict.*

Proposition 1. *The payment function given in Equation 5 is proper.*

The proof is given in [6].

Agent Reporting Strategy. Assume that agent a's report at time t is its final report, then its utility function can be written as $u_j^{a,t} = \sum_{k=1}^t \rho^{a,k} + S(r_j^{a,t}, d^{[1:t]}, \theta_j)$. Then, agent a's expected utility for object type θ_j given its reported belief for object type θ_j, $r_j^{a,t}$, and its true belief about object type θ_j, $b_j^{a,t}$ at time t is

$$EU_j^a(r_j^{a,t}, b_j^{a,t}) = \sum_{i=1}^h P(d_i|\theta_j)b_j^{a,t}u_j^{a,t} = \sum_{i=1}^h P(d_i|\theta_j)b_j^{a,t}\left(\sum_{k=1}^t \rho^{a,k} + S(r_j^{a,t}, d^{[1:t]}, \theta_j)\right), \tag{9}$$

where $P(d_i|\theta_j)$ is the probability that the decision maker takes decision d_i when the object's type is θ_j.

Proposition 2. *If agent a is paid according to Ψ, then it reports its beliefs about the object types truthfully.*

The proof is a straight forward solution to expected utility maximization problem. The complete proof is given in [6].

5   Experimental Results

We have conducted several experiments using our aggregation technique for decision-making within a multi-sensor landmine detection scenario described in Section 1. Our environment contains different buried objects, some of which are landmines. The true types of the objects are randomly determined at the beginning of the simulation. Due to the scarcity of real data related to landmine detection, we have used the domain knowledge that was reported in [3,11,12] to determine object types, object features, sensor agents' reporting costs, decision maker agent's decision set, decision maker agent's utility of determining objects of different types, and, to construct the probability distributions for $P(\theta_j|g)$ and $P(d_i|\theta_j)$. We report simulation results for root mean squared error (RMSE) defined in Section 3 and also for number of sensors over time, cost over object types, and average utility of the sensors over time.

Compared Techniques. For comparing the performance of our prediction market based object classification techniques, we have used two other well-known

Table 1. Parameters used for our simulation experiments

Name	Value
Object types	mine, metallic object(non-mine), non-metallic object(non-mine)
Features	metallic content, object's area, object's depth, sensor's position
Sensor types	MD, IR, GPR
Max no. of sensors	10 (5MD,3IR,2GPR)
Max no. of decisions	14
T (object ident. window)	10
ν (value if $n^{t'=1..t} \leq$ $n^{threshold}$)	5
n_{max} (max no. of reports before value is negative)	20
$n_{threshold}$ (no. of reports before value $< \nu$)	5

Table 2. Different number of sensors and the sensor types deployed over time by a decision maker to classify different types of objects

Object type	Time steps	PM	DDF	D-S
Mine	1	1(1MD)	1(1MD)	1(1MD)
	2	3(1MD, 1IR)	3(1MD, 1GPR)	3(1IR, 1GPR)
	3	4(1GPR)	5(1MD,1IR)	4(1MD)
	4	5(1MD)	6(1IR)	5(1MD)
	5	6(1MD)	7(11MD)	6(1IR)
	6	7(1IR)	8(1MD)	7(1IR)
	7	-	9(1IR)	8(1MD)
Met.	1	1(1MD)	1(1MD)	1(1MD)
or	2	3(1MD, 1IR)	4(1MD,1IR, 1GPR)	3(1IR, 1GPR)
Fr.	3	4(1GPR)	5(1MD)	4(1MD)
D-S	4	5(1MD)	6(1IR)	5(1IR)
	5	6(1IR)	7(11MD)	6(11IR)
	6	7(1MD)	8(1IR)	7(1MD)
	7	8(1IR)	9(1GPR)	8(1MD)
	8	-	9(1MD)	8(1MD)
Non-	1	1(1MD)	1(1MD)	
met.	2	2(1MD)	2(1IR)	
	3	3(1IR)	3(1MD)	
	4	4(1MD)	4(1GPR)	
	5	5(1IR)	5(1MD)	
	6	6(1MD)	6(1IR)	
	7	-	7(1MD)	

techniques for information fusion: (a) Dempster-Shafer (D-S) theory for land-mine classification [11], where a two-level approach based on belief functions is used. At the first level, the detected object is classified according to its metal content. At the second level the chosen level of metal content is further analyzed to classify the object as a landmine or a friendly object. The belief update of the sensors that we used for D-S method is the same one we have described in Section 3.1. (b) Distributed Data Fusion (DDF) [9], where sensor measurements are refined over successive observations using a temporal, Bayesian inference-based, information filter. To compare DDF with our prediction market-based technique, we replaced our belief aggregation mechanism given in Equation 7 with a DDF-based information filter. We compare our techniques using some standard evaluation metrics from multi-sensor information fusion [14]: root mean squared error (RMSE) defined as in Section 3, normed mean squared errors (NMSE) calculated as: $NMSE^t(\hat{\Theta}^t - vec(\theta_j)) = 10\,log_{10} \dfrac{\frac{1}{m}\sum_{j=1}^{m}\left(\hat{\Theta}_j^t, vec(\theta_j)\right)^2}{\frac{1}{m}\left(\sum_{j=1}^{m} vec(\theta_j)^2\right) - \left(\frac{1}{m}\sum_{j=1}^{m} vec(\theta_j)\right)^2}$, and, the

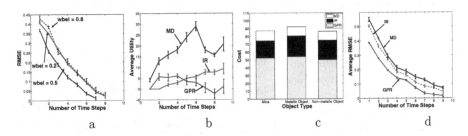

Fig. 2. RMSE for different values of w_{bel}(a), Average sensors' utilities for different sensor types(b), Cost for different object types(c), RMSE for sensors' reports averaged over sensor types(d)

information gain, also known as Kullback-Leibler divergence and relative entropy, calculated as: $D_{KL}^t(\hat{\Theta}^t||vec(\theta_j)) = \sum_{j=1}^m \hat{\Theta}_j^t log\left(\frac{\hat{\Theta}_j^t}{vec(\theta_j)}\right)$.

$\hat{\Theta}^t$ was calculated using D-S, DDF, and our prediction market technique ($\hat{\Theta}^t = \mathbf{B}^t$). Since the focus of our work is on the quality of information fusion, we will concentrate on describing the results for one object. We assume that there are three types of sensors, MD (least operation cost, most noisy), IR (intermediate operation cost, moderately noisy), and GPR (expensive operation cost, most accurate). We also assume that there are a total of 5 MD sensors, 3 IR sensors, and 2 GPR sensors available to the decision maker for classifying this object. Initially, the object is detected using one MD sensor. Once the object is detected, the time window in the prediction market for identifying the object's type starts. The MD sensor sends its report to the market maker in the prediction market and the decision maker makes its first decision based on this one report. We assume that decision maker's decision (sent to the robot/sensor scheduling algorithm in Figure 1) is how many $(0-3)$ and what type (MD,IR,GPR) of sensors to send to the site of the detected object subsequently. We have considered a set of 14 out of all the possible decisions under this setting. From [12], we derive four object features, which are metallic content, area of the object, depth of the object, and the position of the sensor. Combinations of the values of these four features constitute the signal set G and at each time step, a sensor perceiving the object receives a signal $g \in G$. The value of the signal also varies based on the robot/sensor's current position relative to the object. We assume that the identification of an object stops and the object type is revealed when either $\mathbf{B}_j^t \geq 0.95$, for any j, or after 10 time steps. The default values for all domain related parameters are shown in Table 1. All of our results were averaged over 10 runs and the error bars indicate the standard deviation over the number of runs. For our first group of experiments we analyze the performance of our technique w.r.t. the variables in our model, such as w_{bel} and time, and, w.r.t. to sensor and object types. We observe that as more information gets sensed for the object, the RMSE value, shown in Figure 2(a), decreases over time. It takes on average $6-8$ time steps to predict the object type with 95% or greater accuracy

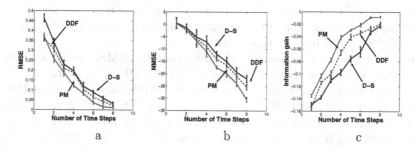

a   b   c

Fig. 3. Comparison of our Prediction Market-based information aggregation with Dempster-Shafer and Distributed Data Fusion Techniques using different metrics: RMSE(a), NMSE(b), Information gain(c)

depending on the object type and the value of w_{bel}. We also observe that our model performs the best with $w_{bel} = 0.5$ (in Equation 2), when the agent equally incorporates its private signal and also the market's aggregated belief at each time step into its own belief update. Figure 2(b) shows the average utility of the agents based on their type. We can see that MD sensors get more utility because their costs of calculating and submitting reports are generally less, whereas GPR sensors get the least utility because they encounter the highest cost. This result is further verified in Figure 2(c) where we can see the costs based on sensor types and also based on object types. We observe that detecting a metallic object that is not a mine has the highest cost. We posit that it is because both MD and IR sensors can detect metallic content in the object and extra cost is due to the time and effort spent differentiating metallic object from a mine. Although most of the mines are metallic [11,12], we can see that the cost of detecting a mine and a non-metallic object are similar because we require a prediction of at least 95%. Due to the sensitive nature of the landmine detection problem, it is important to ensure that even a non-metallic object is not a mine even if we encounter higher costs. However, despite MD's high utility (Figure 2(b)) and low cost (Figure 2(c)), its error of classifying the object type is the largest, as can be seen from Figure 2(d). In Table 2, we show how the decision maker's decisions using our prediction market technique results in the deployment of different numbers and types of sensors over the time window of the object. We report the results for the value of belief update weight $w_{bel} = 0.5$(used in Equation 2) while using our prediction market model, as well as using D-S and DDF. We see that non-metallic object classification requires less number of sensors as both MD and IR sensors can distinguish between metallic vs. non-metallic objects, and so, deploying just these two types of sensors can help to infer that the object is not a mine. In contrast, metallic objects require more time to get classified as not being a mine because more object features using all three sensor types need to be observed. We also observe that on average our aggregation technique using prediction market deploys a total of $6 - 8$ sensors and detects the object type with at least 95% accuracy in $6 - 7$ time steps, while the next best compared DDF technique deploys a total of $7 - 9$ sensors and detects the object type with at least 95% accuracy in $7 - 8$ time steps.

Our results shown in Figure 3(a) illustrate that the RMSE using our PM-based technique is below the RMSEs using D-S and DDF by an average of 8% and 5% respectively. Figure 3(b) shows that the NMSE values using our PM-based technique is 18% and 23% less on average than D-S and DDF techniques respectively. Finally, in Figure 3(c) we observe that the information gain for our PM-based technique is 12% and 17% more than D-S and DDF methods respectively.

6 Conclusions

In this paper, we have described a sensor information aggregation technique for object classification with a multi-agent prediction market and developed a payment function used by the market maker to incentivize truthful revelation by each agent. Currently, the rewards given by the market maker agent to the sensor agents are additional side payments incurred by the decision maker. In the future we plan to investigate a payment function that can achieve budget balance. We are also interested in integrating our decision making problem with the problem of scheduling robots(sensors), and, incorporating the costs to the overall system into the decision-making costs. Another direction we plan to investigate in the future is a problem of minimizing the time to detect an object in addition to the accuracy of detection. Lastly, we plan to incorporate our aggregation technique into experiments with more number of sensors and also with real robots.

References

1. Chen, Y., Dimitrov, S., Sami, R., Reeves, D.M., Pennock, D.M., Hanson, R.D., Fortnow, L., Gonen, R.: Gaming Prediction Markets: Equilibrium Strategies with a Market Maker. Algorithmica J. 58(4), 930–969 (2009)
2. Chen, Y., Kash, I.: Information Elicitation for Decision Making. In: AAMAS 2011, pp. 175–182 (2011)
3. Cremer, F., Schutte, K., Schavemaker, J.G.M., den Breejen, E.: A comparison of decision-level sensor-fusion methods for anti-personnel landmine detection. Information Fusion 2(1), 187–208 (2001)
4. Gros, B., Bruschini, C.: Sensor technologies for the detection of antipersonnel mines: a survey of current research and system developments. In: Proc. of the International Symposium on Measurement and Control in Robotics, pp. 509–518 (1996)
5. Hanson, R.: Logarithmic Market Scoring Rules for Modular Combinatorial Information Aggregation. Journal of Prediction Markets 1(1), 3–15 (2007)
6. Jumadinova, J., Dasgupta, P.: Multi-sensor Information Processing using Prediction Market-based Belief Aggregation. arXiv:1201.2207 [cs.MA]
7. Jumadinova, J., Dasgupta, P.: A Multi-Agent System for Analyzing the Effect of Information on Prediction Markets. International Journal of Intelligent Systems 26(1), 383–409 (2011)

8. Makarenko, A., Durrant-Whyte, H.: Decentralized Bayesian algorithms for active sensor networks. Information Fusion 7, 418–433 (2006)
9. Manyika, J., Durrant-Whyte, H.: Data fusion and sensor management. Prentice Hall (1995)
10. Michiardi, P., Molva, R.: Simulation-based Analysis of Security Exposures in Mobile Ad Hoc Networks. In: Mobile Ad Hoc Networks, Eur. Wireless Conf. (2002)
11. Milisavljevič, N., Bloch, I.: Sensor Fusion in Anti-Personnel Mine Detection Using a Two-Level Belief Function Model, Part C: Applications and Reviews. IEEE Transactions on Systems, Man, and Cybernetics 33(2), 269–283 (2003)
12. Milisavljevič, N., Bloch, I., Acheroy, M.: Characterization of Mine Detection Sensors in Terms of Belief Functions and their Fusion, First Results. In: Proc. of the Third International Conference on Information Fusion, pp. 15–22 (2000)
13. Mukherjee, P., Sen, S.: Comparing Reputation Schemes for Detecting Malicious Nodes in Sensor Networks. The Computer Journal 54(3), 482–489 (2011)
14. Osborne, M., Roberts, S., Rogers, A., Ramchurn, S., Jennings, N.R.: Towards realtime information processing of sensor network data using computationally efficient multi-output gaussian processes. In: IPSN, pp. 109–120 (2008)
15. Othman, A., Sandholm, T.: Decision Rules and Decision Markets. In: AAMAS 2010, pp. 625–632 (2010)
16. Rogers, A., David, E., Jennings, N.R.: Selfish Sensors in Wireless Micro-Sensor Networks. In: Proceedings of AAMAS 2004 (2004)
17. Rosencrantz, M., Gordon, G., Thrun, S.: Decentralized sensor fusion with distributed particle filters. In: IPSN 2003, pp. 55–62 (2003)
18. Srinivasan, A., Teitelbaum, J., Wu, J., Cardei, M., Liang, H.: Reputation-and-Trust-Based Systems for Ad Hoc Networks. In: Algorithms and Protocols for Wireless, Mobile Ad Hoc Networks. Wiley (2008)
19. Stone, P., Kaminka, G.A., Rosenschein, J.S.: Leading a Best-Response Teammate in an Ad Hoc Teams. In: David, E., Gerding, E., Sarne, D., Shehory, O. (eds.) AMEC 2009. LNBIP, vol. 59, pp. 132–146. Springer, Heidelberg (2010)
20. Vinyals, M., Rodriguez-Aguilar, J., Cerquides, J.: A Survey of Sensor Networks from a Multiagent Perspective. Computer Journal 54(3), 455–470 (2011)
21. Waltz, E., Llinas, J.: Multisensor Datafusion. Artech House (1990)
22. Wolfers, J., Zitzewitz, E.: Prediction Markets. Journal of Econ. Perspectives 18(2), 107–126 (2004)
23. Wu, Q., Rao, N., Barhen, J., Iyengar, S., Vaishnavi, V., Qi, H., Chakrabarty, K.: On Computing Mobile Agent Routes for Data Fusion in Distributed Sensor Networks. IEEE Trans. on Knowledge and Data Engineering 16(6), 740–753 (2004)

Agent Adaptation
across Non-ideal Markets and Societies

Eunkyung Kim, Yu-Han Chang, Rajiv Maheswaran, Yu Ning, and Luyan Chi

Information Sciences Institute, University of Southern California
4676 Admiralty Way, Marina del Rey, CA 90292
{eunkyung,ychang,maheswar}@isi.edu, {yuning,lchi}@usc.edu

Abstract. We address the problem of creating agents that can succeed in environments where adapting to the norms of the market or society is a significant factor to performing well. We focus on the Social Ultimatum Game, a multi-agent multi-round extension of the Ultimatum Game, a classical game-theoretic problem which has been studied for decades due to the variability of human behavior it elicits. We create ten societies of agents based on five classes of agent behavior to create a diverse test environment. We used Amazon Mechanical Turk to evaluate how human participants adapt to these various societies, serving as a baseline for agent-based approaches. Current approaches primarily succeed in societies similar to their own and fail elsewhere. We construct a new type of adaptive agent, based on single-step marginal-value optimization, and show that it outperforms humans across these varying agent societies when playing the Social Ultimatum Game.

1 Introduction

Creating software agents that can negotiate effectively is an important problem that has been studied extensively by agent researchers. In the trading agent competition, a goal is typically to find optimal policies in settings with uncertain and incomplete information, and where policies are typically evaluated in societies of entirely artificial agents [1].

In this paper, we examine a setting where agents must perform within the context of a given market or society, where the behavior of the other individuals within that society is not assumed to be rational (selfish, profit-maximizing). We want to create agents that can perform effectively across different instances of such environments. This will be increasingly necessary as trading agents begin to deal with non-rational humans in new domains, and as the domains themselves increase in complexity. Notions such as reciprocity and fairness become useful heuristics in such cases. Since performance can be highly dependent on the interaction environment, the design of such a negotiation agent is not a straightforward optimization problem. Performance depends on adapting to the norms of that society by learning quickly through interaction.

As context for this investigation, we use the Social Ultimatum Game [2], a multi-agent multi-round extension of the Ultimatum Game. The Ultimatum

E. David et al. (Eds.): AMEC/TADA 2012, LNBIP 136, pp. 90–103, 2013.

Game has a three-decade history in social sciences that shows how cultural and other factors significantly affect behavior/performance. It maps to real-world problems because each interaction splits surplus from a joint activity (a common negotiation issue) and thus abstracts many economic transactions. In the classical Ultimatum Game, an endowment can be shared by a proposer and responder, if the responder agrees to the proposer's split of the endowment. Otherwise, neither the proposer or responder receives any reward. Even in this one-shot interaction, it has been shown through many investigations in a wide-range of research communities that humans exhibit a wide range of behaviors that deviate from a "rational" payoff-maximizing strategy based on factors such as cultural background, occupation and emotional factors among others.

In order to perform well, it is important for the proposer to have an accurate model of the responder. The Social Ultimatum Game allows each player to take the role of the proposer, to pick the responder from the set of all players, to decide to accept or reject any offers it receives from the other players, and to repeat this process for multiple rounds. Thus, players have the chance to learn and adapt to the game population. Also, the game adds an alternate method for generating payoffs: enticing the other players to choose oneself as the responder.

To investigate adaptation in this context, we implemented several behavioral and bargaining approaches, drawn from the wide literature in this area: adaptive fairness, quantal response equilibrium, regret minimization, tit-for-tat, sigmoid acceptance learning, and randomized expected reward. We introduce a new approach called marginal value optimization. Where necessary, models were trained with data gathered from human players. We then created a collection of agent societies and conducted experiments where a single agent of each type was placed into societies of homogeneous agents of varying types. We also conducted experiments using Amazon Mechanical Turk where a single human played against these societies to establish a real-world baseline for performance that required adaptivity to diverse societies. Our contributions in this paper are (1) a study of how various computational agents perform in diverse agent societies, (2) how these agents compare against human performance in these societies and (3) a simple approach based on single-step *marginal-value optimization* that outperforms humans.

2   Related Work

The Ultimatum Game [3] has been studied extensively by many communities under various conditions in order to understand the diverse human behavior it elicits and its divergence from the "rational" Nash equilibrium strategy [4,5,6,7,8,9,10]. There are certain conditions under which people have gravitated towards the payoff-maximizing strategy including autism [9], or being familiar with economics [11] and others [12,13,14,8]. However, there has been significant research showing that behavior varies greatly by culture and the society to which one belongs [15,16,17,18].

Building adaptive agents for economic contexts is an established and prominent research area in the multi-agent systems community, exemplified by the trading agent competition [1] and various similar competitions. For brevity, we only mention the background work that directly affects the agents we created for this investigation. Many of these agents are implemented within our Social Ultimatum Game framework, and are the subject of the comparative study conducted as part of this work.

A seminal work in using agent-based simulation to study human interaction was Axelrod's tournament for Prisoner's Dilemma that yielded the Tit-for-Tat strategy as a simple yet powerful strategy for success [19]. Recently, regret minimization has become a prominent method for modeling human behavior as well as for performing well under multiple scenarios [20]. Quantal Response Equilibrium is a methodology for modeling human behavior that has been used in many settings including game-theoretic agents in security settings [21,22]. A sigmoidal acceptance learning (SIGAL) approach was recently used to model social factors in a revelation negotiation game and outperformed humans and equilibrium agents [23]. An agent that used an adaptive model of fairness along with partial exploration was used to closely replicate human reciprocity over time in an Ultimatum Game context [2].

3   The Social Ultimatum Game

The classical Ultimatum Game is a two-player game where P_1 proposes a split of an endowment $e \in \mathbb{N}$ to P_2 where P_2 would receive $q \in \{0, \delta, 2\delta, \ldots, e - \delta, e\}$ for $\delta \in \mathbb{N}$. If P_2 accepts, P_2 receives q and P_1 receives $e - q$. If P_2 rejects, neither player receives anything. The subgame-perfect Nash or Stackelberg equilibrium has P_1 offering $q = \delta$ (i.e., the minimum possible offer), and P_2 accepting, because a "rational" P_2 should accept any $q > 0$, and P_1 knows this. Yet, humans both make and reject offers that exceed δ.

The Social Ultimatum Game represents that people operate in societies of multiple agents and repeated interactions. Players, denoted $\{P_1, P_2, \ldots, P_N\}$, play $K \geq 2$ rounds, where $N \geq 3$. In each round k, every player P_m receives a new endowment e and chooses a recipient r_m^k and makes them an offer $q_{m,n}^k$ (where $n = r_m^k$). Each recipient P_n then considers the offers they received and makes a decision $d_{m,n}^k \in \{0, 1\}$ for each offer $q_{m,n}^k$ to accept (1) or reject (0) it. If the offer $q_{m,n}^k$ is accepted by P_n, then P_n receives $q_{m,n}^k$ and P_m receives $e - q_{m,n}^k$, where e is the endowment to be shared. If the offer $q_{m,n}^k$ is rejected by P_n, then both players receive nothing for that particular offer in round k. Thus, P_m's reward in round k, U_m^k, is the sum of the offers they receive and accept (if any are made to them) and their portion of the proposal they make, if their proposal was accepted. Thus, the utility to the m-th agent in the k-th round is: $U_m^k = (e - q_{m,n}^k)d_{m,n}^k + \sum_{j=1\ldots N, j \neq m} q_{j,m}^k d_{j,m}^k$. The total rewards for P_m over the game is the sum of per-round winnings, $U_m = \sum_{k=1}^{K} U_m^k$.

Figure 1 shows our Social Ultimatum Game interface. The given example is a 5-person 20-round game. The screen on the left is where players choose their responder and offer amount for a given round. The screen on the right is where players see the offers they have received and can choose whether to accept or reject them. Players are given avatars to preserve anonymity so that they cannot identify each other even when playing next to each other. The player on the right screen's self-viewed avatar and username does not appear to the player on the left screen.

4   Autonomous Agents

To investigate various agent-based strategies as well as create diverse agent societies we considered a wide range of established approaches. We also present a new approach. We first summarize the approaches below and later provide more details about how they were adapted to the Social Ultimatum Game context.

- **Tit-for-Tat:** This is a fully reciprocal agent that chooses responders who previously made them offers, and offers an amount that reciprocates that previous offer. This is a standard approach based on its success in [19].
- **Regret Minimization:** This agent minimizes worst-case regret by hedging among a set of available actions. It hedges by increasing the weights associated with high payoff actions, and probabilistically chooses actions based on these weights, which are initialized using human data [20].
- **Expected Reward QRE:** This agent learns the expected rewards of various actions based on human play data and acts using a quantal response equilibrium strategy based on these rewards [21,22]
- **SIGAL QRE:** This agent also uses a quantal response equilibrium strategy but the utility is based on the sigmoid acceptance learning approach which incorporates a model of social utility into the rewards [23].

 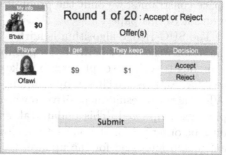

Fig. 1. The Social Ultimatum Game web interface for a 5-person 20-round game. The left screen shows the responder and offer selection interface and the right screen shows the acceptance/rejection interface. Players are given avatars to preserve anonymity so that they cannot identify each other even when playing next to each other.

- **Adaptive Fairness:** This agent is characterized by a fairness threshold which is dynamically updated based on an adaptability parameter and an exploration parameter. It accurately replicates human dynamic reciprocity behavior and is used as a stand-in for various human-like behaviors that are learned from data [2].
- **Marginal Value Optimization:** This agent chooses an action based on the marginal value of being seen as the preferred partner of each agent in the society. The value is a product of the expected value of the offer received from a particular agent and the marginal increase of the likelihood of receiving an offer. This new approach is a contribution of this paper.

Tit-for-Tat: The Tit-for-Tat agent chooses the agent that made it the highest offer in the previous round as a responder and makes it an offer of the same value. If no one made it an offer in the previous round it chooses an agent at random and makes an offer of a preset value. As an agent society, we chose the preset value to be $2.

Regret Minimization (Hedging): The Hedging agent treats the game as a multi-armed bandit problem and uses a novel extension of the EXP3 Hedging algorithm first described by Auer et al. [20] that we call SUG-Hedge. By playing according to the SUG-Hedge algorithm, the agent can guarantee that its *expected regret* will be minimized, with an upper bound on expected regret of $2\sqrt{e-1}\sqrt{KT\ln K}$, where K is the number of possible actions and T is the number of time periods played. Here we use the usual definition of expected weak regret:

$$\max_{1 \le j \le K} E_{a_1,\ldots,a_T}\left[\sum_{t=1}^{T} x_j(t)\right] - E_{a_1,\ldots,a_T}\left[\sum_{t=1}^{T} x_{a_t}(t)\right],$$

that is, the difference between the reward that *could have* been obtained had a different action been chosen over the T rounds of the game, and the reward that was actually obtained using the strategy determined by our algorithm. Due to space constraints, we omit the proof of the regret bound since it is not directly relevant to this paper.

The SUG-Hedge algorithm is fairly straightforward, and is shown below. We maintain weights for each of the possible actions $A_{i,j}$, with each action corresponding to a choice of player i to make an offer to, and a choice of the amount j to offer. Actions are chosen by sampling a distribution defined by these weights. When actions result in positive rewards, the weight for that action is multiplicatively updated. This update takes into account the fact that rewards can only be observed for the one action actually chosen; thus an expected reward is calculated and used for the update. By using an expected reward, we are able to adjust the weights appropriately, as if we had observed the reward resulting from each action at each time period.

We make a few further assumptions to increase the use of the information we gain from each action choice. This is easily seen by considering an example: Assume the SUG-Hedge algorithm makes an offer of $4 to player i, who accepts,

---

Algorithm 1. SUG-Hedge

Parameters: $\gamma \in (0, 1]$, K is total number of actions
Initialization: $\{w_{m,n}\}$

Repeat for round $t = 1, 2 \ldots$ until game ends
1. Get the probability of each action $A_{i,j}$: $P_{i,j}^t = (1 - \gamma)\frac{w_{i,j}}{\sum_{i,j} w_j} + \frac{\gamma}{K}$
2. Choose an action A_{i_t, j_t} randomly according to the distribution $P_{1,1}^t, ..., P_{4,10}^t$
3. For $i = i_t, j \geqslant j_t$,

Revise reward of action $A_{i,j}$: $\widehat{X_{i,j}^t} = \frac{X_{i,j}^t}{\sum_{j' \leqslant j} P_{i,j'}^t}$

Update weight of action $A_{i,j}$: $w_{i,j}^{t+1} = w_{i,j}^t exp\left(\gamma \frac{\widehat{X_{i,j}^t}}{K}\right)$

---

and thus a reward of \$6 is received. Then, we can assume that offers $\geq$ \$4 to player i would also have been accepted. SUG-Hedge thus updates not only $w_{i,4}$ but also $w_{i,j}$ where $j > 4$. This extension enables us to significantly tighten the bound described above. We also consider further extensions to SUG-Hedge that account for rewards due to player reciprocation, but the results are similar, and thus we omit them here. To initialize the weights $\{w_{m,n}\}$, we calculate the probabilities of different offer values based on the game data collected from human experiments (see Section 4), and initialize the weights to reflect the distribution of offer values exhibited in the data.

Expected Reward QRE: The quantal response equilibrium (QRE) model captures the fact that humans do not always choose the option that yields the highest expected utility. Instead, they follow a probabilistic, noisy decision process. Our QRE agent learns a static model of human action selection, using data from previous experiments where we collected data from games with five human players. This action selection model is then used at each round of the game. Thus, the agent does not adapt during game play.

The QRE model states that an action a is chosen with probability $p(a)$, where $p(a) = e^{\lambda U(a)}/\sum_{a \in A} e^{\lambda U(a)}$. We calculate the utilities $U(a)$ as the expected utility of playing an action a. To derive this quantity, we calculate the acceptance rate r_a of each offer amount a from our human game-play data. The expected utility for action a is thus $U(a) = r_a(10 - a)$.

The parameter λ enables us to tune the amount of noise in the action choice. For example, $\lambda = 0$ results in uniform action choice, and $\lambda = \infty$ results in a best response action choice. Tuning λ is thus an important step in creating the QRE agent. We use maximum likelihood estimation (MLE) to fit λ using our human game-play data. The log likelihood of λ is $\log L(\lambda|a) = \lambda \sum_{a \in A} N_a U(a) - N \log\left(\sum_{a \in A} e^{\lambda U(a)}\right)$, where N_a is the number of times action a was chosen in our data set. Since $\log L(\lambda|a)$ is a concave function, it has only one global maximum. Based on our human game-play dataset, the MLE of λ is 0.1020.

SIGAL QRE: The Sigmoidal Acceptance Learning (SIGAL) agent introduced by Peled et al. [23] uses a social utility function instead of a selfish profit-maximizing utility function, and combines that with a sigmoidal acceptance function to determine action choice. The agent was shown to perform well relative to humans in two-agent negotiation tasks. Here we adapt the SIGAL agent to operate in the Social Ultimatum Game, which can be thought of as a multi-agent negotiation task. In fact, the Ultimatum Game was originally referred to as the Ultimatum Bargaining Game.

To adapt SIGAL for the Social Ultimatum Game, we first modified the set of features used to calculate the social utility. The features we used were:

- BEN_p^k: Proposer's benefit on the current round k,
- $P.BEN_p^k$: The benefit gained by the current proposer during the last interaction between the current proposer and decider, where the current proposer was also the proposer during that interaction,
- $P.BEN_d^k$: The benefit gained by the current decider during the last interaction between the current proposer and decider, where the current decider was the proposer during that interaction.

Thus we have the feature vector at round n: $x^k = (BEN_p^k, P.BEN_p^k, P.BEN_d^k)$. Coefficients were learned using logistic regression after a standard normalization procedure: $\hat{x} = (x - std(X))/mean(X)$, where X is the set of all feature vectors in our dataset. Table 1 shows the coefficient values learned in this way.

Table 1. SIGAL Parameters

Feature	BEN_p^k	$P.BEN_p^k$	$P.BEN_d^k$	Free Parameter
Value	7.6034	-7.3302	1.7826	-0.5819

Since the original SIGAL agent was designed for a two-agent negotiation game, we also need to extend the agent to handle our multi-agent (five-person) game. We maintain the spirit of the agent by using a QRE model to select which of the four opponents to make an offer. Similar to the expected reward QRE agent, we estimate the λ parameter from data, using the expected social utility instead of the expected reward. In this case, the MLE of λ is 1.030.

Adaptive Fairness: The full description of the adaptive fairness approach is described in [2]. For clarity in understanding this work, we give a short description of the agent here. Each player P_m is characterized by three parameters: α_m^0 : P_m's initial acceptance threshold, β_m : P_m's reactivity and γ_m : P_m's exploration likelihood.

The value of $\alpha_m^0 \in [0, e]$ is P_m's initial notion of what constitutes a "fair" offer and is used to determine whether an offer to P_m is accepted or rejected. The value of $\beta_m \in [0, 1]$ determines how quickly the player will adapt to information during the game, where zero indicates a player who will not change anything from their initial beliefs and one indicates a player who will solely use the last data point. The value of $\gamma_m \in [0, 1]$ indicates how much a player will deviate from their "best" play in order to discover new opportunities where zero indicates a player who never deviates and one indicates a player who always does.

An important emergent property of this agent is that it can replicate the reciprocity dynamics of human players, without explicitly being coded to do so. This indicates that these agents, while not perfectly aligned, are a reasonable substitute for human-like agents and we can use them to create various societies.

Parameters Learned from Human Data: As mentioned in the prior sections, we used a set of human experiments to learn the parameters of several of the described agents. These experiments were performed under two different settings: (1) University: Undergraduates and staff at a U.S. university, and (2) Conference: Attendees at an international conference with primarily computer science doctoral students and faculty.

We collected 40 game traces for the University setting, and 80 game traces for the Conference setting. Each game was a five-person, 20-round Social Ultimatum Game, with a \$10 endowment given to each player in each round. Payouts were given relative to performance, with a conversion rate of US\$0.025 for each Ultimatum Game dollar. From this data we estimated α, β and γ parameters for the adaptive fairness agents, using different subsets of humans for the different experiment settings described in the next section. These experiments include using the top 25% scorers in the Conference dataset, the top 25% scorers in the University dataset, two clusters of the human population based on offer value entropy (people who spread their offer values out the most and the least) and four humans drawn randomly from the populations. The learned parameters are shown in Table 2. The SIGAL-QRE, ER-QRE and Regret Minimization agents were also initialized with parameters learned from the same University and Conference datasets.

Table 2. Parameters

Agent	Conference Top 25%	University Top 25%	Cluster 1	Cluster 2	Humans			
					#2	#16	#18	#39
α	2.950	4.125	3.075	3.875	7	4	4	2
β	0.349	0.390	0.287	0.528	0.482	0.330	0.598	0.631
γ	0.0675	0.0562	0.0737	0.1475	0.1	0.1	0.05	0.15

Marginal Value Optimization: One of the fundamental gaps in the other approaches is that they do not leverage the possibility that the act of making an offer is also an opportunity to affect the mental model of other agents. An offer is not simply an opportunity for an agent to obtain a payoff but can also serve to increase the likelihood that another member of the society will choose the agent as a partner, or to possibly affect their notion of what is a fair offer if that society member is also adaptive.

We introduce the marginal value optimization (MVO) agent, which considers its offer as an opportunity to influence other agents. On each round it will make an offer value that it believes will make the target agent believe it is the most generous agent in the society.

Let us denote this value as the *top target value*. It chooses the target agent by calculating the marginal value of making that particular agent believe that it is the most generous agent in the society as follows. Let v_n^k be the marginal value of making the top target value to the n-th agent in the k-th round. Let $\hat{q}_n^k$ be the estimate of the offer value that the n-th agent would make to its target in k-th round. Let $p^*(q_{n,m}^k > 0)$ be the likelihood that the n-th agent will make the MVO agent an offer in the next round if the MVO agent offers it the top target value in the k-th round. Let $p(q_{n,m}^k > 0)$ be the likelihood that the n-th agent will make the MVO agent an offer in the next round if the MVO agent does not make it an offer in the k-th round. The marginal value of making the n-th agent a top target value offer in the k-th round is the estimate of the offer that the n-th agent will make back to the MVO agent multiplied by the marginal increase in the likelihood that the MVO agent will receive an offer:

$$v^k(n) = \hat{q}_n^k \cdot \left(p^*(q_{n,m}^k > 0) - p(q_{n,m}^k > 0) \right) \tag{1}$$

This approach actually describes a space of possible approaches that are characterized by the functions that (1) determine the top target value, (2) estimate the value of the returning offer, (3) estimate the likelihood of an offer being reciprocated if the top target value offer is made and (4) the decay in that likelihood if an offer is not made.

Here, we make very simple assumptions for these functions as follows: (1) the top target value is the best offer received in the last two rounds, (2) the estimate of the value of the returned offer is the last known offer from that agent, (3) the likelihood of reciprocation of a top target value offer is 1, and (4) the decay is linear such that it reaches zero when the number of non-offer rounds is the number of players. All value estimates are set to $5 until we receive data during game play. All offers made to the MVO agent are accepted.

5   Experiments

The experiments evaluate the adaptiveness of the various agents, when playing against a society of other players. In each experiment, we create a five-player game, where a given *test* player is evaluated when playing with four other *society* agents drawn from a single society type. Each game is 20 rounds, with a $10 endowment provided to each player in each round. The agent types for the test player were described in the previous section. The ten different societies are as follows:

– **AF-Conf-Top25:** 4 Conference Top 25% AF-agents. This represents the top scoring human strategies in the Conference dataset.

- **AF-Univ-Top25:** 4 University Top 25% AF-agents. This represents the top scoring human strategies in the University dataset.
- **AF-Cluster-1:** 4 Cluster 1 AF-agents. The Conference data was clustered into two sets: one which exhibited high offer value entropy, and one which exhibited low offer value entropy. Cluster 1 represented 40 humans who did not change their offer values very much over time.
- **AF-Cluster-2:** 4 Cluster 2 AF-agents. Cluster 2 represented 40 humans who spread out their offer values.
- **AF-4Types:** AF-agents fit using Human #2, #16, #18, #39. This society is the only one which is composed of a mix of agents. We selected four random humans, and fit one AF agent for each of them. As shown in Table 2, the players varied in terms of initial offer acceptance threshold, and had generally reasonable rates of adaptiveness and exploration, with some variation exhibited across the four players.
- **AF-Alpha-7:** 4 AF-agents, all fit using Human #2. This society was chosen to stress the adaptiveness of the test agents by exposing them to a relatively unusual society. Here the human player would initially only accept offers of at least $7.
- **SIGAL-QRE:** 4 SIGAL-QRE agents.
- **ER-QRE:** 4 ER-QRE agents.
- **Regret:** 4 Regret Minimization agents.
- **TFT-2:** 4 Tit-for-Tat agents with baseline $2 offers.

We evaluate six different types of test agents: (1) Human, (2) Regret, (3) SIGAL-QRE, (4) ER-QRE, (5) Tit-for-Tat, and (6) Marginal Value Optimization (MVO). We also evaluated other variations of these test agent types, as well as test agents based on Adaptive Fairness, but omit the results here for brevity and because they do not add additional insight to this discussion. Here we present the results of the sixty different pairings of one test agent with one society. For each pairing of one artificial agent and one society, we run 1000 games in simulation to obtain an estimate of the performance in each setting. For each pairing of one human and one society, we use Amazon's Mechanical Turk service to obtain the results, obtaining 20 trials for each such pairing.

In total, we ran 200 games using the Mechanical Turk service. Each game was created as a Human Intelligence Task (HIT) inside Turk. In each game, the human players were paid according to their performance, with a conversion rate of US$0.01 for each $1 earned in the Social Ultimatum Game. Most players earned between $1.50 and $2 per game. If it was the first time that a player accepted one of our HITs, the player would be asked to complete a compliance test before starting an actual game. This ensures that the experiment subjects understood our game rules and would provide useful data. The compliance test first described the game rules, provided the user with a chance to play a sample 3-round game, and ended with four short true/false questions to verify that the player understood the rules of the game. If the answers were wrong, the player had to restart the process by reviewing the game rules again. After successfully finishing the compliance test, we also gave the user a short survey to get background information including gender, occupation, age, and education.

Players could then play the 20-round games described above, paired against a society of four agents. They used the interface shown in Figure 1. The type of society was not revealed to the human player, and in fact, the human players were not told that they were actually playing against artificial agents. A random delay introduced between the rounds fostered the perception that they were playing against other humans, who might take varying amounts of time to decide on offer amounts and acceptances.

6   Results

The experiment data is summarized in Figure 2. This table shows the mean and standard deviations of payoffs for the test players in the 10 different agent societies. We can draw a couple conclusions from this data.

Marginal Value Optimization (MVO) Agent Outperforms Human Players: The main result of the paper is that the marginal value optimization (MVO) agent outperforms human players in 9 out of 10 societies. In 7 out of 10 societies the differences in the mean payoff were very high; the MVO test agent outperformed the human test agent payoff by 16.6, 17.9, 24.5, 35.9, 41.6, 42.1, and 65.7. The only society where it does not outperform humans is the ER-QRE society, where humans obtained an average score that was $11.70 higher. The ER-QRE society is made up of agents which follow a static policy, i.e., what transpires during the execution of the game does not affect ER-QRE agent decisions at all - it is a static randomizer.

20 Round game		Society											
		AF-Conf-Top25		AF-Univ-Top25		AF-Cluster-1		AF-Cluster-2		AF-4Types		AF-Alpha-7	
		mean	stdev	mean	stdev	mean	stdev	mean	stdev	mean	stdev	mean	stdev
Test Player	Human	199.2	50.2	193.5	60.6	149.7	60.7	173.1	60.7	211.6	37.3	86.9	33.0
	MVO	203.6	43.9	229.3	80.7	215.4	41.5	215.1	63.3	221.3	48.5	111.4	54.0
	SIGAL-QRE	185.7	32.0	109.6	50.4	147.8	35.6	140.1	38.8	168.4	38.0	64.3	31.0
	ER-QRE	146.2	37.4	138.5	56.1	141.5	40.0	131.5	39.7	167.4	41.1	88.0	44.6
	Regret	172.3	37.4	98.4	44.4	143.9	34.2	140.9	39.6	162.1	38.5	62.7	28.0
	TFT-2	93.4	66.5	162.9	74.8	95.7	59.9	113.8	64.4	167.3	54.9	104.8	66.9

20 Round game		Society							
		SIGAL-QRE		ER-QRE		Regret		TFT-2	
		mean	stdev	mean	stdev	mean	stdev	mean	stdev
Test Player	Human	167.4	25.5	186.4	30.6	138.7	43.9	192.0	12.0
	MVO	184.1	14.8	174.7	13.5	180.2	16.6	209.9	5.7
	SIGAL-QRE	200.0	18.0	210.2	19.9	178.3	18.8	205.9	6.3
	ER-QRE	190.8	20.3	200.0	22.2	170.5	20.9	202.7	6.8
	Regret	224.1	21.1	231.3	22.9	200.0	20.8	199.0	8.0
	TFT-2	209.0	11.2	207.5	11.7	199.3	13.5	200.0	11.1

Fig. 2. Mean and Standard Deviation of Payoffs for Test Players in Various Societies

Fig. 3. Total Payoffs (dark grey), Payoffs from Offers Received (light grey) and Payoffs from Offers Made (white) for Human and MVO Test Players in Various Societies

Most Agents Perform Better within Their Own Societies: The other agents (SIGAL-QRE, ER-QRE, Regret, TFT-2) can generally outperform humans and MVO agents when put within their own society. They also outperform humans in societies similar to their own. In particular, these agent types all have an "accept everything" rule, and perform well in societies composed of any of these five types of agents. However, they suffer significant degradation when wandering into societies composed of Adaptive Fairness type agents. This demonstrates the lack of adaptability of these agents, since they only succeed in societies similar to their own, and cannot adapt to societies that have a different social norm. In the societies composed of Adaptive Fairness agents, not all offers are accepted; only fair offers are accepted.

Unlike these agents, humans generally exhibit good adaptability to different societies, such as the societies composed of Adaptive Fairness agents. The results suggest that they are not as adaptive as one might initially hope to observe, however. For example, the AF-society where the fairness threshold is very high causes problems for humans, as does the society composed of regret minimizing agents. In the first case, humans cannot adjust to the high threshold and make many offers which are rejected; in the second case, humans reject some low offers and thus miss out on many future offers (and corresponding payoffs). Even given the limits of human adaptability, the MVO agent is the only approach that can almost uniformly outperform humans.

To investigate why the MVO agent is able to outperform humans, we separate the payoffs received by the humans and MVO agents into payoffs received from offers received and payoffs received by offers made. The results for the various societies are shown in Figure 3. We see that MVO's assumptions about generating payoffs from others by being the top target is validated. The MVO agent is able to generate more payoffs from offers made to it by others, when compared to human players in all societies.

Furthermore, MVO is also able to generate more payoffs from its own offers when compared to humans in 7 out of 10 societies. This is because the generous offer reduces the probability of rejection in several of the societies. However, it pays a price for this in societies where the probability of rejection is low (or zero). In two of the three cases, it is able to overcome this loss from improvement in the number and quality of offers made to it by others.

7   Summary and Future Work

We investigated the efficacy of several negotiation agents with respect to human performance in adapting to diverse societies. We used the Social Ultimatum Game for this investigation and performed human subject experimentation for data gathering. We introduced an approach based on marginal value optimization which leverages the strategic use of generosity to become the favorite partner of other agents in the society. This approach is able to outperform humans in a wide range of settings. This investigation shows a path to creating adaptive agents that perform well in a large set of societies.

There is significant room for improvement. We used simple estimation functions for many components of the MVO methodology. More accurate estimation may lead to greater performance. Also, we plan on testing the various adaptive agents in societies of multiple human agents. There are additional variations including game duration and endowment heterogeneity that are of interest. We also plan on creating social versions of other games such as Prisoner's Dilemma, Trust, Dictator, etc. to investigate if we can create agents that can perform well in multiple games and not just multiple societies.

Acknowledgements. This material is based upon work supported by the AFOSR Award No. FA9550-10-1-0569 and ARO MURI award No. W911NF-11-1-0332.

References

1. Wellman, M.P., Greenwald, A., Stone, P.: Autonomous Bidding Agents: Strategies and Lessons from the Trading Agent Competition. MIT Press (2007)
2. Chang, Y.-H., Levinboim, T., Maheswaran, R.: The social ultimatum game. In: Guy, T.V., Kárný, M., Wolpert, D.H. (eds.) Decision Making with Imperfect Decision Makers. ISRL, vol. 28, pp. 135–158. Springer, Heidelberg (2012)
3. Güth, W., Schmittberger, S.: An experimental analysis of ultimatum bargaining. Journal of Economic Behavior and Organization 3(4), 367–388 (1982)

4. Nowak, M.A., Page, K.M., Sigmund, K.: Fairness versus reason in the ultimatum game. Science 289(5485), 1773–1775 (2000)
5. Brenner, T., Vriend, N.J.: On the behavior of proposers in ultimatum games. Journal of Economic Behavior & Organization 61(4), 617–631 (2006)
6. Frank, R.H., Gilovich, T., Regan, D.T.: Does studying economics inhibit cooperation? The Journal of Economic Perspectives 7(2), 159–171 (1993)
7. Hofbauer, J., Sigmund, K.: Evolutionary Games and Population Dynamics. Cambridge University Press, Cambridge (1998)
8. van't Wout, M., Kahn, R.S., Sanfey, A.G., Aleman, A.: Affective state and decision-making in the ultimatum game. Experimental Brain Research 169(4), 564–568 (2006)
9. Hill, E., Sally, D.: Dilemmas and bargains: Theory of mind, cooperation and fairness. Working Paper, University College, London (2002)
10. Robert, C., Carnevale, P.J.: Group choice in ultimatum bargaining. Organizational Behavior and Human Decision Processes 72(2), 256–279 (1997)
11. Kahneman, D., Knetsch, J.L., Thaler, R.H.: Fairness and the assumptions of economics. The Journal of Business 59(4), S285–S300 (1986)
12. Blount, S.: When social outcomes aren't fair: The effect of causal attributions on preferences. Organizational Behavior and Human Decision Processes 63(2), 131–144 (1995)
13. Rilling, J.K., Sanfey, A.G., Aronson, J.A., Nystrom, L.E., Cohen, J.D.: The neural correlates of theory of mind within interpersonal interactions. Neuroimage 22(4), 1694–1703 (2004)
14. Sanfey, A.G., Rilling, J.K., Aronson, J.A., Nystrom, L.E., Cohen, J.D.: The neural basis of economic decision-making in the ultimatum game. Science 300(5626), 1755–1758 (2003)
15. Henrich, J., Heine, S.J., Norenzayan, A.: The weirdest people in the world? Behavioral and Brain Sciences 33(2-3), 61–83 (2010)
16. Henrich, J.: Does culture matter in economic behavior? Ultimatum game bargaining among the machiguenga. American Economic Review 90(4), 973–979 (2000)
17. Henrich, J., Boyd, R., Bowles, S., Camerer, C., Fehr, E., Gintis, H., McElreath, R., Alvard, M., Barr, A., Ensminger, J., Henrich, N.S., Hill, K., Gil-White, F., Gurven, M., Marlowe, F.W., Patton, J.Q., Tracer, D.: "Economic man" in cross-cultural perspective: Behavioral experiments in 15 small-scale societies. Behavioral and Brain Sciences 28, 795–815 (2005)
18. Oosterbeek, H., Sloof, R., van de Kuilen, G.: Cultural differences in ultimatum game experiments evidence from a meta-analysis. Experimental Economics 7(2), 171–188 (2004)
19. Axelrod, R., Hamilton, W.D.: The evolution of cooperation. Science 211, 1390–1396 (1981)
20. Auer, P., Cesa-Bianchi, N., Freund, Y., Schapire, R.E.: Gambling in a rigged casino: the adversarial multi-armed bandit problem. In: Proceedings of the 36th Symposium on Foundations of Computer Science (1995)
21. McKelvey, R., Palfrey, T.: Quantal response equilibria for extensive form games. Experimental Economics 1, 9–41 (1998)
22. Yang, R., Kiekintveld, C., Ordonez, F., Tambe, M., John, R.: Improving resource allocation strategy against human adversaries in security games. In: 22nd International Joint Conference on Artificial Intelligence, IJCAI (2011)
23. Peled, N., Gal, Y., Kraus, S.: A study of computational and human strategies in revelation games. In: Ninth International Conference on Autonomous Agents and Multi-Agent Systems, AAMAS (2011)

Incentives in Multi-dimensional Auctions under Information Asymmetry for Costs and Qualities*

Athanasios Papakonstantinou and Peter Bogetoft

Department of Economics, Copenhagen Business School
Porcelnshaven 16 A, 1, 2000 Frederiksberg, Denmark
{ap.eco,pb.eco}@cbs.dk

Abstract. This paper discusses the design of a novel multi-dimensional mechanism which allows a principal to procure a single project or an item from multiple suppliers through a two-step payment. The suppliers are capable of producing different qualities at costs which cannot exceed a certain value and the mechanism balances between the costs faced by the suppliers and the benefit the principal achieves from higher qualities. Iniatially, the principal implements a standard second score auction and allocates the project to a single supplier based its reported cost and quality, while then it elicits truthful reporting of the quality by issuing a symmetric secondary payment after observing the winner's production. We then provide an alternate mechanism in which the principal issues an asymmetric secondary payment which rewards agents for producing higher qualities, while it penalises them for producing lower qualities than they reported. We prove that for both mechanisms truthful revelation of costs and qualities is a dominant strategy (weakly for costs) and that they are immune to combined misreporting of both qualities and costs. We also show that the mechanisms are individually rational, and that the optimal payments received by the winners of the auctions are equal to the payment issued by the standard second score auction.

1 Introduction

The appearance and effectively the dominance of the Internet in many everyday activities has signaled a digital revolution which has thrown some considerable attention to auction mechanisms. Auctions are now playing an instrumental role in a vast number of on-line activities, whether affecting them directly (e.g. on-line trading sites such as ebay and taobao) or behind the scenes (e.g. on-line advertising). Traditional auction theory has been focusing on single-dimensional

---

* This research is undertaken as part of the Danish Council on Strategic Research funded project on Foundations of Electronic Markets (CFEM). This is a collaborative project involving the Universities of Aarhus and Copenhagen, Copenhagen Business School, The Alexandra Institute, DCCA and industrial partners: DONG Energy, Energinet.dk, Inno:vasion, TradeExtension and Patrisia Market Design.

E. David et al. (Eds.): AMEC/TADA 2012, LNBIP 136, pp. 104–118, 2013.

mechanisms which usually allocate a product to a highest bidder or procure a service from the supplier with the lowest cost.

However, single-dimensional auctions focus solely on the price; hence fail to address issues related to the quality or the characteristics of the auctioned good. This is very important in cases where the auctioned good is not a well defined item, but instead it is a contract or a service in which cost or price is one of many parameters. For example, in a contract for the construction of public infrastructure, the price of the project is a very important parameter but it should not be the only one. In this case, the quality of the materials, the design and possible effects on the people and the environment are serious factors that should be taken into consideration when deciding the allocation[1] of the contract. Likewise, in a e-commerce application which for example may involve the purchase of web services, often parameters such as bandwidth, responsiveness, or even the reliability of the provider play a significant role with prospective clients not necessarily aiming for the cheapest service.

Against this background, Che in his seminal paper [1] has designed a series of auctions (first score, second score and second preferred score) to address the cases where the quality of a product is of equal importance to its cost. In these auctions, the suppliers report the quality of the item they are asked to provide and the costs involved in its production at the reported quality, which the mechanism maps into a single dimensional quantity, named as 'score'. All three auctions incentivise agents to truthfully report their costs, and result to an equal expected utility for the buyer, under the assumption that costs are independently distributed. This assumption was relaxed by Branco [2] who introduced a two-stage optimal multi-dimensional auction in a setting in which there was correlation among suppliers' costs. Bogetoft and Nielsen [5] propose more complex cost structures through the introduction of Data Envelopment Analysis (DEA [6,7]) based competition. In this mechanism, and as opposed to second score auctions, all agents' bids determine the winner's payment.

Now, references to multi-dimensional auctions can be found in literature related to Computer Science and in particular multi-agent systems and e-commerce [8]. In particular, Bichler in [9] after comparing single and multi-dimensional auctions in an experimental web-based setting, showed that multi-dimensional auctions resulted in significant higher utility which paves the way for possible e-commerce applications. Furthermore, Beil and Wein [3] propose an iterative mechanism in which the buyer sequentially estimates each bidder's cost function through a series of score auctions. However, they assume that agents are truthful and hence do not address strategic behaviour. Parkes and Kalagnanam [4] propose an iterative multi-attribute procurement price-based auction in which suppliers at each round submit their bids and a winner which maximises the buyer's preference is selected. They show that their mechanism terminates with an outcome of modified Vickrey-Clarke-Groves allocation. Furthermore, multi-dimensional auctions

---

[1] A typical example is the European Union which has introduced a procurement directive based on two criteria: best economic value and lowest cost[11]. Examples include other government authorities, such as the US Department of Defense [1].

can also be applied in settings where multiple suppliers can satisfy the principal's demand [10], although this exceeds the scope of this paper.

However, in all the above approaches there is a rather significant underlying assumption. It is assumed that the principal will enforce through the use of external and artificial means that the suppliers will report their truthful qualities. The above papers either do not include in their models the possibility of the participating agents having control on their reported qualities, or explicitly mention that the auction will be canceled, or an extremely heavy fine will be issued to the winner of the auction if the observed quality deviates from the reported one. We find this un-systematic approach to be unrealistic for most cases. For example, in state procurement auctions the government will face public scrutiny if an obviously incompetent supplier is selected and there may be a cost in the repetition of the auction, while in e-commerce a web content provider who fails to secure the required resource by its suppliers and consequently deliver it to its clients will lose credibility. In both cases, it is more important to create incentives that will motivate the suppliers to report their true quality and based on that for the buyer to decide, instead of canceling the auction or destroying the supplier in case there is a deviation between the reported and observed values.

It is this challenge we address in this paper with the design of two mechanisms which initially allocate the contract to a specific supplier, while guaranteing that the reported qualities and costs are the true ones through an additional payment after the contract is fulfilled and the outcome is observed. In more detail, we extend the state of the art in the following ways:

- We present a procurement mechanism in which the principal issues a two-step payment. The principal initially asks the agents to report their cost and quality, and based on these reports selects a single agent to allocate the contract of providing a service. The selected agent receives an initial payment based on its reports. After that agent fulfils its contract by providing a service at a specific quality which is observed by the principal, the principal issues an additional payment. The second payment balances between possible misreporting of quality in the beginning of the mechanism and the actual production in the final step of the mechanism.
- We introduce a second mechanism in which the principal issues an asymmetric second payment based only on the deviation between the reported and produced qualities. The agents producing more than they reported receive a positive payment, while those producing less than they reported receive a negative payment.
- We prove that for both our mechanisms truthful revelation of qualities and costs is a dominant and a weakly dominant strategy respectively and that they are immune to the combined misreporting of both qualities and costs. We also show that both mechanisms are individually rational. Finally, we show that both mechanisms result to optimal payments for the winning agent, equal to the optimal payment the agent receives in the standard

second score auction. That is, the principal can elicit the agents' true qualities, without facing additional costs and without relying on artificial means (such as terminating the auction).

The rest of the paper is organised as follows: In Section 2 we introduce the notation and describe our setting in detail, while in Section 3 we discuss the traditional second score auction in order to provide some necessary background in multi-dimensional auctions. In Section 4 we introduce, analyse our mechanism and provide the proofs of its economic properties, while in Section 5 we introduce the asymmetric payments extension. Finally, in Section 6 we conclude and provide our future work.

2   The Context

We now introduce and describe our setting in more detail. We consider a principal interested in procuring a project, a service or an item from one of n rational and risk neutral agents, $i \in I = \{1, \ldots n\}$. The project depends on multiple parameters (e.g. bandwidth, latency, space in a data storage Cloud application). The parameters of a project undertaken by agent i are defined by an s-dimensional vector of qualities $y_i \in \mathbb{R}_0^s$. To simplify the analysis, and without lose of generality, we assume that for each agent the parameters of its service can be aggregated in one variable. Hence, each agent has a single quality profile denoted by y_i. In line with existing literature [1,2], we assume that the agents have a prior knowledge of their quality, which as opposed to existing literature, may choose to misreport to the principal if they expect to increase their utility by doing so. The true quality is unknown to the principal, who does not have any means of verifying it before the fulfilment of the project. Therefore, the principal makes its decision based on the report of the agent.

Furthermore, agents are capable of producing different levels of qualities, but in order to produce the quality y_i agent i needs inputs. These inputs represent the cost in production and depend on each agent's efficiencies. The costs are private information to each agent and cannot be verified by any third party (i.e. the principal or other agents). The cost agent i faces in the production of its quality is modeled as a function of quality y_i and can be denoted as $x_i(y_i, c_i)$, where c_i represents the agent's private information about the cost of the project. We assume that the cost function is increasing in both quality and cost parameter and that is convex regarding the quality. These assumptions are realistic in all cases where we expect diminishing returns as the quality increases, for example due to limitations in production methods where significant resources are demanded for a small increase in production. Finally, while agents are aware of their cost parameters, the principal has only access to their distribution. We assume that c_i is independently and identically distributed over $[\underline{c}, \bar{c}]$ with $0 < \underline{c} < \bar{c} < +\infty$ according to a distribution with positive and continuously differentiable density function.

3   The Standard Second Score Auction

As previously mentioned, the second score auction has been widely used in order to procure goods or services while taking into consideration both price and quality, as opposed to standard auctions (i.e. English, Vickrey auctions) which focus solely on the prices. Despite this dual nature of the second score auctions, they only consider agents' strategic behaviour with respect to their reported costs and not their reported qualities. They rely on the assumption that the auction will either be canceled, or the winner of the auction will face an extremely heavy fine if the promised quality is not delivered. Before we proceed to the analysis of our mechanisms which relax this assumption through a more rational and systematic approach, we provide the essential background for the understanding of the second score auction.

A second score auction maps the multi-dimensional bid (costs and qualities) into a single-dimensional variable (score). Effectively, for agent i: $(x_i, y_i) \mapsto S_i(x_i, y_i)$, with $S_i = V(y_i) - x_i(y_i, c_i)$, where $V(.)$ is the principal's value function. The value function is modeled as an increasing and concave function of the quality. The interpretation of the above process is that an agent is willing to produce y_i if its paid at least x_i, with the principal's satisfaction is measured to be $V(y_i)$.

The mechanism proceeds as follows:

1. Principal asks n agents to submit their cost-quality bids $(\widehat{x}_i, \widehat{y}_i)$ with $i \in \{1, ..., n\}$
2. Each bid is assigned with a score $\widehat{S}_i = S(\widehat{x}_i, \widehat{y}_i) = V(\widehat{y}_i) - \widehat{x}_i$.
3. The agent with the highest score wins the auction and is allocated the project[2].
4. The winner agent receives its payment by the principal: $\widehat{P}_{(1)} = V(\widehat{y}_{(1)}) - \widehat{S}_{(2)}$, with subscripts (1) and (2) representing the winner and runner-up agent respectively.

In order to demonstrate how this mecanism works, let us consider a buisness owner who is interested in profesional web presence. The candidate firms have received a list with the specifications she requires i.e. bandwidth, storage and CPU availability, access to multiple email accounts etc[3]. We assume that she has received three offers and that the corresponding bids are $(72.9, 9), (16, 4), (224, 16)$ where the first element is the provider's cost denoted by $x(y) = c_i * y^2$ with $c_i = \{0.9, 1, 0.875\}$. If her value function is $V(y) = 50 * \sqrt{(y)} + 25$ then the corresponding scores will be $S_i = \{102.1, 109, 1\}$. The second offer will be chosen and the payment will be equal to $125 - 102.1 = 22.9$.

The above mechanism has some very important properties. Most notably, truthful revelation of costs is a dominant strategy. Second, the mechanism is

---

[2] Ties are ignored, although standard practices (i.e. random selection) may be applied. Che suggests in his paper that a random tie-breaking rule does not affect the expected payment in equilibrium [1].

[3] We also assume that all these specifications can be aggregated into one quantity (referred as quality).

individually rational as it is easy to prove that the utility of the winner agent is always larger or equal (in case of tie-break) to 0. Finally, the optimal outcome maximises the socially efficient one, since the winner agent is the agent with the highest social welfare: $V(y_{(1)}) - x_{(1)}$ given that the mechanism is incentive compatible regarding cost and truthful reporting of the quality is assumed (the auction is canceled and a harsh penalty is issued to those who do not achieve the reported quality).

4   A Mechanism for Eliciting Both Costs and Outputs

We now relax the assumption regarding the guaranteed truthful reporting of qualities. In doing so, the principal faces the challenge of having to address an additional element of strategic behaviour on behalf of the agent. Indeed, in addition to misreporting its cost, now the agent can manipulate the principal by not delivering the promised quality.

We address the above challenge by designing a mechanism based on a two-step payment which promotes truthful reporting of both costs and qualities without relying on artificial means (i.e. cancellation of the auction). The proposed mechanism balances between two equally important concepts. That is, the agent must receive a reward for its actual production, while penalised for a possible misreporting of its costs and qualities.

Initially a standard second score auction is implemented in order to allocate the project to a specific agent who also receives its first payment. After the principal observes the actual outcome, secondary payment is issued to the selected agent. The first part of this additional payment consists of a symmetric penalty for the agent deviating from its reported quality, while in the second part it receives a compensation for its actual production.

In more detail the mechanism proceeds as follows:

1. Principal asks n agents to submit their cost-quality bids $(\widehat{x}_i, \widehat{y}_i)$ with $i \in \{1, ..., n\}$.
2. Each bid is assigned with a score $\widehat{S}_i = S(\widehat{x}_i, \widehat{y}_i) = V(\widehat{y}_i) - \widehat{x}_i$.
3. The agent with the highest score wins the auction and is allocated the project.
4. The winner agent receives its **first payment** by the principal: $\widehat{P}_{(1)} = V(\widehat{y}_{(1)}) - \widehat{S}_{(2)}$.
5. Winning agent produces quality $y_{(1)}$ (not necessarily equal to $\widehat{y}_{(1)}$).
6. Principal observes winning agent's quality production and issues the **second payment**:

$$B(\widehat{y}_{(1)}, y_1) = d(\widehat{y}_{(1)}, y_1) \times [V(\widehat{y}_{(1)}) - \widehat{S}_{(2)}] + [V(y_{(1)}) - \widehat{S}_{(2)}] \quad (1)$$

where $d(\widehat{y}_{(1)}, y_1)$ is the function that measures the effect of winner's misreporting and consequently the amount of the initial payment the agent has to return back. In the following section we discuss the properties such a function should have and we proceed to define it.

4.1   Definition of d() Function

The secondary payment consists of two parts. In the first part the principal penalises the selected agent for a possible deviation between the reported and produced quality, while in the second part the selected agent receives a payment for its actual production. The d() function is designed to guarantee that the selected agent will be penalised for not being able to meet its initial claims. The penalty is symmetric, that is the selected agent is penalised for its mis-reporting even if its misreporting results to an increase of the principal's value (through over-production). This will be necessary for applications in which over-production has negative effect. For example, over-production may be unwanted due to limitations in storage or transport capacity, or market conditions (over-supply). Alternatively, there may be more complex cases where agents may have to provide costly estimates of their qualities. In these cases, it will be unaccept-able if the same amount of misreporting resulted to a different type of payment (i.e. penalty vs reward).

Therefore, the properties we seek in d() function are the following:

1. The first part of the payment must be a penalty, hence d() must be negative for every $\widehat{y}_{(1)} \in [0, +\infty)$.
2. The penalty must be proportional of the misreporting, that is minor de-viation should result to a minor penalty, with the penalty increasing as misreporting increases.
3. There should be no distinction between agents which under or over reported their qualities, hence function d() must be symmetrical.
4. The secondary payment must be maximised at truthful reporting $\widehat{y}_{(1)} = y_{(1)}$ in order to guarantee incentives.

A function which satisfies the above assumption is the following[4]:

$$d(\widehat{y}_{(1)}, y_{(1)}) = -\left[\frac{(\widehat{y}_{(1)} - y_{(1)})^2}{y_{(1)}^2}\right] - 1 \tag{2}$$

4.2   Proof of Economic Properties

Having described in detail the mechanism, we now identify and prove its eco-nomic properties. Specifically we show that:

1. Truthful revelation of agents' qualities is a dominant strategy.
2. Truthful revelation of agents' costs is a weakly dominant strategy.
3. The mechanism is immune to combined strategic behaviour of both qualities and costs.

---

[4] We are aware that the choice of the d() function appears to be arbitrary. It should be noted that a more complicated analysis of the function exceeds the scope of this paper. This analysis will be central in future work where we consider agents facing costs in the process of identifying their qualities.

4. The mechanism is individually rational.
5. The optimal payment is equal to the optimal payment of a standard second score auction mechanism.

Lemma 1. *Truthful revelation of the agents' qualities is a dominant strategy given that they truthfully reported their costs.*

Proof. We prove that truthful revelation of agents' qualities is a dominant strategy by showing that winner's utility is maximised at truthful reporting (i.e. $\widehat{y}_{(1)} = y_{(1)}$).

The winning[5] agent's utility[6] is equal to:

$$U(\widehat{y}) = V(\widehat{y}) - S_2 + d(\widehat{y})[V(\widehat{y}) - S_2] + V(y) - S_2 - x(y) \qquad (3)$$

With its derivative being equal to:

$$U'(\widehat{y}) = [1 + d(\widehat{y})]V'(\widehat{y}) + d'(\widehat{y})[V(\widehat{y}) - S_2] \qquad (4)$$

For $\widehat{y} = y$ and since $d(y) = -1$ and $d'(y) = 0$ the derivative is equal to 0.

The second derivative for the utility function is:

$$U''(\widehat{y}) = d'(\widehat{y})V'(\widehat{y}) + [1 + d(\widehat{y})]V''(\widehat{y}) + d''(\widehat{y})[V(\widehat{y}) - S_2] + d'(\widehat{y})V'(\widehat{y}) \qquad (5)$$

For $\widehat{y} = y$ and given that $d(y) = -1$ and $d'(y) = 0$ the second derivative is equal to $U''(y) = d''(y)[V(y) - S_2]$ which is negative given that $d''(y) < 0$ and $V(y) - S_2 > 0$. Regarding $V(y) - S_2$, for a selected agent who has truthfully reported its cost: $S_1 = V(y) - x(y) > S_2 \Rightarrow V(y) > S_2$. Finally, the selected agent's utility is equal to $S_1 - S_2$ which positive (unless there is a tie between the first and second agent's scores). $\qquad \square$

Lemma 2. *Truthful revelation of the agents' costs is a weakly dominant strategy given that they truthfully reported their qualities.*

Proof. We prove this by contradiction. Let x and y be an agent's true cost and quality, and S the score that corresponds to these true values, while $\widehat{x}, \widehat{y}, \widehat{S}$ the reported ones. Furthermore, let x_2, y_2, S_2 be the bids and score of the runner up agent (i.e. $\widehat{S} > S_2$).

First, let the agent's misreporting have an effect on the outcome of the auction. We consider the following two cases:

1. Agent wins by misreporting while it would have lost if truthful.
2. Agent loses by misreporting while it would have won if truthful.

- In Case (1) agent reports its cost s.t $\widehat{S} > S_2$ given that $S < S_2$. The agent achieves this by reporting a lower cost than its actual one i.e. $\widehat{x} < x$. Under optimal reporting of quality, the utility of an agent misreporting its cost in Case (1) will be negative i.e. $U(y) = V(y) - x(y) - S_2 = S - S_2 < 0$.

---

[5] From this point we omit subscript (1) for notational convenience.
[6] After the actual quality y has been observed, function $d(\widehat{y}, y)$ can be simplified to $d(\widehat{y})$, since $\widehat{y}$ is the only unknown variable.

- In Case (2) agent reports its cost s.t. $\widehat{S} < S_2$ given that $S > S_2$. The agent would have won the auction, but instead reports a cost greater than its actual one i.e. $\widehat{x} > x$. As a result, the agent loses the auction and consequently receives zero utility.

Second, we assume that the agent misreports its cost without this affecting whether he wins the auction or not. If the agent had already lost the auction misreporting would have no additional effect as the utility would be zero. Had the agent won the auction, misreporting would not result to additional benefits. Specifically, both payments depend on the second lower score and the reported and actually produced (for the second stage) quality. □

Theorem 1. *The mechanism is immune to combined misreporting of both qualities and costs.*

Proof. In the above proofs we showed that truthful reporting of quality is an optimal strategy if the agent reports truthfully its cost, and that the same holds for an agent's costs, given that it truthfully reported its quality. However, given the multi-dimensional nature of the bids an agent could attempt to manipulate the principal by misreporting both costs and qualities. Specifically, we consider these two general cases:

1. Agent wins the auction by misreporting both its quality and cost
2. Agent wins the auction with the misreporting having no effect on the auction's outcome
3. Agent loses the auction despite or due to its misreporting

- In Case (1) the agent reports its quality and cost s.t. $\widehat{S} > S_2$, while $S < S_2$. For example, an agent may be inclined to report both lower cost and higher quality than its true values in order to guarantee that it will win the auction. Let an agent's reported quality be $\widehat{y} = ky$ with $k \in [0, +\infty)$ being the coefficient of under-reporting ($k \leq 1$) or over-reporting ($k > 1$), while the reported cost remains $\widehat{x}$. The utility derived by that agent is:

$$U = V(ky) - S_2 - [(k-1)^2 + 1][V(ky) - S_2] + V(y) - S_2 - x(y) \Rightarrow$$
$$U = -(k-1)^2[V(ky) - S_2] + S_1 - S_2$$

Now since the agent misreported both its cost and quality and won the auction while it should not have won $k \neq 1, S < S_2$ and $\widehat{S} > S_2$ the above expression is negative given that $\widehat{S} = V(ky) - \widehat{x}(ky) > S_2 \Rightarrow V(ky) > S_2$. This type of combined misreporting leads to negative utility.
- In Case (2) the agent would have won the auction anyway, and although misreporting of cost and quality will have no impact on the outcome of the auction, it may have on the secondary payment. In this case, $S > S_2$, and although it is possible that $U > 0$, we know from Lemma 1 that the agent's utility is maximised at $\widehat{y} = y$ if $V(y) - S_2 > 0$. Now, given that in this case the agent has already won the auction: $S - S_2 = V(y) - x(y) - S_2 > 0 \Rightarrow V(y) - S_2 > 0$. So misreporting would deviate from the optimal outcome.

– In Case (3) the agent does not win the auction after misreporting its cost and quality. This may have happened as a result of the misreporting (the agent would have won otherwise), or despite the misreporting. In both those cases, the utility the agent will receive will be equal to zero.

We have showed that combined misreporting of both costs and qualities leads either to negative utility or to a non-optimal outcome, hence the mechanism is immune to this type of strategic behaviour.   □

Theorem 2. *The mechanism is individual rational.*

Proof. We have shown in the above proofs that for truthful reporting of qualities the selected agent's utility is equal to $V(y) - S_2 - x(y)$, which is positive for truthful reporting of costs. This is also the optimal payment the agent receives for reporting its true cost and quality in the standard second score auction. It can be seen, that the principal can elicit agents' true quality without additional cost on its behalf and without relying on artificial means such as cancellation of the auction.   □

Corollary 1. *The agent's optimal payment for reporting its true cost and quality is equal to the payment issued in a standard second score auction.*

5   A Mechanism with Asymmetric Secondary Payment

In the previous section, we introduced a mechanism in which the principal penalises the winning agent for failing to provide the quality it reported. The principal does not discriminate among those agents who under or over reported and balances the fine with a fixed payment equal to the payment the agent would have received in the original second score auction. We focused on the case where the principal's primary focus is the quality's misreporting even if it ends up receiving value higher than it initially expected. Although this may be necessary in several cases (i.e. limited storage capacity, flooding of market through over-supply) or in more complex settings (i.e. costly estimates of qualities), it is natural to assume that in a setting with no special conditions or uncertainty regarding the quality, over-production should not be penalised.

Against this background, in this section we introduce a mechanism in which the principal does not directly penalise those agents who end up producing more than they reported without necessarily incentivising them to do so. The principal values truthful reporting the most, however it is not willing to equally penalise all agents to achieve it. The first payment for this mechanism is identical to the previous one, while the payment issued after the actual production rewards a selected agent which has produced a good or a service of quality higher than the one it reported initially in the mechanism, and issues a fine to a selected agent with the exact opposite behaviour.

In more detail the payment issued by the principal after observing the agent's production $y_{(1)}$ (not necessarily equal to $\widehat{y}_{(1)}$), is the following:

$$B(\widehat{y}_{(1)}, y_1) = d(\widehat{y}_{(1)}, y_1) \times [V(y_1) - V(\widehat{y}_{(1)})] \tag{6}$$

where $d(\widehat{y}_{(1)}, y_1)$ is the function that measures the effect of winner's misreporting. As opposed to Mechanism 1, in this mechanism function d() may reward an agent even if it is misreporting its quality. In the following section we discuss the design of this function and how the additional payment can be balanced in order to guarantee incentives in this mechanism.

5.1 Definition of d() Function

In this mechanism, the winner of the auction is not necessarily directly penalised for choosing to produce a good at a different quality than the promised one. In this case the selected agent will not be asked to return a part of its initial payment if the principal has benefited from the agent's misreporting. We take this into consideration by designing d() function so that an agent will not be directly penalised for causing an increase in principal's value (through over producing), although it may still be far from doing the best it can. Hence, it is important to differentiate between the misreporting that inflicts losses and that one which causes gains for the principal. In order to do so, function d() must have the following properties:

- **For the agent who reported less than it produced and thus created a surplus, $\widehat{y} \in [0, y]$:**
  1. Given that $V(y) - V(\widehat{y}) > 0$, d() must be positive for every $\widehat{y} \in [0, y]$ so the secondary payment is in fact a reward.
  2. The agent should receive a portion of the principal's surplus $V(y) - V(\widehat{y})$.
  3. The agent should not be inclined to under-report systematically, hence it should receive a small portion of that surplus for significant under-reporting.
  ** *Hence, for $\widehat{y} \in [0, y]$, $d(\widehat{y})$ should be an increasing and positive function taking values in $[0, 1]$.*

- **For the agent who reported more than it produced and thus created a deficit, $\widehat{y} \in (y, +\infty)$:**
  1. Given that $V(y) - V(\widehat{y}) < 0$, d() must be positive for every $\widehat{y} \in (y, +\infty)$ so the secondary payment is in fact a penalty.
  2. The agent's penalty should increase as the principal's deficit in quality $V(y) - V(\widehat{y})$ increases. The agent possibly manipulated the first payment of the mechanism by reporting high quality, but it turned out it could not deliver it.
  3. The agent should not be over-penalised for a small amount of misreporting, hence it should receive a fine proportional to the deficit of principal's value.
  ** *Hence, for $\widehat{y} \in (y, +\infty)$, $d(\widehat{y})$ should be an increasing and positive function taking values in $(1, +\infty)$.*

A function which satisfies all the above properties is:

$$d(\widehat{y}_{(1)}, y_{(1)}) = \frac{(\widehat{y}_{(1)} - y_{(1)})^3}{y_{(1)}^3} + 1 \tag{7}$$

5.2 Proof of Economic Properties

Having described in detail the mechanism, we now identify and prove its economic properties. Specifically we show that:

1. Truthful revelation of agents' qualities is a dominant strategy.
2. Truthful revelation of agents' costs is a weakly dominant strategy.
3. The mechanism is immune to combined strategic behaviour of both qualities and costs.
4. The mechanism is individually rational.
5. The optimal payment is equal to the optimal payment of a standard second score auction mechanism.

Lemma 3. *Truthful revelation of agents' qualities is a dominant strategy, given that they truthfully reported their costs.*

Proof. We prove that truthful revelation of agents' qualities is a dominant strategy by showing that winner's utility is maximised at truthful reporting (i.e. $\widehat{y}_{(1)} = y_{(1)}$ or after simplifying the notation $\widehat{y} = y$).

The selected agent's utility after the a project of quality y has been produced and observed, is given by:

$$U(\widehat{y}) = V(\widehat{y}) - S_2 + d(\widehat{y})[V(y) - V(\widehat{y})] - x(y) \tag{8}$$

With its derivative being equal to:

$$U'(\widehat{y}) = [1 - d(\widehat{y})]V'(\widehat{y}) + d'(\widehat{y})[V(y) - V(\widehat{y})] \tag{9}$$

For $\widehat{y} = y$ and since $d(y) = 1$ and $d'(y) = 0$ the derivative is equal to 0.

The second derivative of the utility function is:

$$U''(\widehat{y}) = [1 - d(\widehat{y})]V''(\widehat{y}) + d''(\widehat{y})[V(y) - V(\widehat{y})] - 2d'(\widehat{y})V'(\widehat{y}) \tag{10}$$

For $\widehat{y} = y$ and given that $d(y) = 1$ and $d'(y) = d''(y) = 0$ the second derivative is equal to 0], hence the second derivative test is inconclusive for the stationary point y. We will show that y is a maximum point by examining the sign of the derivative of the utility function for $y \in [0, +\infty)$. Indeed, for Equation 9 it can be said that it is positive for $\widehat{y} \in [0, y]$, while it is negative for $\widehat{y} \in (y, +\infty)$. Hence the utility function is increasing in $[0, y]$, while it is decreasing in $(y, +\infty)$. That is $\widehat{y} = y$ is a maximum point with $U(y) = S_1 - S_2 > 0$ (unless there is a tie), hence truthful revelation of agents' reported quality is a dominant strategy. □

Lemma 4. *Truthful revelation of agents' reported costs is a weakly dominant strategy given that they truthfully reports their qualities.*

Proof. The proof for this theorem is identical to the proof of Lemma 2. Despite the fact that in this mechanism there is a different secondary payment, under optimal reporting of quality, the agent derives an identical utility, equal to $V(y) - S_2 - x(y) = S - S_2$, where S_t is the score that corresponds to truthful reporting of quality and its cost.   □

Theorem 3. *The mechanism is immune to combined misreporting of both qualities and costs.*

Proof. In the above proofs we showed that truthful reporting of quality is an optimal strategy if the agent reports truthfully its cost, and that the same holds for an agent's costs, given that it truthfully reported its quality. However, given the multi-dimensional nature of the bids an agent could attempt to manipulate the principal by misreporting both costs and qualities. An additional complication appears given that there may be a positive secondary payment for a $\widehat{y}^* \in [0, y]$, and hence it is important to determine whether it is possible for an agent to manipulate the reporting of costs early in the mechanism in order to guarantee positive secondary payment. We still consider the two following general cases:

– Agent wins the auction by misreporting both its quality and its cost
– Agent wins the auction with the misreporting having no effect on the auction's outcome.
– Agent loses the auction despite or due to its misreporting

– In Case (1) agent reports both its quality and cost s.t. $\widehat{S} > S_2$, while $S < S_2$. Let $y^* = k^* y$, with k^* being the coefficient of under-reporting ($k^* \leq 1$) or over-reporting ($k^* > 1$), with $k^* y$ maximising the secondary payment $B(\widehat{y}, y)$ (but not the overall agent's utility). The utility derived by that agent is:
$$U = V(k^* y) - S_2 + [(k^* - 1)^3 + 1][V(y) - V(k^* y)] - x(y) \Rightarrow$$
$$U = [S - S_2] + [(k^* - 1)^3 [V(y) - V(k^* y)]]$$

Since the agent misreported both its cost and quality and won the auction while it should have not, the above expression is negative. Indeed $S - S_2 < 0$ and $[(k^* - 1)^3 [V(y) - V(k^* y)]] < 0$ for both $k^* < 1$ and $k* > 1$
– In Case (2) the agent would have won the auction anyway and its possible misreporting of quality and cost had no impact on that outcome. It is important now to examine whether it is still in an agents best interest to report y^*. In this case, $S - S_2 > 0$, and $[(k^* - 1)^3 [V(y) - V(k^* y)]] < 0$. Although, it may be possible that $U > 0$, we know from Lemma 3 that the utility will be maximised at $k = 1$. Hence, it will not be optimal for an agent not to report its true quality, given that it will end up receiving less for misreporting.
– In Case (3) the agent does not win the auction after misreporting its cost and quality. The agent's misreporting has no impact on the auction and the agent's utility will be equal to zero.

We have showed that combined misreporting of both costs and qualities leads either to negative utility or to a non-optimal outcome, hence the mechanism is immune to this type of strategic behaviour.   □

Theorem 4. *The mechanism is individual rational*

Proof. We have shown in the above proofs that for truthful reporting of qualities the selected agent's utility is equal to $V(y) - S_2 - x(y)$, which is positive for truthful reporting of costs. This is also the optimal payment the agent receives for reporting its true cost and quality in the standard second score auction. It can be seen, that the principal can elicit agents' true quality without additional cost on its behalf and without relying on artificial means such as cancellation of the auction.   □

Corollary 2. *The agent's optimal payment for reporting its true cost and quality is equal to the payment issued in a standard second score auction.*

6   Conclusion

In this paper we introduced two novel multi-dimensional mechanisms based on a two-step payment in a setting in which the principal cannot enforce truthful reporting of agents' qualities through artificial means such as the cancellation of the auction or extremely high fines. Initially, the principal procures an item or a service from the winner of a standard second score auction and issues a second score auction payment based on the winner's reported quality and cost. That agent then fulfils its part of the contract and produces an output of a certain quality. The principal, after having observed the production, calculates a second payment based on both the winner's reported and produced quality.

Regarding the secondary payment, in the first mechanism it consists of two parts. In the first part the principal issues a symmetric penalty to the selected agent for misreporting its quality, while in the second part it compensates that agent through a standard second score auction payment based on the agent's produced quality and not its reported. In the second mechanism, the principal issues an asymmetric payment to the selected agent. That is, it rewards that agent if the procured service is of higher quality to the reported one, while it penalises it for the exact opposite. Despite the different approaches, under truthful reporting both mechanisms result to the same total payment which is equal to payment issued to the winner of the standard second auction. Hence, there is no cost in the principal's attempt to guarantee incentives regarding the agents' reported qualities, and therefore no reason at all for enforcing them upon the agents.

For both mechanisms we provided proofs of their economic properties. Specifically, we showed that they are incentive compatible regarding the reported qualities (dominant strategy) and costs (weakly dominant strategy) and individually rational. In addition to this, we showed that they are immune to agents' combined misreporting of their parameters.

In our future work we intend to consider a setting in which the agents are not aware of their specific quality. Agents will only have a probabilistic estimate of their production and based on that estimate the principal will have to make a decision. Agents will face costs in the generation of their estimates and hence they will have to balance between the amount of resources they will invest on generating their estimate and the consequences they may face for providing imprecise or inaccurate estimates. By addressing these issues, we will be able to apply this mechanism in more complex and dynamical domains where there is uncertainty regarding the production. A typical example is the production of electricity through specific renewable sources which depend on weather conditions (i.e. solar, wind power) and hence subject to forecasting. In this case the principal will have to elicit truthful and precise estimates, while the focus of the mechanism remains on the actual production. Also, costs involved in both the estimate and production will have to be balanced so that the whole process is a viable option for both the principal and the participating agents.

References

1. Che, Y.-K.: Design competition through multidimensional auctions. RAND Journal of Economics 24(4), 668–680 (1993)
2. Branco, F.: The design of multidimensional auctions. RAND Journal of Economics 28(1), 63–81 (1997)
3. Beil, D.R., Wein, L.: An inverse-optimization-based auction mechanism to support a multiattribute RFQ process. Management Science 49(11), 1529–1545 (2003)
4. Parkes, D., Kalagnanam, J.: Models for Iterative Multiattribute Procurement Auctions. Management Science 51(3), 435–451 (2005)
5. Bogetoft, P., Nielsen, K.: DEA based auctions. European Journal of Operational Research 184(2), 685–700 (2008)
6. Charnes, A., Cooper, W.W., Rhodes, E.: Measuring the efficiency of decision making units. European Journal of Operational Research 2(6), 429–444 (1978)
7. Charnes, A., Cooper, W.W., Rhodes, E.: Short Communication: Measuring the efficiency of decision making units. European Journal of Operational Research 3, 339 (1979)
8. He, M., Jennings, N.R., Leung, H.-F.: On Agent-Mediated Electronic Commerce. IEEE Transactions on Knowledge and Data Engineering 15(4), 985–1002 (2003)
9. Bichler, M.: An experimental analysis of multi-attribute auctions. Decision Support Systems 29, 249–268 (2000)
10. Bichler, M., Kalagnanam, J.: Configurable Offers and Winner Determination in Multi-Attribute Auctions. European Journal of Operational Research 160, 380–394 (2003)
11. Asker, J., Cantillon, E.: Properties of scoring auctions. RAND Journal of Economics 39(1), 69–85 (2008)

A Model-Free Approach for a TAC-AA Trading Agent*

Mariano Schain, Shai Hertz, and Yishay Mansour

Tel Aviv University
{marianos,shaihertz,mansour}@tau.ac.il

Abstract. We describe a *model-free* approach to bidding in the Ad-Auctions Trading Agents Competition: First, a simple and robust yet high-performing agent using a *Regret Minimization* optimization algorithm for the 2010 competition, followed by our top performing agent for the 2011 competition, still using simplified modeling and optimization methods. Specifically, we model the user populations using particle filters, but base the observations on a Nearest Neighbor estimator (instead of game specific parameters). We implement a simple and effective bid optimization algorithm by applying the equimarginal principle combined with perplexity-based regularization. The implementation of our 2011 agent also remains model-free in the sense that we do not attempt to model the competing agents behavior for estimating costs and associated game parameters.

1 Introduction

During the past few decades, the Internet transformed from an academic information-sharing tool into a world-wide business platform in which people and companies of all sizes conduct an ever-growing portion of their activities. It has become evident that the competitive advantage of many of the Internet companies relies on their ability to apply machine learning algorithms (for example, learning user preferences to improve user experience, learning user interests to increase the effectiveness of web advertisements, and so on). In the Google AdWords setting, for example, advertisers bid on keywords[1] with the goal of maximizing the net revenue[2]. Learning algorithms that allow agents to bid such that profits are optimized constitute significant ingredients of the competitiveness of agents.

Optimization, however, relies on a model of the environment (nature). Therefore, to be successful, agents first have to establish a good approximation of the state of nature. In contrast to parametric methods that are tailored to the specific (usually statistical, but also structural) attributes of a model of nature, in the model-free approach minimal

---

* This research was supported in part by the Google Inter-university center for Electronic Markets and Auctions, by a grant from the Israel Science Foundation, by a grant from United States-Israel Binational Science Foundation (BSF), by a grant from the Israeli Ministry of Science (MoS), and by the Israeli Centers of Research Excellence (I-CORE) program, (Center No. 4/11).

[1] The bidding activity is usually implemented by automated trading agents.

[2] The revenue resulting from purchases made by users who clicked the displayed advertisements, offset by the payments to Google for the clicks, as determined by the outcome of the bidding mechanism.

E. David et al. (Eds.): AMEC/TADA 2012, LNBIP 136, pp. 119–132, 2013.
© Springer-Verlag Berlin Heidelberg 2013

assumptions are made regarding the model of nature. As such, model-free algorithms are usually simpler and more robust to model errors or changes. However, ignoring the parameters and structure of a valid model might limit the achievable performance of an algorithm (compared to algorithms that make use of the model). This is the very tradeoff considered in our work - we explore the extent of using model free methods while maintaining a limited performance hit.

In this paper we describe our model free approach to implement a bidding agent for the Trading Agent Competition [4], a yearly competition that implements a simulated Ad-Auction environment in which competing advertisers bid for sponsored search results of search queries. Specifically, we research the usage of model-free methods to address the main challenge of the advertiser: to control - by setting the bids - its revenues and costs which are determined by the states of the user populations, the behavior of competing advertisers, and a predetermined capacity constraint.

A conceptually similar model-free approach which uses a simulation-based iterative best-response technique is detailed in [9]. Other previous approaches to the TAC-AA bidding optimization problem (e.g., [2]) rely on the game description to accurately estimate the game parameters, model the user populations state and competitors actions. Both [2,1] formulate the bidding optimization problem as a combinatorial (intractable) optimization problem and heuristically search for the best solution. Although such methods do achieve top scores in the given game, they might be sensitive to modeling errors, both parametric (estimation errors) and structural (wrong model used).

Our first attempt, for the TAC-AA 2010 competition, almost entirely ignored the game description and based its (almost trivial) modeling and estimation on simple moving averages. Our optimization scheme used a regret minimization algorithm to perform a fractional allocation of the available capacity. This very simple scheme that only performed top-aiming bids on a subset of the available queries resulted in a very simple agent that was implemented very fast and performed quite well - among the 13 competitors it achieved 6th position in the semifinals (therefore qualifying for the final 8 competitors) and 7th in the finals, scoring $\sim 30\%$ behind the top performers.

For the 2011 competition, following [2], we implemented particle filters to model the states of the user populations. Our implementation however, following the model-free approach, does not use the methods of [2] to compute the particle filter input (those methods are highly tailored to the game specification). We use a *K-Nearest Neighbor* (K-NN) estimator instead, that we train on historical games data (data from 100 games provides 200000 samples) and achieve $\sim 30\%$ relative estimation error. However, using dedicated techniques we were able to keep the overall modeling accuracy (and the overall agent performance) comparable with the model-based methods.

Our optimizer was implemented to search for the equimarginal utility bid (See [1] for motivation, and also Section 5.1). Using simple linear models for estimating cost-bid relation allowed for an efficient implementation of the optimization as a simple one-dimensional search. Furthermore, to mitigate the risk of under-utilized capacity resulting from over-estimation of the sales potential in a user population we introduced a tunable regularization factor that favors allocations across a high number of queries (i.e., allocations of high perplexity).

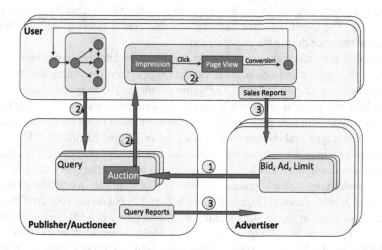

Fig. 1. The Ad-Auctions game dynamics: The competing agents (the advertisers) submit bid bundles which are used by the platform to run auctions for queries performed by simulated searching users. The users may click on ads and purchase products from the winning advertisers. Reports regarding past performance are provided daily to the advertisers so they can adjust their future actions.

All the above resulted in a top performing agent, achieving the third place in the final round of the TAC-AA 2011 competition, scoring within 3% of the winner.

2   The TAC Ad-Auctions Game

The Ad-Auctions game, one of several games run yearly by the Trading Agents Competition (TAC) forum, is a simulated Ad-Auction environment in which competing advertisers (specifically, software agents implementing the advertisers behavior) bid for their Ads to be displayed alongside search results of queries performed by a set of user populations. All the queries and related auctions are managed by a publisher. The competing agents interact with a game server that simulates the user populations and the publisher actions.

As illustrated in Figure 1, the ad-auctions game dynamics are such that each advertising agent is required to provide a daily bid bundle to the publisher. The publisher uses the advertiser's bids during the following day to run an auction for every search query performed by a user. The auction result determines the advertiser's ad positions and the price to be paid to the publisher upon a user click on the ad. An advertiser collects a fixed revenue for every user query in which the advertiser got his ad displayed (an *impression*) and the user clicked and further made a purchase (*convert*). The advertiser problem is therefore to maximize his accumulated net revenue (during 60 simulated days) by providing bid bundles while considering the potential costs and revenues for each query (affected mainly by the user populations size and state, and by the competing agents bids). The agent may use daily reports that reveal information regarding the agent's performance during the previous day.

Each simulated user, making a query per day, has a predetermined preference to one of three manufactures and one of three product types (therefore, there are 9 products and 9 respective user populations). The game simulates 10000 users of each population. To keep the game simple, user's queries are limited to a choice of manufacturer and product type. The user may also choose not to mention in his query any manufacturer or product type and therefore there is a total of 16 possible queries. The specific query made by a user depends on his *state*, reflecting his tendency to search, click, and make a purchase and his *focus level* - the agreement between the query to be made and the user's underlying state and product preference. For example, in one of the states (*Informational Search*, denoted *IS*), users only click on Ads but do not convert. Obviously, the portion of users in the *IS* state making a specific query is a key factor influencing the potential profitability of a query in the eyes of the advertiser that should optimize his bid accordingly. The user's state transition probabilities are governed by an almost-Markovian model that is available to the competing agents.

Finally, inter-query dependencies are introduced through a predefined capacity constraint that is revealed to each competing agent at the beginning of the game session. An advertiser that sells over his capacity (during a moving window of five days) suffers a significant decrease of the users conversion probability (upon an impression), which in turn reduces the ROI (since the cost per click remains the same). See [4] for a complete specification of the game.

3   The Agent Structure

We schematically partition our agent to three main components: A *Modeler* responsible to assess and predict the state of the changing environment (in the TAC-AA game this includes the user population and competitors state, in past, current, and future days), an *Estimator* responsible to discover the game parameters (this includes reserve prices, continuation probability etc') and an *Optimizer* that uses the services provided by the estimator (and indirectly, the modeler) to come up with optimal actions (the daily bids).

Our baseline agent for 2010 included a trivial implementation of the modeler and estimator, combined with a simple optimization scheme over a restricted actions space. Our subsequent agent for 2011 significantly enhanced the modeling algorithm (while - along the lines of our 'model-free' approach - keeping as much of its mechanisms independent of the game specification), and implemented an enhanced (yet simple) optimization scheme over a significantly richer action space. Both optimizer implementations however are based on the following template daily capacity allocation scheme. The target daily capacity allocated for the following day $\hat{Q}_{t+1}$ (total to be further allocated across queries) is set such that it complements the units sold during the previous days $S_{t-3}, S_{t-2}, S_{t-1}$ and the estimation of units to be sold today $\hat{S}_t$ to a γ-increase of the 5-day capacity C (the slight addition over the capacity is to allow for operation over the capacity at a range that will not hurt the conversion rates significantly). In addition, the allocation is never less than a minimal amount which is half the average daily sales required to achieve the capacity quota:

$$\tilde{Q}_{t+1} = \max\{\frac{C}{10}, (1+\gamma)C - \hat{S}_t - \sum_{i=1}^{3} S_{t-i}\}.\tag{1}$$

Finally, the estimate for *today* sales $\hat{S}_t$ is the average of the quota allocated for today $\tilde{Q}_t$ and the actual allocation[3] $\check{Q}_t$.

4   A simple Model-Free Agent for TAC-AA 2010

Our first agent, taking part in the 2010 tournament, completely ignored the user popu-lations model. It merely used the previously observed profits of queries to fractionally allocate the daily quota calculated by (1). Specifically, we significantly reduced the ac-tion space by only bidding high on queries. Furthermore, we only bid for queries that have either our agents' specialty component or specialty manufacturer or both (a total of seven queries) - This is since such queries carry the highest profit potential for our agent and therefore are best suitable to our *high bid* strategy. As a result, setting the capacity allocation of each query, subject to the overall daily quota set by (1), was the only remaining daily decision do be made. We use a *regret minimization* scheme [8] to fractionally allocate the overall capacity across queries. Based on estimates of the cost per click and the conversion rate for each query, we set the daily budget limit parameter of each query accordingly[4].

Noting that our problem may be interpreted as a setting of learning from expert advice using *regret minimization* algorithms [5], our query quota allocation is based on the Randomized Weighted Majority (RWM) algorithm [6]. That is, the different queries are the experts, the gains are the observed profits gained by bidding at each of the queries, and the portion of the overall daily quota to be allocated to each query is the weight w_i^t of expert (query) i on day t. Specifically, we apply a regret minimization scheme by fractionally allocating the available capacity based on a running average of the profits per unit sold of each query: let v_q^t be the value (i.e., costs subtracted from revenue) per unit sold reported for query q for day t. Upon receiving reports for day $t-1$ on day t, a daily score for each query q is set $s_q^{t-1} = e^{\eta v_q^{t-1}}$, where η is a predefined constant learning rate parameter. The overall (adjusted) score of query q for day $t-1$ is:

$$\hat{s}_q^{t-1} = \hat{s}_q^{t-2} + \alpha(s_q^{t-1} - \hat{s}_q^{t-2}),$$

where α is also a predefined constant learning rate parameter. The portion of the es-timated available capacity for day $t+1$ allocated to query q is the query's portion of the total score on day $t-1$. Therefore, the following units quantity will be allocated to query q for day $t+1$:

$$u_q^{t+1} = \frac{\hat{s}_q^{t-1}}{\sum_q \hat{s}_q^{t-1}} \tilde{Q}_{t+1}.$$

On day t, we maintain an estimate for the upcoming cost per click $\hat{c}_q^{t+1}$ of each query q. The estimate is an adjustment of the previous estimate $\hat{c}_q^t$ based on the actual figure

---

[3] Note that the actual allocation for day t was set at day $t-1$.

[4] Such that the budget is exhausted upon selling the allocated amount of units.

reported for day $t-1$: $\hat{c}_q^{t+1} = \hat{c}_q^t + \tau(c_q^{t-1} - \hat{c}_q^t)$, where the learning rate τ is constant. We maintain similar estimates for the conversion rate $\hat{v}_q^{t+1}$ (the fraction of actual sales out of the total clicked ads).

Once we have $\hat{c}_q^{t+1}$, the bid b_q^{t+1} of query q for day $t+1$ is $b_q^{t+1} = \hat{c}_q^{t+1} + \delta \hat{p}_q^{t-1}$, where $\hat{p}_q^{t-1}$ is the average position of our bid for query q in day $t-1$ and δ is randomly chosen such that our position is kept high (the bid increases if our position deteriorates).

Finally, the spend limit l_q^{t+1} for each query q is set to control the number of units to be actually sold for each query on day $t+1$:

$$l_q^{t+1} = \frac{u_q^{t+1} c_q^{t-1}}{v_q^{t-1}}$$

5 Tau Agent for TAC-AA 2011 – User Modeling and Regularized Equimarginal Optimization

Our target for the 2011 competition was to improve our agent's performance as much as possible while still employing model free methods. Observing the methods and results reported in [1] and [2] we concluded that a good model of the user populations is essential for top performance. We therefore implemented particle filters to model the user populations states. Our particle filter input however does not rely on specification-tailored computations of the total impressions as in [2]. Instead, we estimate this quantity using the KNN model-free method. Architecture-wise, the service provided by the modeler is an assessment of the number of users submitting each of the queries [5]. Our modeler also provides an assessment of the number of users that may submit a query but never convert. As will become evident, those two quantities (specifically, their ratio) are the key metric in evaluating the potential profitability of bidding on a query[6]. The estimator maintains estimates of the game parameters for each query (reserve prices, click through and continuation probabilities), and also the two-way mappings of bids to resulting costs and ad positions. As it turns out, a simple linear relation between bids and costs suffices (as an alternative to modeling the competitors' bids behavior) to achieve top scores. Finally, The service provided by the estimator to the optimizer is an estimate of the total achievable sales (and the related bid required) given a target profit per unit. As described in detail below, this is done by using the modeler assessments to figure out the cost per click that will result in the required profit per unit, and then using the continuation probability and related position to estimate the total number of conversions.

The agent's optimizer uses the equimarginal principle to replace a multidimensional search over all bids combinations by a simple one dimensional search for the highest profit level (equal over all queries) that achieves the daily quota. This optimal uniform profit level directly induces the required bids for each of the queries. To reduce variability and address the inherent uncertainty, our profit level optimization is regularized by the number of queries that take part in the bid (i.e. we give preference to profit levels

---

[5] For past, current, and future days (the estimate for future days is based on the estimate for the current day and applying the user transition model).

[6] Users that click but never convert may result in significant loss to the advertiser.

that result in the daily quota spread over queries). We now turn to describe in detail each of our agent's components.

5.1 Optimizer

The optimizer's task is to find at every day t an optimal (highest profits) bid bundle for day $t + 1$ that achieves the daily allocation $\tilde{A}_{t+1}$ of (1). Denote (for some fixed day t and query q, therefore omitted from the notation) by m_b the number of users submitting query q and converting (with some positive probability), and by m_n the number of users submitting query q and never converting. We now show that the following relation holds:

$$U(m) = m \left(R - \frac{CPC(b(m))}{CVR}(1 + \frac{m_n}{m_b}) \right) , \qquad (2)$$

where m is the number of units sold to the users, R is the revenue associated to a unit sold, $U(m)$ is the total profit from selling m units, $b(m)$ is the bid level that results in m units sold, $CPC(\cdot)$ is the mapping of the bid level to the cost per click, and CVR is the conversion rate. Indeed, the sales for a query are achieved by $m_b \cdot CTR$ clicks from the 'buying' population and (since the users are simulated in a random order) $m_n \cdot CTR$ clicks from the 'non-buying' population. Therefore, $m_b \cdot CTR \cdot CVR$ sales requires $(m_b + m_n)CTR$ clicks and the number of clicks required to achieve a sale is $\frac{1}{CVR}(1 + \frac{m_n}{m_b})$. We conclude that when m units are sold, the cost of making a sale is $\frac{CPC(b(m))}{CVR}(1 + \frac{m_n}{m_b})$ and the relation (2) follows. Note that since $b(m)$ (the bid resulting in at least m sales) is a step function, $U(m)$ is pieacewise linear in m. Moreover, the slope of $U(m)$ negatively depends on $CPC(b(m))$ and is therefore decreasing in m.

We can now formalize the optimizer problem of finding the optimal bid bundle subject to the capacity constraint as the following program:

$$\max_{\{b_q\}} \sum_q U_q(m_q(b_q)) , \text{ subject to } \sum_q m_q(b_q) \leq \tilde{Q} , \qquad (3)$$

where $m_q(b_q)$ is the assumed number of units to be sold when bidding b_q on query q, and $\tilde{Q}$ is the daily sales quota as set using (1). Now, making the simplifying assumption that $U_q(\cdot)$ are concave[7] for every q, it is easy to see that for an optimal solution $\{m_q^*\}$ of (3) all the marginal utilities $\frac{dU_q}{dm}(m_q^*)$ are equal.

Since $U_q(m)$ is piecewise linear, equating marginal utility is equivalent to equating utility. Therefore, the optimization problem (3) is solved by a simple linear search for the maximal utility u for which the resulting total sales achieve the quota: $\{(m_q(u))\}$ such that $\sum m_q(u) \geq \tilde{A}$, where $m(u)$ is the inverse mapping of the marginal utility $u(m) = R - \frac{CPC(b(m))}{CVR}(1 + \frac{m_n}{m_b})$ and is provided to the optimizer by the estimator. Note that a decrease in the utility per unit sold occurs when the related cost per unit sold increases (reflecting a better ad position for the query), which leads to a higher number of conversions. Therefore $m(u)$ decreases with u.

---

[7] $U_q(m)$ is of course not concave, since $U_q(m)$ has a discontinuity precisely at the discontinuity points of $b(m)$, but this assumption will give the "right" intuition.

Algorithm 1. Optimize $(\tilde{Q}, \{m_q(\cdot)\}, \{b_q(\cdot)\})$

$u \leftarrow u_h$
while $(\sum_q m_q(u) \leq \tilde{Q})$ AND $(u \geq u_l)$ **do**
    $u \leftarrow u - \Delta$
end while
return $\{b_q(u)\}$

As a result, our simple search for the optimal utility starts at a predefined constant high utility level u_h and decreases it repeatedly (in Δ sized steps) until our total estimated sales reaches the target daily allocated quota (or until a predefined constant low utility u_l is reached - this is to avoid the risk of negative utility, and to ensure that our algorithm stops even in cases where the total potential sales are lower than the allocation).

Regularization was added to preclude quota underutilization[8]:

The regularization is based on the perplexity of the allocation[9]. Denote by $\overline{m}(u) \in \Delta_{16}$ the normalized vector of units allocated to the queries.. The perplexity of $\overline{m}$ increases with the number of queries taking part in the allocation represented by $\overline{m}$ (and the other way around).

Now, in the regularized optimization algorithm we discount the estimated sales for a given utility level using a logistic function of the allocation perplexity. Specifically, by a factor $\frac{1}{1+\beta \cdot e^{-p(\overline{m})}}$. We used a parameter β to tune the regularization degree, where a high β represents a high preference to spreading the allocation across queries. Now, as u decreases, $m_q(u)$, the perplexity $p(\overline{m}(u))$, and the regularization factor increases. Therefore, our regularized algorithm (which is identical to Algorithm 1, but with $(1 + \beta \cdot e^{-p(\overline{m}(u))})$ multiplying $\tilde{Q}$ in the while condition) will result in the highest uniform utility level that achieves a regularized quota (higher - since the regularization factor is smaller than 1).

5.2 Estimator

The estimator provides an estimation of sales (and related bid) given a target utility level. To do so, the estimator uses the modeler assessments m_n and m_b and estimates the other quantities appearing in the following relation, which is based on (2)

$$u(m) = R - \frac{CPC(b(m))}{CVR}\left(1 + \frac{m_n}{m_b}\right). \tag{4}$$

Specifically, the estimator first solves (4) to find the required *CPC*, then it finds the target position that results in the required *CPC*, and finally it estimates the resulting sales figure (using the estimates of the continuation parameter and conversion rate). A similar computation is done (upon finding the optimal allocation) to set the bids. The bid for each query is set such that it results in the target number of units $m(u)$. We now

---

[8] Resulting from a combination of sales estimation errors and allocation to very few queries.
[9] The perplexity of a probability distribution $\overline{d} \in \Delta_n$ is defined as $p(\overline{d}) = 2^{H(\overline{d})}$, where $H(\cdot)$ is the entropy.

Fig. 2. The estimation of CPC (left) and position (right) as a function of the bid

describe in detail the methods used by the estimator for estimating each of the required quantities.

CPC and Bid Relation. We make the simplifying assumption that the CPC and the bid are linearly related. Therefore, the estimator maintains the ratio and the upper and lower thresholds (i.e., the bid threshold beneath which our ad is not shown at all, and the bid threshold above which our ad is the first ad shown).

The ratio estimation as well as the lower and upper thresholds are initialized based on previous games and are updated after each query report. Namely, when a bid lower than our minimal bid results in showing our ad we lower our minimal bid towards it. When a bid higher than our maximal bid doesn't result in our bid shown first we raise our maximal bid. The ratio estimation is updated by averaging with the previous estimate. Figure 2 illustrates the CPC and position relations with the bid.

Position and Bid Relation. First the estimator maintains *num_bidders*, an estimate of the number of bidders for each query. The number is initialized to the maximal value (i.e., 5) and updated after each query report by averaging with the previous estimate (this time a weighted average that prefers the latest estimate). As before, we assumed an underlying linear relation and used the minimal bid and the maximal bid estimates.

Click through Rate and Reserve Prices. The CTR for every query q is determined by three factors: the parameter e_q^a (a baseline value randomly chosen by the server for each competing advertiser at game start), whether the ad is placed in a promoted slot or not (f_{pro}), and whether the ad targeting matches the user population (f_{target}). For games that have at least one promoted slot, we find e_q^a together with the two reserve prices ρ_{reg} and ρ_{pro} by solving the following three relations:

$$\rho_{pro} = \rho_{reg} + 0.5, \quad cpc_r = \frac{\rho_{reg}}{(e_q^a)\chi}, \quad cpc_p = \frac{\rho_{pro}}{(e_q^a)\chi},$$

where cpc_r and cpc_p are the minimal cost per click observed on regular slots and promoted slots, respectively. The first relation is a simplifying assumption since by the game specification we always have $\rho_{reg} \leq \rho_{pro} \leq \rho_{reg} + 0.5$. The second and third are due to the generalized second price auction, the minimal price that an advertiser would have to bid in order to to get his ad shown is the squashed reserve price for the minimal regular or promoted position, respectively. The squashing parameter χ is given at game start so we can easily solve the three unknown variables and get estimates for both reserve prices and for $e_q^a = (2(cpc_p - cpc_r))^{-\frac{1}{x}}$. As this value is an approximation, it is averaged with the previous approximation whenever recomputed. Now, given the bid level we can assess whether our ad will be placed in a promoted slot or not. This allows us to use a good approximation of the true f_{pro}. Finally, knowing our ad type and the relevant population sizes we set f_{target} and get the desired approximation of the click through rate.

For games with no promoted slots we calculate the CTR iteratively. Given our reported position, the estimation of the continuation probability γ (as detailed in the next section) and the modeler assessment of the number of impressions on clicking users ($imps$), we first calculate the effective number of impressions - the number of users that actually considered clicking our ad (after passing higher positioned higher ads and continue without clicking), and then simply estimate the click through rate:

$$imps_{\text{eff}} = imps \cdot [\gamma(1 - CTR_{\text{old}} \cdot CVR)]^{position-1} \;,\; CTR_{\text{new}} = \frac{clicks}{imps_{\text{eff}}} \quad (5)$$

Continuation Probability. For a game with promoted slots, once we have an estimate of the CTR we use the reported position and clicks and the modeler assessment of $imps$ to solve (5), where γ and $imps_{\text{eff}}$ are the only unknowns. Otherwise (to overcome the circular dependency between estimating CTR and continuation probability), we first calculate the CTR based on the previously calculated continuation probability and then calculate the new continuation probability.

Sales and Bid. Sales estimation is the main service of the estimator provided to the optimizer. Given a target utility (profit) level for a query, the estimator returns the number of conversions (sales) that will result by bidding on the query such that the requested profit is attained. First, the target cost per click is recovered using (4) and the modeler assessments of m_n and m_b. Next, the bid relations with cost and position are used to find the position related to the target cost per click (this is our target position). Then, the modeler assesment of total impressions and the estimation of the continuation probability are used to calculate using (5) the effective number of impressions for the target position. Finally, the estimates of click and conversion probabilities are used to provide the estimate of the number of conversions when bidding for the target position.

A related service provided by the estimator is the required bid level to achieve a target profit in a query (this is used by the optimizer once the optimal profit level is decided). To find the required bid level, the estimator does the first two steps of the sales estimation, returning the bid level that pertains to the target cost per click (using the bid and cost relation).

5.3 Modeler

The modeler provides upon request $m_b^q(d)$ and $m_n^q(d)$, the maximal (potential) number of *buying* impressions and the maximal number of *non-buying* impressions (respectively) for query class q on day d. As detailed above, $m_b^q(d)$ and $m_n^q(d)$ (specifically, their ratio) are a key metric in evaluating the utility of selling a unit by bidding on query

q and as a consequence a key parameter to the bid optimization algorithm. Denote by $n_s^p(d)$, the number of users in state s for population p on day d (recall that there are 9 user populations, one for each combination of manufacturer and product type). For clarity, in what follows we omit from the notation the dependence on the day d unless required to avoid ambiguity. Now, by the users behavior as described in the game specification, for each level-2 query $q = (M, C)$ we have

$$m_b^{(M,C)} = n_{F2}^{(M,C)}, \text{ and } m_n^{(M,C)} = \frac{1}{3} n_{IS}^{(M,C)} ,$$

for each level-1 query $q = (M, \phi)$ or $q = (\phi, C)$ we have

$$m_b^{(M,\phi)} = \frac{1}{2}(n_{F1}^{(M,C1)} + n_{F1}^{(M,C2)} + n_{F1}^{(M,C3)})$$

$$m_n^{(M,\phi)} = \frac{1}{6}(n_{IS}^{(M,C1)} + n_{IS}^{(M,C2)} + n_{IS}^{(M,C3)})$$

$$m_b^{(\phi,C)} = \frac{1}{2}(n_{F1}^{(M1,C)} + n_{F1}^{(M2,C)} + n_{F1}^{(M3,C)})$$

$$m_n^{(\phi,C)} = \frac{1}{6}(n_{IS}^{(M1,C)} + n_{IS}^{(M2,C)} + n_{IS}^{(M3,C)})$$

and finally, for the (only) level-0 query (ϕ, ϕ) we have (summing over the 9 populations):

$$m_b^{(\phi,\phi)} = \sum_p n_{F0}^p, \text{ and } m_n^{(\phi,\phi)} = \frac{1}{3} \sum_p n_{IS}^p$$

Also, each user makes a query every simulated day and each query results in an impression for each of the winning advertisers. Therefore, by modeling $n_s^p(d)$, the number of users in state s for population p on day d, the modeler is able to provide upon request $m_b^q(d)$ and $m_n^q(d)$ for any query q.

We therefore maintain a particle filter for each of the 9 populations (each providing an estimate of $n_s^p(d)$). Each particle filter is a collection of particles, where each particle represents a distribution of the population over the possible states. The distribution represented by the particle filter is the weighted average of the distributions of its particles, and the weight assigned to each particle reflects the plausibility of an observed quantity (in our case, as suggested by [2], the estimated total number of impressions in the level-2 query that corresponds to the population) given its represented distribution.

The particle filter algorithm is therefore the following: we maintain a separate set of particles for each day *yesterday*, *today*, and *tomorrow*. When a new day starts, the particle set for *yesterday* is discarded, and the previous particle set for *today* is used for creating the new particle set for *yesterday* by reweighing and resampling it (upon receiving the query report and having an estimate of the total number of impressions). The new particle sets for *today* and *tomorrow* are created by advancing the new particle set for *yesterday* once and twice respectively. All this creates an updated estimate of $n_s^p(d-1)$, $n_s^p(d)$ and $n_s^p(d+1)$ at every day d of the game, allowing the modeler to service requests for m_b^q and m_n^q for days $d-1$, d, and $d+1$.

In the rest of the section describing our modeler we review in more detail the particle filter update steps and related implementation concers. Of special interest (w.r.t. our model free approach) is the usage of nearest neighbor learning to estimate the particle filter input (in contrast to the direct calculation described by [2]).

Reweighting. Given an observation of T estimated total impression, the weight $w(P|T)$ assigned to a particle representing a users distribution

$$P = (N_{NS}, N_{IS}, N_{F0}, N_{F1}, N_{F2}, N_{TR})$$

is computed as the probability of a total of $T - N_{F2}$ successes in N_{IS} binomial experiments, each with success probability $\frac{1}{3}$ (this is because each of the N_{F2} users results in an impression for the related L2 query, and with probability $\frac{1}{3}$ each of the N_{IS} users results in an impression for the related L2 query). In practice, we use the normal probability approximation for the distribution with average $\frac{N_{IS}}{3}$ and variance $\frac{2N_{IS}}{9}$ and set

$$w(P|T) = \phi(\frac{3(T - N_{F2}) - N_{IS}}{\sqrt{2N_{IS}}}), \tag{6}$$

where $\phi(\cdot)$ is the normal probability density. Upon re-weighting, the weights are normalized such that they sum to 1.

In some situations it may happen that the probability (6) is negligible for all particles. This may be caused by estimation errors of the total number of impressions (the particle filter *observation*) or by competitors behavior: if all advertisers reach their spending limit within the day then the total number of impressions is no longer equal to the total number of users in searching states, a condition that violates a fundamental assumption of the derivation of (6). A naive computation of (6) in such cases results in zeroing of the weights of all the particles, a situation that should be avoided to enable the subsequent resampling (that depends on the weights summing to 1). Therefore, the reweighing algorithm avoids a direct computation of (6) and instead computes for each particle the ratio of its probability to the maximal particle's probability (and subsequently normalize such that the weights sum to 1).

Resampling. Given a re-weighted particle set (the *baseline* set), resampling involves creating a new particle set in which the number of times each particle appears in the new set (the *resampled* set) is relative to its weight in the baseline set. Once resampled, the weights are discarded and weighted averages over the baseline set are equivalent to uniformly averaging over the resampled set. In some situations we implement selective resampling (only reweigh and resample a randomly chosen portion of the particles [10], leaving the rest of the particles unchanged regardless of the observation). This allows for quick readjustment in case of estimation errors.

Advancing Particles. Advancing a set of particles consists of advancing each particle of the set, simulating the daily change of state of the users. A particle representing a users distribution $P = (N_{NS}, N_{IS}, N_{F0}, N_{F1}, N_{F2}, N_{TR})$ is advanced by applying a transition model (which defines the state transition probabilities) to the

---

[10] The portion of the particles that is kept unchanged depends on our level of confidence in the observation.

represented user population, resulting in an *adnavced* users distribution P^a = $(N_{NS}^a, N_{IS}^a, N_{F0}^a, N_{F1}^a, N_{F2}^a, N_{TR}^a)$. The transition model is given as part of the game definition, and is constant except for the transitions from focused searching states to the transacted state (which depend on competing advertisers actions, and therefore is no longer Markovian). Furthermore, the transition probabilities depend on the presence of a burst (effecting the probability of transitioning from *NS* to *IS*, an effect that lasts for a sequence of days) and therefore each particle also maintains a burst-status which is used to select the appropriate transition model to use.

The particle advance algorithm is the following: First the appropriate transition model (*burst* or *regular*) is selected - this is a random choice (the probability of a burst depends on the current burst status). Second, the users N_S of each state S are transitioned according to the transition model (we use successive binomial sampling to implement a multinomial random generator, and we compute the conversion probability based on estimates of the number of bidders for each query). Finally, N_S^a (the advanced population of state S) is set as the aggregation of all users transitioned to state S.

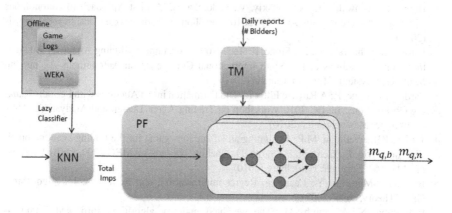

Fig. 3. Modeler architecture: particles are advanced using the transition model (TM) which is regularly updated with the recent estimates of the number of bidders for each query. Also, a K-Nearest Neighbor estimator that was trained off-line is used to provide the input (total number of impressions) to the particle filter.

Using KNN for Total Impressions Estimation. The input (observation) of the particle filter is the total number of impressions during a simulated day. This quantity is not directly provided to the agent, however, a dedicated algorithm (presented by the TacTex team in [2]) may be used to find a value that is consistent with the reported data Instead of using TacTex's algorithm, we use a nearest neighbor estimator that uses training samples from past games logs to train a weka-based [10] K-Nearest-Neighbor estimator that is then used to provide (on-line, given the reported data) an estimation of the total number of impressions to the particle filter. Figure 3 illustrates the modeler architecture. Using 200000 samples with $K = 3$ resulted in an average relative error of 30%. However, our experiments indicate that no significant influence on the overall performance of the agent was noticed at this error rates (compared to the 'exact' computation of the total number of impressions).

6   Conclusion

Our 2011 agent's results (compared to our 2010 agent's results) show that implementation of both modeling and optimization methods are required to achieve top TAC-AA scores. However, game-spec tailored modeling is not mandatory. Our simple and efficient optimization scheme compensates for the inaccuracies of our model-free methods, and achieves scores comparable to those of model-based agent implementations employing mathematical programming optimization schemes.

References

1. Berg, J., Greenwald, A., Naroditskiy, V., Sodomka, E.: A First Approach to Autonomous Bidding in Ad Auctions. In: ACM EC 2010 Workshop on Trading Agent Design and Analysis (2010)
2. Pardoe, D., Chakraborty, D., Stone, P.: TacTex09: A Champion Bidding Agent for Ad Auctions. In: Proceedings of the Ninth International Conference on Autonomous Agents and Multiagent Systems, Toronto, Canada (2010)
3. Pardoe, D., Stone, P.: A Particle Filter for Bid Estimation in Ad Auctions with Periodic Ranking Observations. In: EC 2010 Workshop on Trading Agent Design and Analysis (TADA), Cambridge, Massachusetts (2010)
4. Jordan, P.R., Wellman, M.P.: Designing an ad auctions game for the trading agent competition. In: David, E., Gerding, E., Sarne, D., Shehory, O. (eds.) AMEC 2009. LNBIP, vol. 59, pp. 147–162. Springer, Heidelberg (2010)
5. Blum, A., Mansour, Y.: Learning, Regret minimization, and Equilibria. In: Algorithmic Game Theory, ch. 4 (2007)
6. Littlestone, N., Warmuth, M.: The weighted majority algorithm. Info. and Computation 108(2), 212–261 (1994)
7. Freund, Y., Schapire, R.: A decision-theoretic generalization of on-line learning and an application to boosting. Journal of Comp. and System Sciences 55(1), 119–139 (1997)
8. Cesa-Bianchi, N., Lugosi, G.: Prediction, learning, and games. Cambridge University Press (2006)
9. Vorobeychik, Y.: A Game Theoretic Bidding Agent for the Ad Auction Game. In: Third International Conference on Agents and Articial Intelligence (2011)
10. Hall, M., Frank, E., Holmes, G., Pfahringer, B., Reutemann, P., Witten, I.H.: The WEKA Data Mining Software: An Update. SIGKDD Explorations 11(1) (2009)

Ad Exchange – Proposal for a New Trading Agent Competition Game*

Mariano Schain and Yishay Mansour

Tel Aviv University
{marianos,mansour}@tau.ac.il

Abstract. Brand advertising through web display ads, aimed at driving up brand awareness and purchase intentions, is the cornerstone of the Internet economic ecosystem. The ever increasing penetration of the Internet and recent technological advances allow for cost effective targeting and gave rise to an array of new interconnected entities - e.g., the pivotal Ad Exchange (AdX) - offering added value to publishers and advertisers.

We propose a new game for the Trading Agent Competition (TAC), to be launched in 2013, reflecting the challenges faced by an Ad Network (AdN) as it bids for display ads opportunities. Those settings are new and conceptually different than those modeled by existing TAC games: the key conflict that AdNs face is to fulfill advertising contracts at minimum cost while sustaining and attracting advertisers by achieving high quality targeting. Therefore, efficient marketing effectiveness is the main concern of an agent implementing the AdN strategy.

In our proposed AdX game, which significantly differs from the TAC Ad Auctions (TAC-AA) game setting, we also consider the following key elements of the AdX setting: the method in which reserve prices are set by publishers, the mechanism for discovering the value of cookie matching services, and the ways the targeting quality of ad networks effects their long term earnings prospects.

Keywords: Trading Agents, Ad Exchange, Competition.

1 Introduction

Similarly to traditional communication platforms such as radio and television, online advertising is the most significant business paradigm of the Internet. Most business models for Internet-based services depend on online advertising revenues to enable the huge investments that are needed in order to provide their services at attractive (and usually no) cost to users.

The Internet as an advertising platform is used by advertisers during the different stages of the purchase funnel: Display ads (the ads displayed alongside web content)

---

* This research was supported in part by the Google Inter-university center for Electronic Markets and Auctions, by a grant from the Israel Science Foundation, by a grant from United States-Israel Binational Science Foundation (BSF), by a grant from the Israeli Ministry of Science (MoS), and by the Israeli Centers of Research Excellence (I-CORE) program, (Center No. 4/11).

E. David et al. (Eds.): AMEC/TADA 2012, LNBIP 136, pp. 133–145, 2013.

are mostly used to strengthen brands by creating awareness and interest, while sponsored search ads (the ads displayed alongside search results) are mainly used to directly induce sales of products or services. This difference also results in different pricing schemes for the ads: while advertisers pay a *cost per click* (CPC) for sponsored search, the display ads are usually priced per thousand impressions - *Cost Per Mille* (CPM). The effectiveness of both schemes however (from the advertiser's perspective) relies on the ability to target the right audience.

While the effectiveness of sponsored search advertising is straightforward to measure (direct effect on sales), the situation is more challenging for brand advertising where brand awareness and purchase intentions may only be indirectly deduced. Nevertheless, brand advertising accounts for the majority of the Internet advertising activity (see [5]). It is therefore not surprising that with the advent of some key enabling technologies[1] the ecosystem has evolved from direct advertiser-publisher interaction for setting (upfront) the price of the impressions inventory, to an interconnected network of entities[2] (each adding value to the advertisers, publishers, or both) in which the inventory prices are dynamically set.

As the number of interactions between advertisers and publishers increased, Supply Side Platforms (SSPs) were introduced to assist the publishers optimize their inventory allocation decisions (e.g., by dynamically assigning each ad impression opportunity to one of several contracted advertisers). Ad Exchanges were introduced in turn to increase ad value to publishers, offering liquidity of inventory (e.g., impression opportunities that did not fit any ongoing campaign) and value discovery (i.e., impressions that may be sold for higher value than the contracted price) through a platform that enabled interested advertisers (or ad networks and agencies acting on their behalf) to bid for impression opportunities. Similarly to SSPs and Ad Exchanges, Demand Side Platforms (DSPs) were introduced to assist the ad agencies and networks in optimizing their decisions (e.g., budget allocation of the advertising campaigns across publishers and ad exchanges, and impression opportunities bid levels) such that market targeting goals are met. Finally, audience classification is key both for publishers and advertisers (the former may get higher prices for impressions in which the audience attributes are specified, the latter uses the audience attributes to ensure proper targeting). Therefore, user classification services are also provided by dedicated entities based on cookie matching technologies.

As noted, the Ad Exchange (AdX) is a pivotal entity in the display ad ecosystem. It interacts with most interested entities, provides added value both to the publishers and the advertising agencies, and is best positioned to extract value from the aggregated information that flows through it as bidding takes place (e.g., the true value of ad impressions to different advertisers, the orientation of the audience of different publishers, etc.).

Naturally, this has spawned research activity aimed at analyzing and establishing the methods used by the different entities involved (as surveyed in [1]): e.g, the auction

---

[1] Mainly user profiling and real-time bidding.

[2] Some other entities (such as ad delivery servers and content distribution systems) take part in the display ad ecosystem but are less relevant to the proposed setting, and are omitted from the game.

mechanism at the AdX [2], the reserve price decision by the publisher (or more gener-ally, the decision whether to submit an impression opportunity to an AdX or consume a prepaid inventory) [3], and, in a somewhat different setting, the bid price decision by the ad network [4].

We consider a reality in which advertisers (or ad agencies, on advertisers' behalf) contract ad networks upfront to execute advertising campaigns with agreed-upon total budget and *reach*[3] (thereby effectively setting the CPM upfront). An ad network may conduct several campaigns simultaneously. A key problem for the ad network in this setting is therefore the choice of advertising campaign to serve for each impression opportunity. This is a fundamental new conflict faced by ad networks (e.g., with respect to the problem of ad networks in the sponsored search setting) which are now required to balance the long term profitability goal (attracting advertisers by providing sustainable high quality targeting) with the short term campaign profitability goal (which depends on its ability to win properly targeted impression at low cost, compared to the agreed upon CPM). We decided to take the ad network perspective and design the AdX game around this conflict, while simulating many of the new above-mentioned methods and mechanisms of the other entities involved.

As typical in the Trading Agent Competition[4] the whole setting (i.e., users popula-tion, web sites, ad exchange, and advertisers) is simulated by a game server. The com-peting agents implement (each) the ad network functionality, bidding for impression opportunities by the AdX in order to fulfill the targeting goals specified in their ad-vertising contracts, subject to the budget constraints. This significantly differs from the TAC Ad Auctions[5] (TAC-AA) setting [6], where targeting effectiveness only matters in the short term and is only affecting immediate conversion rates. Our proposed game also introduces budget constraints[6]. Furthermore, our proposed game differs from the TAC-AA setting in the concerns of other entities, and therefore by the mechanisms and strategies they employ (e.g., the separation of the publisher and the auctioning platform functionality to two autonomous entities, and the separation of the advertiser and the ad bidding function).

All in all, this new game may serve as a test bed for methods employed by ad net-works in an AdX setting, when combined with contemporary mechanisms and methods employed by the other involved entities (as simulated) and with our proposed concep-tual model of campaign targeting effectiveness. An overview of the game is provided in section 2. A detailed description of the game elements and flow is provided in sections 3 and 4, respectively.

2   Game Overview

The proposed game setting is illustrated in Figure 1. The game consists of a sequence of periods (30 days long each). Advertising campaign contracts are assigned to Ad

---

[3] The *reach* of an advertising campaign is the size of unique users exposed to the campaign.
[4] See www.sics.se/tac
[5] See aa.tradingagents.org/
[6] Budget constraints are optional in TAC-AA, but in a different context.

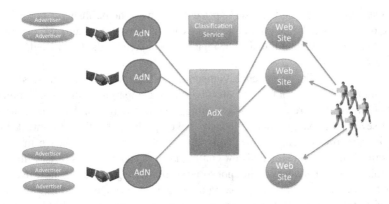

Fig. 1. AdX game entities: *Users* visits to *Web sites* result in impression opportunities that are auctioned by the *Ad Exchange*. Bids for the impression opportunities are submitted by *Ad Networks* in order to execute their contracts with *Advertisers*.

Networks at the beginning of each period. During a period the competing agents (implementing the Ad Network functionality) bid daily for user impression opportunities at web sites (auctioned by the Ad Exchange).

All functionality (except the Ad Network, which is implemented by the competing agents) is implemented by a game server:

- *Audience*: The user population visiting the publishers' web sites. We maintain user populations based on several attributes (e.g. Age, Gender, Income). Each attribute has a small set of possible values (e.g., *male* and *female* for Gender). Each day every user may visit one or more web sites: After each visit of a user to a web site, a continuation parameter determines whether the user continues to visit web sites or stops until the next day.
- *Publishers*: The web sites that are submitting impression opportunities to the Ad Exchange upon users' visits. Each web site has a predefined orientation level toward the attributes, which is reflected in a probability of a user of a certain type visiting each web site. With every user visit, the web site (the *publisher*) submits one or more Ad Requests to the AdX (each reflecting an impression opportunity), accompanied with a user identification reference and a reserve price (the requested minimal price to be paid by a winning advertiser).
- *Ad Exchange*: Auction platform for the impression opportunities. Upon an Ad Request from a web site, the AdX solicits the competing Ad Networks to bid for the potential impression. Together with the Bid Request indication, the AdX passes the id of the web site and part of the attribute values of the user (depending on a *cookie matching* service that each ad network may choose to purchase). The Ad Networks may submit bids for the display ad. The AdX implements the mechanism for selecting the winning bid and related price[7] and notifies the web site regarding the actual ad to be displayed.

---

[7] A second price auction, as detailed later.

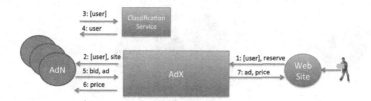

Fig. 2. Real Time Bidding sequence: A user visit to a web site results in (1) an impression Bid Request sent to the AdX. The AdX notifies (2) the Ad Networks, which in turn may use (3) a user classification service to retrieve the actual user attributes (4). Ad Network submit (5) bids for the impression opportunity, and the winning ad and related price are then selected by the AdX and notified to the ad network (6) and web site (7).

- *User classification service provider*: Using cookie matching technologies, user classification services allow the ad networks to target the required audience of their advertising campaigns. The price of the service and its accuracy are set by a dedicated auction.
- *Advertisers*: At the beginning of each period, Advertisers are matched to Ad Networks to carry out their advertising campaigns. The matching depends in part on the quality rating of the ad networks (the rating reflects the ability of ad networks to achieve campaign targeting goals, and is based on past period's performance). Another part of the matching is done by auction, where Ad Networks bid for the CPM of marketing campaigns with required reach.

Finally, *Ad Networks* are implemented (each) by a competing agent. The Ad Networks are periodically matched with advertising campaigns. The competing agents bid periodically for the user classification service level, and bid daily for impression opportunities. In reality, real-time bidding (i.e., the agents are consulted for a bid for each impression opportunity) takes place (as illustrated in Figure 2). However, this is too communication-intensive for our simulated game and is replaced here by a daily bid bundle that reflects the average allocation decision of the agent over all possible impressions (see Figure 3). The ad network profits from a campaign are the total revenues from the advertisers less the total costs of paying for impressions and classification services. The Ad Network problem is therefore to set the advertiser and bid for each impression (based on the context: user segment, web site, and campaign contracts status), such that its long term profits are maximal. The Ad Network has to balance short term (current campaign) profits and the need to maintain a high quality rating (to secure profits from future campaigns). Periodic reports that include bidding, impressions, and costs statistics are provided to the competing agents to assist them in their decision making.

3   Game Elements

3.1   Users

A user is characterized by a value from each of three attribute sets: *Age* = {*child, teen, adult, retired*}, *Gender* = {*male, female*}, and *Income* = {*low, medium, high*}.

Fig. 3. Daily Bidding sequence: To overcome the communication intensive nature of real-time bidding, our game implements the following scheme: Every day each Ad Network submits a *Bid Bundle* to the AdX. The bid bundle is a mapping from user and web site pairs to a bid and ad pair. The AdX uses the bid bundle throughout the day to simulate the sequence 2 to 5 of Figure 2. The accumulated results and prices are sent daily to each ad network in a dedicated report.

A population of 100000 users (the audience) is created at the beginning of each game according to a given[8] probability distribution $P_U \in \Delta_{Age \times Gender \times Income}$ over the possible attribute values. We use available statistical data[9] to set the audience distribution P_U upfront.

3.2   Web Sites and Access Devices

We define a distribution $P_W \in \Delta_W$ over the set of 16 web sites W. $P_W(w)$ represents the relative popularity of web site w, i.e., the probability of an arbitrary user visiting the web site. We also set upfront the conditional probability distributions $P_{Age}(\cdot|w)$, $P_{Gender}(\cdot|w)$, and $P_{Income}(\cdot|w)$. Those may be interpreted as the orientation of web site w toward each of the user attributes values. For example, $P_{Age}(\cdot|w)$ is the distribution over age among all users accessing web site w. A web site w is also characterized by the probability distribution $P_{Device}(\cdot|w)$ over the set *Devices* $=\{PC, Mobile\}$ of access device types used by visiting users. Again, we use available statistical data to set the prior device distribution $P_D \in \Delta_{Devices}$ and the conditional distributions $P_{Device}(\cdot|w)$ upfront.

Now, every day, each user visits web sites. User $u = $ (age, gender, income) chooses to visit a web site $w \in W$ using device d, according to $P(w|u,d)$. Using Bayes rule, and a conditional independence assumption, we have

$$P(w|u,d) = \frac{P_{Age}(age|w) P_{Gender}(gender|w) P_{Income}(income|w) P_{Device}(d|w) P_W(w)}{P_U(u) P_D(d)}.$$

Upon visiting web site w, a user may continue visiting web sites that day with probability $P_{Continue}(w)$.

---

[8] This prior distribution is known to all competitors.

[9] e.g., from web information services such as www.alexa.com

3.3 Impressions and Ad Types

Every user visit to a web site w results in one or more impression (i.e., *ad*) opportunities [10] according to a predefined probability distribution $P_{\text{Impressions}}(\cdot|w)$. The type of each ad is adtype $\in \{Video, Text\}$. The preference of ad type is another characteristic of a web site, reflected in a probability $P_{\text{Adtype}}(\cdot|w)$ of ad type choice for a visited web site w. The web site submits sequentially every impression opportunity to the Ad Exchange (see next section) detailing the device type and ad type, the user reference, and a reserve price [11]. We simulate an adaptive method of setting reserve prices by publishers. The initial average reserve price is randomly chosen, and reserve prices in subsequent days (for ads with the similar attributes) are adaptively set to maximize the publisher's profits [12]. This is done by randomly generating reserve prices r_t^i during day t around a daily baseline average b_t and updating the baseline for the next day in the direction of the reserve price $b_t^{\max}$ that resulted in the highest profits during the day:

$$r_t^i = b_t + \epsilon_i$$
$$b_{t+1} = \eta b_t + (1 - \eta) b_t^{\max} ,$$

where the perturbation ϵ_i is normally distributed with zero mean and predefined constant variance.

3.4 Ad Exchange

The Ad Exchange operates a second-price auction among the Ad Networks for every impression opportunity: A bid request accompanied with the impression opportunity details (as indicated by the publisher, and maybe augmented with specific user attributes, depending on the cookie matching service level of the agency, as described below) is sent to every Ad Network and the highest bidder wins the impression [13], paying the bid of the second highest bidder (or the reserve price, if his bid was the only bid above the reserve price).

3.5 Market Segments

We define a set of marketing segments, each a subset of the possible values of user attributes (e.g., teen to adult male , or female of high earnings, etc'). The segments may overlap (i.e., a user may belong to multiple segments, or to none of those predefined). The segments serve as the key elements of defining the advertising campaign targeting goals, as detailed in section 3.6. Formally, a marketing segment is a subset of the user

---

[10] Since Ad Networks are rewarded by *unique* impressions (as detailed in Section 3.6), the multiple appearance of the same ad in a web page is discouraged.

[11] The reserve price is the minimum payment the web site (the publisher) is willing to accept for the impression.

[12] A too high reserve price might result in unsold impressions and therefore unrealized potential profits.

[13] Only if the bid was at least as high as the reserve price, otherwise, the impression opportunity is lost.

space $Age \times Gender \times Income$. Our game setting consists of a set S of 16 predefined segments, each defined as the product of attribute subsets (e.g., female of medium or high income).

3.6 Advertisers and Marketing Campaigns

We define a set D of 32 advertisers, each advertiser $d \in D$ having a targeting preference $T_d \in \Delta_S$, where $T_d(s)$ reflects the relative (w.r.t. the other segments) inclination of advertiser d to marketing segment $s \in S$. Periodically, each advertiser contracts one of the advertising agencies to execute an online brand-related marketing campaign (i.e., with the purpose of strengthening its brand among its targeted audience). A campaign is characterized by the required *reach* (the size of total audience impressed) and total budget[14]. In the contract, the advertiser also specifies an ad type preference factor (video vs. text) and access device preference factor (mobile vs. PC). Those factors represent the marketing value the advertiser assigns to an impression from one ad type (or access device) over the other. Formally, a contract by advertiser d has the following attributes (see section 4.3 for the mechanism of establishing their values):

- B_d: *Budget.* Maximal total campaign payment by the advertiser to the ad network. This reflects a budget allocation[15] of $B_d(s) = B_d \cdot T_d(s)$ to segment s.
- R_d: *Reach.* Total effective number of unique user impressions during the period. This reflects a requirement of $R_d(s) = R_d \cdot T_d(s)$ effective number of unique users for each segment s.
- D_d: *Device factor.* A unique *Mobile* impression is counted as D_d effective impressions. A *PC* impression is counted as one effective impression.
- M_d: *Media factor.* A unique *Video* impression is counted as M_d effective impressions. A *Text* impression is counted as one effective impression [16].

For an impression on user u, let $d(u)$ be the advertiser chosen by the ad network for the potential impression on u, and let $D_d(u)$ be $D_{d(u)}$ if u is using a mobile device and 1 otherwise. Similarly, let $M_d(u)$ be $M_{d(u)}$ if u is being impressed by video and 1 otherwise. The effective number of unique impressions on segment s achieved by the ad network is

$$I_d(s) = \sum_{d(u)=d \text{ and } s(u)=s} D_d(u) \cdot M_d(u) \,, \tag{1}$$

where $s(u)$ indicates the actual[17] segment to which user u belongs, and the sum is over all unique impressions on users u that belong to segment s.

---

[14] In a sense, this sets the effective CPM to be paid by the advertiser to the ad network.

[15] With flexibility, as described below.

[16] A user that is impressed more than once during a period is counted according to the highest effective value of the impressions.

[17] Note that the ad network may not have complete information to exactly compute $I_d(s)$. The game server computes this value, mimicking a marketing survey that may take place in reality upon the conclusion of a campaign. After all, the actual segment to which the user belongs carries the true marketing value for the advertiser!

Now, to encourage ad networks achieving the required reach levels of the contract with advertiser d, the effective reach ratio $\text{ERR}_d(s)$ of segment s is set as a function of the effective number of unique impressions in segment s:

$$\text{ERR}_d(s) = \frac{2}{a}\left[\arctan\left(a\frac{I_d(s)}{R_d(s)} - b\right) - \arctan(-b)\right],$$

where a and b are set[18] such that when when $I_d(s) = R_d(s)$ we have $\text{ERR}_d(s) = 1$ and the marginal payment per impression is exactly $\frac{B_d(s)}{R_d(s)}$. This monotone relation is illustrated in Figure 4.

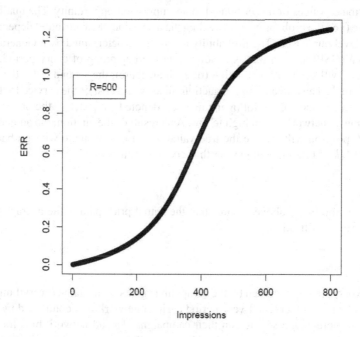

Fig. 4. The Effective Reach Ratio (ERR) as a function of the effective number of unique impressions achieved by the ad network, for a contract requiring a reach $R = 500$

Now, the baseline payment $E_d(s)$ to the ad network from advertiser d for impressions on users from segment s is set

$$E_d(s) = \text{ERR}_d(s) \cdot B_d(s).$$

At the end of every period, the total payment C_d from advertiser d to the ad network is set to

$$C_d = \min\{B_d, \sum_s E_d(s)\}. \tag{2}$$

---

[18] For example, $a = 4.08577$ and $b = 3.08577$. Actually, for any nonzero k, the unique b satisfying $\frac{\arctan(k)-\arctan(-b)}{1+b} = \frac{1}{1+k^2}$, and $a = b + k$ may apply. In this case we use $k = 1$.

Finally, the performance of the ad network at executing the campaign of advertiser d is the average effective reach ratio achieved:

$$Q_d = \frac{1}{|S|} \sum_{s \in S} \mathrm{ERR}_d(s) \ . \tag{3}$$

3.7   Cookie Matching Service

When a potential impression is announced to an ad network, the actual attributes of the associated user are only provided with a probability that depends on a prepaid cookie matching service[19]. The cookie matching service provides to the ad networks the true attributes values of a user related to an impression opportunity. The quality of the matching (i.e., the probability of providing the true value of an attribute) depends on the service level purchased. The probability and cost are determined by a Generalized Second Price (GSP) auction that is conducted at the beginning of every period. The highest bidder will get 100% revelation (of each attribute), the second 90%, the third 80%, and so on[20]. The outcome of the auction (quality and cost of the service to the ad networks) is determined in the following manner: denote by $c_{i_1}, .., c_{i_m}$ the ordering of the bids of the ad networks from high to low. As a result of the auction, the ad network n in the kth position will receive the true value of a user's attribute with probability $p_k = (1 - 0.1(k - 1))$, and will pay for the service the amount of,

$$K_n = p_k \cdot c_{i_{k+1}} \ . \tag{4}$$

The normalization by p_k above ensures that the actual price paid is the average price for correct user classification.

3.8   Ad Networks

The ad networks are implemented by the competing agents of the game (everything else is simulated by a game server). Every period each ad network n is contracted by a set D_n of one or more advertisers to run their campaigns. The ad network bids for each impression opportunity on user u (on behalf of one of its contracted advertisers), and for every impression won and presented to user u pays the auction resulting price $c(u)$. The net earnings N_n of ad network n in every period are therefore:

$$N_n = \sum_{d \in D_n} C_d - \sum_u c(u) - K_n \ , \tag{5}$$

where K_n is set by (4). At the end of every period, the average campaign quality

$$\overline{Q}_n = \frac{1}{|D_n|} \sum_{d \in D_n} Q_d = \frac{1}{|D_n| \cdot |S|} \sum_{s \in S, d \in D_n} \mathrm{ERR}_d(s) \ ;$$

---

[19] This reflects the situation in which the user reference (i.e., cookie) provided by the Ad Exchange has to be matched to a real user, using a dedicated third-party service.

[20] Otherwise, a uniformly randon user attribute value is indicated.

is calculated for every ad network n, and the quality factor Q_n^{new} of each ad network n (to be used during the subsequent period for contract matching - as detailed below) is updated using η learning rate:

$$Q_n^{\text{new}} = (1 - \eta)Q_n + \eta\overline{Q}_n \,.$$

4 Game Flow

The game consists of twelve or more periods of one month (30 days) each (the ending period is randomly chosen) of online marketing campaigns conducted by eight competing ad networks. The target of the ad network is to maximize its total accumulated profits. During each period, each ad network conducts one or more campaigns. The earnings potential of an ad network in every period depends on the targeting effectiveness of its past campaigns. Therefore, the ad network problem is to maximize its campaign profits while delivering high targeting value to the advertisers. To achieve its goals, each ad network bids daily for users' impression opportunities and selects for each impression which of its contracts to serve. The ad networks base their daily and periodic decisions on daily and periodic reports.

4.1 Monthly Contracts Assignment

All elements of the contract of each advertiser are fixed except the budget[21]. At the beginning of each period, the advertisers are randomly split into two groups. In one group, each advertiser d randomly selects the budget B_d for his period's contract, and the contracts are allocated in decreasing budget order to agencies by decreasing quality rating. The other group of contracts is auctioned among the agencies, where each agency bids for the contract budget[22]. This scheme rewards the highly rated Ad Networks by allocating them contracts of higher budgets (so they can proportionally increase their earnings), while giving all the Ad Network agents an opportunity to execute marketing campaigns and improve their rating [23].

4.2 Monthly Bidding for Cookie Matching Service

Concurrently with the contract allocation, an auction for the cookie matching service level takes place. Each agency bids for the payment to the service provider, and pays according to the outcome of the auction as detailed in section 3.7.

4.3 Daily Bidding for Impression Opportunities

Every bid request announced by the AdX to an ad network includes identifications of the associated web site, device, media, and (depending on the matching service level

---

[21] This is to ensure a balance between the user segments sizes and the required reach targets.

[22] Lower budget bids are obviously preferred by the advertisers. A Generalized Second Price (GSP) auction is employed.

[23] The way the advertisers are split and their budgets randomly selected is set such that the game balance is maintained.

purchased) the user attributes values. Every ad network may return to the AdX a bid and a related advertiser. To overcome the intensive communication rate required to implement real-time bidding in our game, every ad network submits to the AdX upfront a daily bid bundle. The bid bundle is used by the AdX throughout the day to map bid requests to ad networks' bid/advertiser pairs. The daily bid bundle of an ad network n is a list that details the following information for each segment $s \in S$ and site $w \in W$ combination:

- $P_n(w, s) \in \Delta_{D_n}$: A probability distribution over the advertisers associated with the ad network (through campaign contracts) for the current period.
- $B_n(w, s) \in \Re^{D_n}$: A vector of bid amounts (for each potential advertiser $d \in D_n$) indicating the bid level of the ad network given an impression opportunity of a user in segment s visiting web site w. Four such vectors are provided, for each combination of access device and medium (e.g., video and/or mobile device impressions).

The way the game simulator implements the daily real-time bidding on behalf of the ad agencies is as follows: Upon a bid request as a result of user u visiting web site w, the user attributes to be revealed to each of the ad agencies are determined according to the cookie matching service level in effect. Based on the revealed attributes, the most likely user segment s_n is chosen[24] for each ad network n. The advertiser d_n of each ad network n is chosen according to the probability distribution $P_n(w, s_n)$. Finally, given the ad type and access device values of the potential impression, the bid level to be used on behalf of the ad network n for the auction is the value for advertiser $d_n \in D_n$ from the relevant bid vector $B_n(w, s_n)$.

4.4 Periodic Reports

The ad networks use daily reports to update their daily bidding decisions. The daily report sent to each ad network n consists of the following elements (detailed for each advertiser, for each web site, for each users segment):

- The number of unique impressions won. Also for the competing ad networks.
- The total cost paid.

Monthly reports provides the ad network with a performance indication regarding its profits and campaign quality. The report includes the following (detailed per advertiser and per user segment):

- Campaign contracts
- Monthly revenues and costs.
- Quality scores. Also for competing ad networks.

4.5 Game Results

Upon game termination (chosen randomly, starting with 0.1 probability at the 12th period, and increased by 0.1 for each period thereafter), each ad network score is its accumulated profits (5) over all periods.

---

[24] The "unknown" segment is chosen if the probability is below a predetermined threshold. Also, multiple segments may be the most probable - in that case one of them is uniformly chosen.

5 Conclusion

We propose a new TAC game in an attempt to bring to the forefront key mechanisms and conflicts of participating entities in the emerging AdX setting. In an attempt to create a realistic game, our design mimics many of the real-world methods employed. However, due to inherent limitations of a game setting[25] and for the sake of simplicity, the modeling of some key aspects such as Real-Time-Bidding, the Ad Exchange business model, and the user classification service, was relaxed. Nevertheless, our proposed game captures the main conflict of Ad Networks in the AdX setting and as such may hopefully serve to investigate related Ad Network strategies and their dependencies on the mechanisms employed by the other modeled elements. A current version of the AdX game specification is maintained at [7].

References

1. Muthukrishnan, S.: Ad exchanges: Research issues. In: Leonardi, S. (ed.) WINE 2009. LNCS, vol. 5929, pp. 1–12. Springer, Heidelberg (2009)
2. Chakraborty, T., Even-Dar, E., Guha, S., Mansour, Y., Muthukrishnan, S.: Selective call out and Real-time Bidding. In: Saberi, A. (ed.) WINE 2010. LNCS, vol. 6484, pp. 145–157. Springer, Heidelberg (2010)
3. Balseiro, S., Feldman, J., Mirrokni, V., Muthukrishnan, S.: Yield Optimization of Display Advertising with Ad Exchange. In: ACM Conference on Electronic Commerce (2011)
4. Feldman, J., Mirrokni, V., Muthukrishnan, S., Pai, M.M.: Auctions with intermediaries. In: Proceedings of the 11th ACM Conference on Electronic Commerce (2010)
5. Magna Global, 2011 Advertising Forecast (2011), http://www.magnaglobal.com
6. Jordan, P.R., Wellman, M.P.: Designing an ad auctions game for the trading agent competition. In: David, E., Gerding, E., Sarne, D., Shehory, O. (eds.) AMEC 2009. LNBIP, vol. 59, pp. 147–162. Springer, Heidelberg (2010)
7. The Ad Exchange Game - Specification,
   http://www.cs.tau.ac.il/~marianos/Research.html

---

[25] Mainly, the interaction of independent agents with a central server over uncontrolled infrastructure.

Competing Intermediaries in Online Display Advertising

Lampros C. Stavrogiannis, Enrico H. Gerding, and Maria Polukarov

University of Southampton
Southampton, SO17 1BJ, UK
{ls8g09,eg,mp3}@ecs.soton.ac.uk

Abstract. Motivated by the emergence of online advertising exchanges, where display advertisements are traded in real time via specialized intermediaries, such as advertising networks and demand side platforms, we analyze a scenario in which a single, indivisible good is auctioned at a central seller via two intermediary auctions, all implementing Vickrey auctions. We study, for the first time, the selection problem faced by the buyers who have to decide in which intermediary auction to bid after observing the set reserve prices. We find that, in case of complete information about the buyers' valuations for the good, an infinite number of Nash equilibria exist for the selection strategies, and that reserve prices are driven up, as opposed to the classical setting without intermediaries. We also illustrate that the reserve price setting problem of the intermediaries admits a symmetric subgame-perfect equilibrium.

1 Introduction

Online advertising is increasingly being conducted using automated, real-time auctions, which take place billions of times per day. Because of their automated and online nature, the problem of designing auctions and autonomous bidding strategies has received growing attention in the field of artificial intelligence [1–4]. Most of this research has focused on sponsored search (where the advertisements appear alongside regular search results), where auctions have been the main tool since the very beginning. By contrast, display advertisements (where third-party banner ads are displayed on websites) were traditionally sold via fixed price, long-term bilateral contracts between publishers of websites and interested advertisers, predominantly through a set of intermediaries, known as *ad networks*, that facilitated transactions and offered access to a larger inventory. Nevertheless, ad networks would usually cooperate with other ad networks in order to fulfill orders in excess, creating lengthy chains that extracted significant amounts of available surplus from the advertisers and publishers, and reduced transparency. More recently, however, this landscape has radically changed with the emergence of *ad exchanges* [5], centralized marketplaces where display advertisements are auctioned in real time, providing advertisers and publishers with increased liquidity and better targeting technologies. This has brought about a significant growth in display advertising revenue. According to a recent report from Forrester Research [6], the display advertising business in the U.S. is expected to triple in the next four years, from $ 10.9 billions in 2011 (accounting for 37% of total online advertising [7]) to $ 27.6 billions in 2016.

E. David et al. (Eds.): AMEC/TADA 2012, LNBIP 136, pp. 146–159, 2013.
© Springer-Verlag Berlin Heidelberg 2013

At the same time, the introduction of these markets has resulted in increased complexity for advertisers, who often lack the expertise or are not allowed to bid directly in the central exchange, but can only participate via specialized intermediaries, such as demand side platforms and ad networks. These intermediaries typically run their own auction before forwarding the winning bid on behalf of the advertiser onto the exchange. Against this background, in this paper we apply game theoretic concepts to the problem of how an advertiser should choose an intermediary, and how this decision affects the policies (in particular, the reserve prices) of the intermediaries. To the best of our knowledge, this is the first work that considers the problem of competing intermediaries where advertisers are *non-captive* (i.e. can choose an intermediary). More specifically, we study an abstracted setting where buyers are willing to buy a single indivisible good (the banner space) from a central auctioneer (the ad exchange) by placing a bid at one of two intermediaries, each running a local auction among their delegated buyers. These two intermediaries then compete at the central auction for the good.

Our focus here is on the intermediary selection problem faced by the buyers: after determining their valuations for the good and observing the reserve prices of the intermediaries, they must simultaneously select one of them to bid in. This is a natural assumption for a qualitative analysis on the effect of intermediary competition, given that advertisers incur an implicit cost of managing each campaign that prohibits them from bidding in all intermediary auctions. In addition to the impact on the buyers' revenue, their strategy has also important implications for the design of the auctions, both at the level of the intermediaries, and at the center, who are all interested in maximizing their revenue by setting appropriate reserve prices.

Our contributions are as follows. We identify resulting equilibria of the intermediary selection subgame when buyers have complete information about other buyers' preferences, which can be learned if the interactions are repeated sufficiently often, as is usually the case in online advertising. We find that an infinite number of Nash equilibria exist and show that reserve prices are driven up because of the inherent pressure of the competition at the center between intermediaries. More specifically, there is a symmetric subgame-perfect equilibrium for the intermediaries where they both set reserve prices equal to the second highest valuation of the buyer population. This contrasts with existing work on competing auctions without intermediaries, where reserve prices are driven downwards.

The paper is structured as follows. In the second section, we provide an overview of related work on competing auctions and ad exchanges. Then, the third section provides a formal description of our model and details of the game being played. We define the intermediary selection problem and detail our results in the fourth section. Finally, the fifth section concludes.

2   Related Work

Our model is an extension to that of Feldman et al. [8], who study the reserve price setting problem faced by the exchange, and multiple intermediaries implementing Vickrey auctions. The authors show that intermediaries will use a stochastic reserve price over an interval in equilibrium, whereas the central auctioneer maximizes its profit by setting a reserve price that decreases with increasing number of intermediaries, but remains strictly positive. However, crucially, they assume that buyers are *captive* (i.e. they cannot move between the intermediaries), and that the number of buyers in each intermediary and their type distributions are exogenously determined and identical for all intermediaries. By contrast, we assume that the buyers can choose their intermediary, and so the distribution at an intermediary is endogenously defined by the buyers' selection strategies.

Competition between auctions that are independent and do not involve intermediaries in a non-captive setting has first been studied by McAfee [9] and Peters and Severinov [10]. They identify a symmetric equilibrium where buyers randomize equally between the auctions and reserve prices equal sellers' production cost. Their results are based on a 'large market hypothesis', i.e. require a large (infinite) number of sellers, so that buyers' expected profit is unaffected by changes in a single auction, and naturally break down in the case of oligopolies which naturally arise in our setting. Given this, Burguet and Sákovics [11] studied the competition between two sellers implementing Vickrey auctions when buyers are privately informed. The authors identify a unique Bayes-Nash equilibrium for the selection problem faced by the buyers, where there is a cut-off point, w, so that buyers with valuations less than w always prefer the low-reserve auction, whereas buyers with higher types randomize equally between the two auctions. Hernando-Veciana [12] extends these results to more than two auctions, assuming a finite set of strategies for the auctioneers. Based on this work, Gerding et al. [13] studied the duopoly competition between auctions in presence of a mediating institution and identified a pure-strategy Nash equilibrium for the sellers when production costs are asymmetric. Furthermore, competing auctions in the context of sponsored search was studied by Ashlagi et al. [14]. However, none of these works considers the problem of competing intermediaries, whose presence fundamentally changes the nature of the problem. More specifically, the competing auctions are no longer independent, as they have to compete additionally as bidders at the central auction for the same good, and so the buyers' intermediary selection affects both the intermediaries' as well as the exchange's revenue. Finally, intermediary auctioneers face the same tradeoff as the buyers: the lower their reserve price (hence their bid in expectation) the smaller is their probability of obtaining the item at the center.

3   Model

Suppose there is a unique indivisible good (corresponding to a single-slot impression) for sale by a single auctioneer, c, called the *center* (i.e. the ad exchange). There is also a population of $n \in \mathbb{N}, n \geq 3$, ex ante symmetric, purely profit maximizing (risk-neutral) buyers (the advertisers) that compete for this good, but are allowed to participate only via two qualified intermediaries (i.e. the ad networks), s_1, s_2. The center and the intermediaries are also profit maximizing but have no value for the good itself. The preferences of buyers and auctioneers are described by von Neumann and Morgenstern utility functions.

Each buyer i has a private valuation $v_i, i \in \{1, ..., n\}$, for the good to be traded over a compact support V normalized to be a subset of $[0, 1]$. Without loss of generality, the ordering of the advertisers is determined by the order of their valuations, i.e. for any two buyers $i, j \in \{1, ..., n\}$, $i < j$ if and only if $v_i \geq v_j$. The expected utility for a buyer i with valuation v_i is $\Pi_\ell(v_i) = \alpha_\ell(v_i)(v_i - \rho_\ell)$, where $\alpha_\ell : V \mapsto [0, 1]$ is the probability of obtaining the item in intermediary s_ℓ's local auction ($\ell = 1, 2$), and $\rho_\ell \in [0, 1]$ the price to be paid to the intermediary.

In our setting, each intermediary, s_ℓ, $\ell = 1, 2$, runs a second-price sealed-bid (i.e. Vickrey) auction with a minimum reserve price, r_ℓ, $\ell = 1, 2$, respectively[1]. Without loss of generality, for the remainder of this paper we will assume that $r_1 \leq r_2$. The center runs a Vickrey auction without a reserve price[2] and a fair tie-breaking rule, and each intermediary is allowed to submit a single bid[3]. In our extended model, buyers are not captive, but must select their (single) intermediary after learning their valuations based on the announced reserve prices and available information. We note that the selection problem is independent of the actual bidding. Thus, after selecting their desired intermediary, it is a weakly dominant strategy for the buyers to submit their true valuations.

Each intermediary, s_ℓ, $\ell = 1, 2$, runs a contingent auction among its set of buyers, denoted K_ℓ, to determine the winning bid, $w_\ell = \max_{i \in K_\ell}\{v_i\}$, the price to be paid from the winning buyer conditional on its winning at the central auction, $\rho_\ell = \max\{v_{\arg\max\{v_i \in K_\ell \setminus \{w_\ell\}\}}, r_\ell\}$, as well as the bidding amount to be submitted to the center. Given that the auction at the center is dominant-strategy incentive compatible, it is a weakly dominant strategy for the intermediaries to bid their contingent payments (i.e. ρ_ℓ, $\ell = 1, 2$), which correspond to their equivalent valuations. Hence, the expected profit of an intermediary s_ℓ is $\Pi_{s_\ell}(\rho_\ell) = \alpha_c(\rho_\ell)(\rho_\ell - \rho_m)$, $m \neq \ell$, where $\alpha_c : V \mapsto [0, 1]$ is the probability of obtaining the item at the center. In more detail, the game proceeds as follows:

1. Buyers learn their valuations for the good.
2. Intermediaries simultaneously announce their reserve prices, r_1, r_2.
3. Buyers simultaneously select their preferred (single) intermediary s_ℓ, $\ell = 1, 2$.
4. Buyers submit a bid (i.e. their valuation) to their selected intermediary.
5. Intermediaries run their auctions for the good among their local buyers.
6. Intermediaries submit their bids, ρ_ℓ, $\ell = 1, 2$, to the center.
7. The center runs its auction given the bids submitted by the intermediaries, transfers the good to the winning intermediary and receives payment.
8. The winning intermediary transfers the good to its winning buyer and receives payment.

4   The Intermediary Selection Problem

In the above setting, we study the problem faced by the buyers who must select one of the intermediaries in order to maximize their expected utility from obtaining the good.

---

[1] This is the mechanism implemented in large, automated ad networks, such as Google AdWords.

[2] This is done for simplification reasons. We could also assume that the center sets a reserve price, but this has no effect on the buyers' choice of intermediary.

[3] This mechanism is currently used in Google (http://www.google.com/doubleclick/) and Microsoft (http://advertising.microsoft.com/exchange) ad exchanges.

More specifically, we characterize Nash equilibria when each buyer knows not only his valuation but also the valuations of the others. As has been pointed out in [15], this is a realistic assumption when the auctions are repeated often, as is usually the case in online advertising, and so the buyers can learn the valuations of their opponents. We now begin our analysis with the following proposition.

Proposition 1. *Given that buyers are rational and bid their true valuations, the profits of the winning buyer and the intermediaries are determined exclusively by the strategies of the three buyers with the highest valuations. Moreover, the buyer with the third highest valuation never gets the item.*

To see this, note that, whenever the two buyers with the highest valuations both select the same intermediary, buyer 1 gets the good and pays v_2. Otherwise, consider the two local second highest bids that are submitted by the intermediaries and hence compete at the center. The winning bid at the center will always be equal to v_3 if both reserve prices are less than v_3, or equal to r_2 otherwise. However, the winner can be either buyer 1 or buyer 2, depending on the strategy of buyer 3. This means that buyer 3 never obtains the good but his strategy affects the strategies of buyers 1 and 2. This has also important implications on the reserve prices of the intermediaries. In summary, valuations and reserve prices less than v_3 have no impact on the intermediary selection and reserve price setting games.

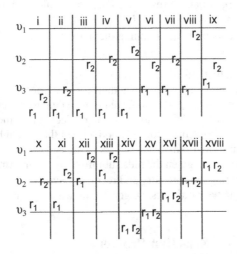

Fig. 1. Figure showing all possible cases for analysis of the intermediary selection problem

Proposition 1 allows us to reduce the intermediary selection problem to a 3-player game and identify all its Nash equilibria. We obtain 18 possible scenarios (there are 3 intervals, $[0, v_3)$, (v_3, v_2), (v_2, v_1), and two degenerate intervals, v_3, v_2, yielding 15 combinations for $r_1 < r_2$ and $r_1 = r_2$ respectively, and 3 more cases for $r_1 = r_2$ in the former intervals), as Figure 1 illustrates. However, some of these scenarios share the same payoff matrix, so we can summarize all Nash equilibria in 7 final cases below.

More specifically, if $p_1, p_2, p_3 \in [0,1]$ are the probabilities of selecting the low-reserve intermediary, s_1, for buyers 1, 2 and 3 respectively, the intermediary selection game admits the following Nash equilibria (NE):

1. $r_1 \leq r_2 < v_3$. In this situation the following sub-cases arise:
   - If buyer 3 follows a pure strategy ($p_3 = 0$ or $p_3 = 1$), or if $p_3 = \frac{1}{2}$ and $v_1 - v_2 = v_2 - v_3$, there are an infinite number of NE, where buyer 1 selects the same intermediary as buyer 3 (i.e. $p_1 = p_3$) and obtains the good, whereas buyer 2 can follow any strategy $p_2 \in [0,1]$.
   - If $\frac{v_1 - v_2}{v_1 - v_3} \leq p_3 \leq \frac{v_2 - v_3}{v_1 - v_3}$, there are two pure-strategy NE (PSNE) where buyers 1 and 2 select different intermediaries.
   - If $0 < p_3 \leq \frac{v_2 - v_3}{v_1 - v_3}$ and $0 < p_3 < \frac{v_1 - v_2}{v_1 - v_3}$, it is a PSNE for buyers 1 and 2 to select s_2 and s_1 respectively.
   - If $\frac{v_2 - v_3}{v_1 - v_3} < p_3 < 1$ and $\frac{v_1 - v_2}{v_1 - v_3} \leq p_3 < 1$, it is a PSNE for buyers 1 and 2 to select s_1 and s_2 respectively.
   - If $\min\{\frac{v_1 - v_2}{v_1 - v_3}, \frac{v_2 - v_3}{v_1 - v_3}\} \leq p_3 \leq \max\{\frac{v_1 - v_2}{v_1 - v_3}, \frac{v_2 - v_3}{v_1 - v_3}\}$ and $v_1 - v_2 \neq v_2 - v_3$, then there exists a mixed-strategy NE (MSNE) where $p_1 = p_3$ and $p_2 = \frac{v_1 - v_2 - p_3(v_1 - v_3)}{v_1 - 2v_2 + v_3}$.
2. $r_1 < r_2 = v_3$. In this situation the following sub-cases arise:
   - If $p_3 = 0$ (i.e. buyer 3 selects the high-reserve intermediary, s_2), there are an infinite number of MSNE where buyer 1 also selects s_2 ($p_1 = 0$) whereas buyer 2 can follow any strategy $p_2 \in [0,1]$.
   - If $p_3 = 1$:
     - If $v_1 - v_2 \leq v_2 - v_3$, there are two PSNE where buyers 1 and 2 select different intermediaries.
     - If $v_1 - v_2 \neq v_2 - v_3$, it is a MSNE for both buyers 1 and 2 to randomize equally ($p_1 = p_2 = \frac{1}{2}$).
     - If $v_1 - v_2 = v_2 - v_3$, there are an infinite number of MSNE where $p_1 = \frac{1}{2}$ and $p_2 \in [0,1]$.
   - If $p_3 \in (0,1)$:
     - If $\frac{2(v_1 - v_2)}{v_1 - v_3} \leq p_3 < 1$, there are two PSNE where buyers 1 and 2 select different intermediaries.
     - If $0 < p_3 \leq \frac{2(v_2 - v_3)}{v_1 - v_3}$ and $0 < p_3 < \frac{2(v_1 - v_2)}{v_1 - v_3}$, it is a PSNE for buyers 1 and 2 to select s_2 and s_1 respectively.
     - If $v_1 - v_2 \neq v_2 - v_3$ and $\min\{\frac{2(v_1 - v_2)}{v_1 - v_3}, \frac{2(v_2 - v_3)}{v_1 - v_3}\} \leq p_3 < 1$, there is a MSNE where $p_1 = \frac{p_3}{2}$ and $p_2 = \frac{v_1 - v_2 - \frac{p_3}{2}(v_1 - v_3)}{v_1 - 2v_2 + v_3}$.
3. $r_1 < r_2 < v_2$ and $r_2 > v_3$. There are an infinite number of NE where buyer 1 selects the high-reserve intermediary, s_2, and always gets the item, whereas buyer 2 selects s_1 with any probability $p_2 \in [0,1]$.
4. $v_3 \leq r_1 = r_2 \leq v_2$. In this situation the following sub-cases arise:
   - If $v_2 = r_1$, there are an infinite number of MSNE where $p_1 \in [0,1]$ and $p_2 = \frac{1}{2}$. There are also two PSNE where buyers 1 and 2 select the same intermediary.
   - Otherwise, if $v_1 - v_2 \neq v_2 - r_1$, there is a unique MSNE where $p_1 = p_2 = \frac{1}{2}$, whereas if $v_1 - v_2 = v_2 - r_1$, there are an infinite number of MSNE with $p_1 = \frac{1}{2}$ and $p_2 \in [0,1]$. Moreover, if $v_1 - v_2 \leq v_2 - r_1$, there are also two PSNE where buyers 1 and 2 select different intermediaries.

5. $r_1 < r_2 = v_2$. There is a PSNE where both buyers 1 and 2 select the low-reserve intermediary, s_1, and an infinite number of NE where buyer 1 selects the high-reserve intermediary, s_2, whereas buyer 2 selects s_1 with a probability $p_2 \in [0, 1]$. In all these NE, buyer 1 obtains the item.

6. $r_1 \leq v_2 < r_2 < v_1$ or $v_2 < r_1 < r_2 < v_1$. There exists a unique PSNE where both buyers 1 and 2 select the low-reserve intermediary, s_1 and buyer 1 obtains the item.

7. $v_2 < r_1 = r_2 < v_1$. There are an infinite number of NE where buyer 1 selects s_1 with probability $p_1 \in [0, 1]$ and gets the item.

Theorem 1. *Cases (1) - (7) above fully characterize the Nash equilibria of the intermediary selection game in the complete information setting.*

Proof. The proof is done by solving the corresponding games in all the aforementioned cases.

Figure 2 illustrates the normal form representation of the selection game when $r_1 \leq r_2 < v_3$ (case (1)). If $p_3 = 0$ or $p_3 = 1$, it is a dominant strategy for buyer 1 to select the same intermediary as buyer 3, whereas buyer 2 always gets zero utility, so the latter can follow any strategy $p_2 \in [0, 1]$. If $0 < p_3 < 1$, buyer 2 expects non-zero utility in the anti-diagonal elements of the payoff matrix, and zero utility otherwise. Hence, PSNE only exist in these two situations. For the existence of the $(p_1, p_2) = (0, 1)$ PSNE, we need that $(1 - p_3)(v_1 - v_3) \geq v_1 - v_2 \Rightarrow p_3 \leq \frac{v_2 - v_3}{v_1 - v_3}$. The condition for the existence of the $(p_1, p_2) = (1, 0)$ PSNE is $p_3 \geq \frac{v_1 - v_2}{v_1 - v_3}$. Hence, if both conditions hold, the intermediary selection game involves the two corresponding PSNE. Otherwise, if the first condition is true but the second is not, there is only a single PSNE $(p_1 = 0, p_2 = 1)$. Finally, if the second condition is true and the first is not there is also a single PSNE $(p_1 = 1, p_2 = 0)$.

Under a MSNE, the expected utilities from s_1, s_2 for buyers 1 and 2 should be equal. This condition for buyer 2 yields:

$$p_3(v_2 - v_3)(1 - p_1) = p_1(1 - p_3)(v_2 - v_3) \Rightarrow p_1 = p_3 \ .$$

Similarly, for buyer 1:

$$p_2(v_1 - v_2) + (1 - p_2)p_3(v_1 - v_3) = p_2(1 - p_2)(v_1 - v_3) + (1 - p_2)(v_1 - v_2) \Rightarrow$$
$$p_2(v_1 - 2v_2 + v_3) = v_1 - v_2 - p_3(v_1 - v_3) \Rightarrow$$

$$\begin{cases} (v_1 - v_2 \neq v_2 - v_3 \wedge p_2 = \frac{v_1 - v_2 - p_3(v_1 - v_3)}{v_1 - 2v_2 + v_3} \wedge \\ \wedge \min\{\frac{v_1 - v_2}{v_1 - v_3}, \frac{v_2 - v_3}{v_1 - v_3}\} \leq p_3 \leq \max\{\frac{v_1 - v_2}{v_1 - v_3}, \frac{v_2 - v_3}{v_1 - v_3}\}) \ . \\ \vee \\ (v_1 - v_2 = v_2 - v_3 \wedge p_3 = \frac{v_1 - v_2}{v_1 - v_3} = \frac{1}{2}) \ . \end{cases}$$

In the first case ($v_1 - v_2 \neq v_2 - v_3$), the requirement that $0 \leq p_2 \leq 1$ provides the constraints for p_3. Figure 3 illustrates the normal form representation of the resulting game for the case when $v_1 - v_2 = v_2 - v_3$ and $p_3 = \frac{1}{2}$, where, solving the game for MSNE gives $p_1 = \frac{1}{2}$ and $p_2 \in [0, 1]$.

Buyer 2

	s_1	s_2
Buyer 1 s_1	$v_1 - v_2, \quad 0$	$p_3(v_1 - v_3),$ $(1 - p_3)(v_2 - v_3)$
s_2	$(1 - p_3)(v_1 - v_3),$ $p_3(v_2 - v_3)$	$v_1 - v_2, \quad 0$

Fig. 2. Normal form representation of the intermediary selection game when $r_1 \leq r_2 < v_3$. Row player is buyer 1 and column player is buyer 2.

Buyer 2

	s_1	s_2
Buyer 1 s_1	$1, \quad 0$	$1, \quad \frac{1}{2}$
s_2	$1, \quad \frac{1}{2}$	$1, \quad 0$

Fig. 3. Normal form representation of the intermediary selection game when $r_1 \leq r_2 < v_3$, $v_1 - v_2 = v_2 - v_3$ and $p_3 = \frac{1}{2}$. Row player is buyer 1 and column player is buyer 2.

Figure 4 shows the normal form representation of the selection game when $r_1 < r_2 = v_3$ (case (2)) and buyer 3 has selected the low-reserve intermediary, s_1, i.e. $p_3 = 1$. For this setting, if $v_1 - v_2 \leq v_2 - v_3$, there are two PSNE (corresponding to the antidiagonal elements of the payoff matrix) where buyers 1 and 2 select different intermediaries. Moreover, if $v_1 - v_2 \neq v_2 - v_3$, there exists a unique MSNE where both buyers 1 and 2 randomize equally between the intermediaries, i.e. $p_1 = p_2 = \frac{1}{2}$. If not $(v_1 - v_2 = v_2 - v_3)$, an infinite number of MSNE arise where $p_1 = \frac{1}{2}$ and $p_2 \in [0, 1]$.

On the other hand, Figure 5 shows the normal form representation of the selection game in this case, when buyer 3 selects the high-reserve intermediary, s_2, i.e. $p_3 = 0$. As can be seen, there are an infinite number of MSNE, where $p_1 = p_3 = 0$ and $p_2 \in [0, 1]$.

If $p_3 \in (0, 1)$, then Figure 6 shows the corresponding normal form representation of the selection game. We consider three cases: (i) $v_1 - v_2 = v_2 - v_3$, (ii) $v_1 - v_2 < v_2 - v_3$ and (iii) $v_1 - v_2 > v_2 - v_3$.

Figure 7 shows the simplified normal form representation of the intermediary selection game when $v_1 - v_2 = v_2 - v_3$. As can be seen, in this case a single PSNE arises, where buyer 1 selects s_2 and buyer 2 selects intermediary s_1.

If $v_1 - v_2 < v_2 - v_3$, the following PSNE arise:

- If $\frac{2(v_1 - v_2)}{v_1 - v_3} \leq p_3 < 1$, there are two PSNE (corresponding to the antidiagonal elements of the payoff matrix) where buyers 1 and 2 select different intermediaries.

Buyer 2

	s_1	s_2
Buyer 1 s_1	$v_1 - v_2, 0$	$(v_1 - v_3)/2, (v_2 - v_3)/2$
s_2	$(v_1 - v_3)/2, (v_2 - v_3)/2$	$v_1 - v_2, 0$

Fig. 4. Normal form representation of the intermediary selection game when $r_1 < r_2 = v_3$ and buyer 3 selects intermediary s_1. Row player is buyer 1 and column player is buyer 2.

Buyer 2

		s_1	s_2
Buyer 1	s_1	$v_1 - v_2, 0$	$0, v_2 - v_3$
	s_2	$v_1 - v_3, 0$	$v_1 - v_2, 0$

Fig. 5. Normal form representation of the intermediary selection game when $r_1 < r_2 = v_3$ and buyer 3 selects intermediary s_2. Row player is buyer 1 and column player is buyer 2.

Buyer 2

		s_1	s_2
Buyer 1	s_1	$v_1 - v_2, 0$	$(p_3/2)(v_1 - v_3),$ $(1 - p_3/2)(v_2 - v_3)$
	s_2	$(1 - p_3/2)(v_1 - v_3),$ $(p_3/2)(v_2 - v_3)$	$v_1 - v_2, 0$

Fig. 6. Normal form representation of the intermediary selection game when $r_1 < r_2 = v_3$. Row player is buyer 1 and column player is buyer 2.

- If $0 < p_3 < \frac{2(v_1 - v_2)}{v_1 - v_3}$, there is a PSNE where buyer 1 selects the high-reserve intermediary, s_2, and buyer 2 selects the low-reserve intermediary, s_1.

On the other hand, when $v_1 - v_2 > v_2 - v_3$, whenever $0 < p_3 \leq \frac{2(v_2 - v_3)}{v_1 - v_3}$, there is a unique PSNE where buyer 1 selects the high-reserve intermediary, s_2, and buyer 2 selects the low-reserve intermediary, s_1.

For the existence of a MSNE when $v_1 - v_2 \neq v_2 - v_3$, the expected utilities from the two intermediaries s_1 and s_2, $\Pi_1(v_i), \Pi_2(v_i), i = 1, 2$ for buyers 1 and 2 respectively should be equal:

$$
\Pi_1(v_2) = \Pi_2(v_2) \Rightarrow (1 - p_1)\frac{p_3}{2}(v_2 - v_3) =
$$
$$
= p_1(1 - \frac{p_3}{2})(v_2 - v_3) \Rightarrow p_1 = \frac{p_3}{2} . \tag{1}
$$

$$
\Pi_1(v_1) = \Pi_2(v_1) \Rightarrow p_2(v_1 - v_2) + (1 - p_2)\frac{p_3}{2}(v_1 - v_3) =
$$
$$
= p_2(1 - \frac{p_3}{2})(v_1 - v_3) + (1 - p_2)(v_1 - v_2) \Rightarrow
$$
$$
\Rightarrow (2p_2 - 1)(v_1 - v_2) = (p_2 - \frac{p_3}{2})(v_1 - v_3) \Rightarrow \tag{2}
$$
$$
\Rightarrow p_2 = \frac{v_1 - v_2 - \frac{p_3}{2}(v_1 - v_3)}{v_1 - 2v_2 + v_3} .
$$

Buyer 2

		s_1	s_2
Buyer 1	s_1	$1, 0$	$p_3, 1 - p_3/2$
	s_2	$2 - p_3, p_3/2$	$1, 0$

Fig. 7. Normal form representation of the intermediary selection game when $r_1 < r_2 = v_3$ and $v_1 - v_2 = v_2 - v_3$. Row player is buyer 1 and column player is buyer 2.

The requirement that $0 \le p_2 \le 1$ gives us the following restrictions:

$$\begin{cases} p_2 \ge 0 \\ \wedge \\ p_2 \le 1 \end{cases} \Rightarrow \begin{cases} v_1 - v_2 - \frac{p_3}{2} \cdot (v_1 - v_3) \ge 0 \wedge v_1 - 2 \cdot v_2 + v_3 > 0 \ . \\ \vee \\ v_1 - v_2 - \frac{p_3}{2} \cdot (v_1 - v_3) \le 0 \wedge v_1 - 2 \cdot v_2 + v_3 < 0 \ . \\ \wedge \\ |v_1 - v_2 - \frac{p_3}{2} \cdot (v_1 - v_3)| \le |v_1 - 2 \cdot v_2 + v_3| \ . \end{cases} \Rightarrow$$

$$\Rightarrow \begin{cases} \frac{2(v_2 - v_3)}{v_1 - v_3} \le p_3 \le 1 \wedge v_1 - v_2 > v_2 - v_3 \ . \\ \vee \\ 1 \ge p_3 \ge \frac{2(v_1 - v_2)}{v_1 - v_3} \wedge v_1 - v_2 < v_2 - v_3 \ . \end{cases}$$

(3)

As shown in the payoff matrix of Figure 8, when $r_1 < r_2 < v_2$ but r_2 is higher than v_3 (case (3)), buyer 1 always selects the high-reserve intermediary and obtains the item at equilibrium, no matter what is the strategy of buyer 2, and $p_2 \in [0, 1]$.

Buyer 2

		s_1	s_2
Buyer 1	s_1	$v_1 - v_2, 0$	$0, v_2 - r_2$
	s_2	$v_1 - r_2, 0$	$v_1 - v_2, 0$

Fig. 8. Normal form representation of the intermediary selection game when $r_1 < r_2 < v_2$ and $r_2 > v_3$. Row player is buyer 1 and column player is buyer 2.

If $v_3 \le r_1 = r_2 = r \le v_2$ (case (4)), buyers 1 and 2 expect utilities resulting in the intermediary selection game of Figure 9. In this case, whenever $v_1 - v_2 > v_2 - r$ (i.e. buyer 1 prefers the diagonal elements of the payoff matrix), there are 2 PSNE only if $v_2 = r$ where both buyers 1 and 2 select the same intermediary. On the other hand, if $v_1 - v_2 \le v_2 - r$, then there are 2 PSNE where buyers 1 and 2 select different intermediaries.

For the existence of MSNE, it should be that:

$$\Pi_1(v_1) = \Pi_2(v_1) \Rightarrow p_2(v_1 - v_2) + (1 - p_2)\frac{v_1 - r}{2} =$$

$$= p_2 \frac{v_1 - r}{2} + (1 - p_2)(v_1 - v_2) \Rightarrow (2p_2 - 1)(v_1 - v_2) = (2p_2 - 1)\frac{v_1 - r}{2} \ .$$

(4)

Buyer 2

		s_1	s_2
Buyer 1	s_1	$v_1 - v_2, 0$	$(v_1 - r)/2, (v_2 - r)/2$
	s_2	$(v_1 - r)/2, (v_2 - r)/2$	$v_1 - v_2, 0$

Fig. 9. Normal form representation of the intermediary selection game when $v_3 \le r_1 = r_2 \le v_2$. Row player is buyer 1 and column player is buyer 2.

This means that $p_2 = \frac{1}{2}$ when $v_1 - v_2 \neq v_2 - r$ or $p_2 \in [0, 1]$ otherwise. Moreover, for buyer 2:

$$\Pi_1(v_2) = \Pi_2(v_2) \Rightarrow (1 - p_1)\frac{v_2 - r}{2} = p_1\frac{v_2 - r}{2} \ . \tag{5}$$

So, $p_1 = \frac{1}{2}$ if $v_2 \neq r$, or $p_1 \in [0, 1]$ otherwise.

When $r_1 < r_2 = v_2$ (case (5)), there is a PSNE where both buyers 1 and 2 select the low-reserve intermediary, s_1, as well as an infinite number of NE where buyer 1 selects the high-reserve intermediary, s_2, and buyer 2 follows any strategy $p_2 \in [0, 1]$, as the normal form representation of the intermediary selection game in Figure 10 shows. We should note that buyer 1 always gets the item at equilibrium and it is in fact a weakly dominant strategy for him to select the high-reserve intermediary.

Buyer 2

		s_1	s_2
Buyer 1	s_1	$v_1 - v_2, 0$	$0, 0$
	s_2	$v_1 - v_2, 0$	$v_1 - v_2, 0$

Fig. 10. Normal form representation of the intermediary selection game when $r_1 < r_2 = v_2$. Row player is buyer 1 and column player is buyer 2.

When $r_1 \leq v_2 < r_2 < v_1$ or $v_2 < r_1 < r_2 < v_1$ (case (6)), the intermediary selection is a one-player game, that of buyer 1, where he will always select the low-reserve intermediary, s_1, yielding him a utility of $v_1 - max\{r_1, v_2\}$.

Finally, when $v_2 < r_1 = r_2 < v_1$ (case (7)), which is also a one-player game, buyer 1 can follow any strategy, $p_1 \in [0, 1]$, as he will always win and pay the reserve price. $\square$

A closer look at the equilibrium strategies of buyers shows that the winning buyer selects the intermediary whose reserve price is closer to v_2 from below. This means that intermediaries have incentives to increase their reserve prices up to v_2. After our equilibrium analysis of the intermediary selection strategy, we are now able to make the following statement about the equilibrium behaviour of the competing intermediaries.

Theorem 2. *There always exists a symmetric subgame-perfect equilibrium among the intermediaries where they both set a reserve price equal to the second-highest valuation of the buyers.*

Proof. If both intermediaries set reserve prices $r_1 = r_2 = v_2$, then each intermediary's profit equals v_2 if both two buyers with the highest valuations visit him or her, and zero otherwise, as Table 1 depicts. Given the mixed-strategy equilibrium behaviour of the buyers (Theorem 1, case (6)), the expected profit for the intermediaries, under a fair tie-breaking rule at the central auction, is $\mathbb{E}[u_{s_1}] = \frac{p_1 v_2}{2}$, $\mathbb{E}[u_{s_2}] = \frac{(1-p_1)v_2}{2}$, which are both positive if we limit p_1 in $(0, 1)$. Now, suppose that one of the intermediaries, say s_2, increases his or her reserve price beyond v_2 by a strictly positive amount ϵ, i.e. $r_2 = v_2 + \epsilon$. Then, as we have shown, buyer 1 has an incentive to select intermediary s_1, giving the former a utility of $v_1 - v_2$. So, the deviating intermediary expects zero profit.

On the other hand, suppose that the deviating intermediary, s_1, sets a reserve price lower than v_2, i.e. $r_1 = v_2 - \epsilon$. Then, from Theorem 1, case (5), there is a PSNE where both buyers 1 and 2 select the low-reserve intermediary and an infinite number of NE where buyer 1 selects the high-reserve auction. It is actually a weakly dominant strategy for buyer 1 to select the high-reserve intermediary, so we can focus on this last situation, where, no matter what is the strategy of buyer 2, s_1 always loses the good at the central auction, yielding him or her zero profit again, as Table 2 and Table 3 illustrate, and so there is no incentive to deviate from $r_1 = v_2$. □

Table 1. Profits, u_{s_1}, u_{s_2}, for intermediaries s_1 and s_2 respectively for given visit decisions of buyers 1 and 2, when $r_1 = r_2 = v_2$

Buyer 1	Buyer 2	u_{s_1}	u_{s_2}
s_1	s_1	v_2	0
s_1	s_2	0	0
s_2	s_1	0	0
s_2	s_2	0	v_2

Table 2. Profits, u_{s_1}, u_{s_2}, for intermediaries s_1 and s_2 respectively for given visit decisions of buyers 1 and 2, when $r_1 \leq v_3 < r_2 = v_2$

Buyer 1	Buyer 2	u_{s_1}	u_{s_2}
s_1	s_1	v_2	0
s_1	s_2	0	$r_2 - v_3$
s_2	s_1	0	$r_2 - v_3$
s_2	s_2	0	$r_2 - r_1$

Table 3. Profits, u_{s_1}, u_{s_2}, for intermediaries s_1 and s_2 respectively for given visit decisions of buyers 1 and 2, when $v_3 < r_1 < r_2 = v_2$

Buyer 1	Buyer 2	u_{s_1}	u_{s_2}
s_1	s_1	v_2	0
s_1	s_2	0	$r_2 - r_1$
s_2	s_1	0	$r_2 - r_1$
s_2	s_2	0	v_2

This last finding has an important implication for the center as well. One of the research questions posed in [5] was whether there is a truthful auction at the center that can extract a sufficient fraction of the book value, i.e. the second highest valuation among all buyers. Here, we have just shown that in this complete information scenario, the current Vickrey auction at the center will extract exactly half of the book value in the aforementioned equilibrium.

5   Conclusions and Future Work

In this paper we have studied, for the first time, the selection problem of buyers in auctions with intermediaries. We have investigated the complete information setting which often arises in online advertising given the large history of interactions between buyers. Our results show that this scenario admits an infinite number of Nash equilibria for the buyers. Moreover, we have shown that, in this case, a symmetric subgame-perfect equilibrium exists for the intermediaries where they both set identical, high-reserve prices, equal to the second highest valuation among the buyers' population.

Our study is a first step towards understanding competition between auctions involving intermediaries. There are many remaining challenges to be addressed. First, we intend to investigate the problem of intermediary selection in a Bayesian setting that often arises due to the long-tail effect of the Internet: a small number of products attracts a large part of the demand, affecting the number of times advertisers meet their competitors (and can learn their preferences). Then we intend to investigate the problem of optimal auction design for the intermediaries and the center. This is an important task in oligopolies, given that a seller's selection of mechanism affects the number and distribution of visiting buyer types, as well as the response of competing sellers, leading to an infinite regress [16]. Moreover, an important aspect of these advertising systems is asymmetric information between buyers (i.e. different ad networks provide different user tracking information that affects the valuations of the advertisers), a problem that has been tackled in [17, 18] but only for settings with no intermediaries. Finally, scenarios with more than one central sellers are another interesting problem for future research.

References

1. Cary, M., Das, A., Edelman, B., Giotis, I., Heimerl, K., Karlin, A.R., Mathieu, C., Schwarz, M.: Greedy bidding strategies for keyword auctions. In: Proceedings of the 8th ACM Conference on Electronic Commerce, EC 2007, pp. 262–271. ACM, New York (2007)
2. Pardoe, D., Chakraborty, D., Stone, P.: TacTex09: A champion bidding agent for ad auctions. In: Proceedings of the 9th International Conference on Autonomous Agents and Multiagent Systems (AAMAS 2010) (May 2010)
3. Kuminov, D., Tennenholtz, M.: User modeling in position auctions: Re-considering the GSP and VCG mechanisms. In: Proceedings of the 8th International Joint Conference on Autonomous Agents and Multiagent Systems, AAMAS 2009, pp. 273–280 (2009)
4. Aggarwal, G., Goel, A., Motwani, R.: Truthful auctions for pricing search keywords. In: Proceedings of the 7th ACM Conference on Electronic Commerce, EC 2006, pp. 1–7. ACM, New York (2006)
5. Muthukrishnan, S.: Ad exchanges: Research issues. In: Leonardi, S. (ed.) WINE 2009. LNCS, vol. 5929, pp. 1–12. Springer, Heidelberg (2009)
6. VanBoskirk, S., Overby, C.S., Takvorian, S.: U.S. Interactive Marketing Forecast, 2011 to 2016 (September 2011)
7. PwC: IAB U.S. Internet Advertising Revenue Report for 2011 First Six Months Results (September 2011)
8. Feldman, J., Mirrokni, V., Muthukrishnan, S., Pai, M.M.: Auctions with intermediaries: extended abstract. In: Proceedings of the 11th ACM Conference on Electronic Commerce, EC 2010, pp. 23–32. ACM, New York (2010)

9. McAfee, R.P.: Mechanism Design by Competing Sellers. Econometrica 61(6), 1281–1312 (1993)
10. Peters, M., Severinov, S.: Competition among sellers who offer auctions instead of prices. Journal of Economic Theory 75(1), 141–179 (1997)
11. Burguet, R., Sákovics, J.: Imperfect competition in auction designs. International Economic Review 40(1), 231–247 (1999)
12. Hernando-Veciana, Á.: Competition among auctioneers in large markets. Journal of Economic Theory 121(1), 107–127 (2005)
13. Gerding, E.H., Rogers, A., Dash, R.K., Jennings, N.R.: Sellers competing for buyers in online markets: reserve prices, shill bids, and auction fees. In: Proceedings of the 20th International Joint Conference on Artifical Intelligence, pp. 1287–1293. Morgan Kaufmann Publishers Inc., San Francisco (2007)
14. Ashlagi, I., Monderer, D., Tennenholtz, M.: Simultaneous ad auctions. Mathematics of Operations Research 36(1), 1–13 (2011)
15. Edelman, B., Ostrovsky, M., Schwarz, M.: Internet advertising and the generalized second-price auction: Selling billions of dollars worth of keywords. The American Economic Review 97(1), 242–259 (2007)
16. Pai, M.M.: Competition in mechanisms. SIGecom Exchanges 9, 7:1–7:5 (2010)
17. Abraham, I., Athey, S., Babaioff, M., Grubb, M.: Peaches, lemons, and cookies: Designing auction markets with dispersed information. Technical Report MSR-TR-2011-68, Micosoft Research (January 2011)
18. McAfee, R.P.: The design of advertising exchanges. Review of Industrial Organization 39, 169–185 (2011)

Author Index